Junior
Worldmark
Encyclopedia of

World Holidays

Junior Worldmark Encyclopedia of World Holidays

VOLUME **4**

New Year, Ramadan and Id al-Fitr, Thanksgiving and Harvest Festivals

U·X·L®

AN IMPRINT OF THE GALE GROUP

DETROIT · NEW YORK · SAN FRANCISCO
LONDON · BOSTON · WOODBRIDGE, CT

Junior Worldmark Encyclopedia of World Holidays

Robert H. Griffin and Ann H. Shurgin

Staff

Kelle Sisung, *Contributing Editor*
Carol DeKane Nagel, *U·X·L Managing Editor*
Thomas L. Romig, *U·X·L Publisher*
Meggin Condino, *Senior Analyst, New Product Development*

Dean Dauphinais, *Senior Editor, Imaging and Multimedia Content*
Shalice Shah-Caldwell, *Permissions Associate, Text and Pictures*

Robert Duncan, *Senior Imaging Specialist*
Randy A. Bassett, *Image Database Supervisor*
Barbara J. Yarrow, *Graphic Services Manager*

Pamela A. E. Galbreath, *Senior Art Director*
Graphix Group, *Typesetting*

Rita Wimberley, *Senior Buyer*
Evi Seoud, *Assistant Manager, Composition Purchasing and Electronic Prepress*
Dorothy Maki, *Manufacturing Manager*

Printed in the United States of America
10 9 8 7 6 5 4 3 2 1

Library of Congress Cataloging-in-Publication Data

Junior worldmark encyclopedia of world holidays/ edited by Robert Griffin.
    p.   cm.
Includes bibliographical references and index.
Summary: Alphabetically arranged entries provide descriptions of celebrations around the world of some thirty holidays and festivals, including national and cultural holidays, such as Independence Day and New Year's Day, which are commemorated on different days for different reasons in a number of countries.
ISBN 0-7876-3927-3 (set). — ISBN 0-7876-3928-1 (vol. 1). — ISBN 0-7876-3929-X (vol. 2). — ISBN 0-7876-3930-3 (vol. 3). — ISBN 0-7876-3931-1 (vol. 4).
1. Holidays—Encyclopedias, Juvenile. 2. Festivals—Encyclopedias, Juvenile. [1. Holidays—Encyclopedias. 2. Festivals—Encyclopedias. 3. Encyclopedias and dictionaries.] I. Griffin, Robert H., 1951–

GT3933 .J86 2000
394.26'03—dc21
                                        00-023425

Contents

Contents

Volume 3:

Volume 4:

Contents
by Country

Contents by Country

Reader's Guide

Ever wonder why children trick-or-treat on Halloween? How Christmas festivities in Italy differ from those in the United States? What the colors of Kwanzaa represent? When will Ramadan come this year? Who creates all those floats in the parades? The answers to these and other questions about holiday traditions and lore can be found in *Junior Worldmark Encyclopedia of World Holidays*. This four-volume set explores when, where, why, and how people from thirty countries around the world celebrate eleven different holidays.

Each chapter in *Junior Worldmark Encyclopedia of World Holidays* opens with a general overview of the featured holiday. The chapter then provides details on one to six countries that observe that holiday. Each overview and country profile is arranged into the following rubrics, allowing for quick scanning or comparisons among the countries and holidays:

- **Introduction:** Offers a brief description and useful background information on the holiday. The introduction in the overview discusses the holiday in general; the country introductions focus on how the holiday is observed in that featured country.

- **History:** Discusses the holiday's development, often from ancient origins through modern times. When a holiday was established to commemorate a historical event, such as a revolution or a nation's declaration of independence, a historical account of the event is given. When a holiday began with the rise of a religion, a discussion of the growth of the religion follows. Each holiday's general history is presented in the overview, while its development in a particular country is the focus of the country history.

- **Folklore, Legends, Stories:** Each holiday has at least a few legends and stories, folklore and superstitions associated with it. These are discussed here, along with literature commonly associated with the holiday. Traditional characters or historical tales can be found, as well as a brief synopsis of a well-known story or an excerpt from a poem. Religious holidays include excerpts or synopses of the scriptural account on which they are based. For some holidays, sidebars listing popular stories and poems are included.

- **Customs, Traditions, Ceremonies:** This section delves into the actual celebration of the holiday, from preparation for its arrival through ceremonies to bid it farewell for another year. Some of the ceremonies and traditions are religious, others are secular. Some are based on beliefs and superstitions so old that no one knows their origin, while others center around the reenactment of historical or religious events. Some are carried out on a grand scale, while others involve a quiet family ceremony. Learn how a European family celebrates a particular holiday while someone in Africa or Asia celebrates it in a very different—or sometimes very similar—way.

- **Clothing, Costumes:** Some holidays, such as Halloween and Carnival, have costumes at the heart of the celebration. For others, such as Independence Days, simply wearing the national colors is enough. In many cultures, people don traditional folk costumes for particular holidays, while others just dress in their "Sunday best." Whether it is a pair of sneakers or a six-foot feather plume, clothing and costumes play an important role in the traditions. This section will explain how people dress for the holiday and why.

- **Foods, Recipes:** What does Christmas dinner mean to an Italian family? What do Chinese youngsters snack on at New Year festivals? What is the main "Thanksgiving dinner" dish in Swaziland? This rubric details the special hol-

iday meals shared by people within a culture. It covers the foods themselves as well as table settings, mealtime ceremonies, and the significance of eating certain foods on special days. For some holidays, picnic or festival foods are also mentioned. For most countries, a favorite holiday recipe is featured.

- **Arts, Crafts, Games:** Described here are famous works of art associated with specific holidays, as well as crafts created by different peoples in connection with the holiday, such as intricate Nativity scenes made by Italian woodcarvers and special pictures created by Chinese artists to bring good luck in the New Year. Holiday decorations and traditional games are also discussed here. Included for some holidays are crafts projects that, in addition to bringing added enjoyment by making one's own decorations, will help foster an appreciation of the art of other cultures.

- **Symbols:** Included in the holiday overviews are discussions of the symbols associated with the holiday and its celebration. A description of each symbol is given, along with its origin, meaning, and significance to the holiday.

- **Music, Dance:** Whether performing classical compositions or folk dancing in a courtyard, people all over the world love to make music and dance during their holidays. This rubric focuses on the music and dance that helps make up holiday celebrations. Some musical performances can be fiercely competitive, like the steel band contests held during Carnival in Trinidad. Others are solemn and deeply moving, like a performance of Handel's *Messiah* in a cathedral at Easter. Here learn about folk instruments, the origins of songs and dances, and famous composers or musicians from many cultures. Excerpts from songs associated with the holiday are also given.

- **Special Role of Children, Young Adults:** Children and young adults often have a special role to play in holiday celebrations. While children may simply participate in family activities during a holiday in some countries, in others children have distinct roles in parades, plays and performances, or customs. Here students can learn how children their own age celebrate holidays in nations thousands of miles away.

- **For More Information and Sources:** Print and electronic sources for further study are found at the end of each holiday overview and again at the end of each country essay. Those following the overview are general sources for the holiday, whereas the others pertain to a particular nation. Books listed should be able to be found in a library, and electronic sources are accessible on the World Wide Web.

Additionally, each chapter contains a Holiday Fact Box highlighting the themes of the specific holiday, while sprinkled throughout the set are boxes featuring recipes, activities, and more fascinating facts. One hundred twenty-five photos help bring the festivities to life. Beginning each volume is a table of contents for the entire set listing the holidays and countries featured, a table of contents by country, an explanation of how the modern calendar developed, a calendar list of world holidays, and a words to know section. Concluding each volume is a cumulative subject index providing easy access to the holidays, countries, traditions, and topics discussed throughout *Junior Worldmark Encyclopedia of World Holidays*.

Advisory Board

Special thanks to the *Junior Worldmark Encyclopedia of World Holidays* advisors for their invaluable comments and suggestions:

- Mary Alice Anderson, Media Specialist, Winona Middle School, Winona, Minnesota.

- Ginny Ayers, Department Chair, Media Technology Services, Evanston Township High School, Evanston, Illinois.

- Jonathan Betz-Zall, Children's Librarian, Sno-Isle Regional Library System, Edmonds, Washington.

- Peter Butts, Media Specialist, East Middle School, Holland, Michigan.

Comments and Suggestions

We welcome your comments on this work as well as your suggestions for holidays to be featured in future editions of *Junior Worldmark Encyclopedia of World Holidays*. Please write: Editors, *Junior Worldmark Encyclopedia of World Holidays*, U•X•L, 27500 Drake Rd., Farmington Hills, MI 48331–3535; call toll-free: 1–800–877–4253; fax: 248–414–5043; or send e-mail via www.galegroup.com.

How the
Modern
Calendar
Developed

The Egyptian Calendar

The earliest known calendar, that of the Egyptians, was lunar based, or calculated by the cycles of the Moon. One cycle is a lunar month, about 29.5 days in length, the time it takes the Moon to revolve once around the Earth. Although the calculations are fairly simple, reliance upon lunar months eventually leads to a problem: a lunar year, based upon 12 lunar cycles, is only 354 days. This is 11 days shorter than the solar year, the time it takes Earth to revolve once around the Sun. In any agricultural society, such as that of ancient Egypt, the solar-based seasons of the year are vitally important: they are the most reliable guide for knowing when to plow, plant, harvest, or store agricultural produce. Obviously, the discrepancy between the lunar and solar year had to be addressed.

The Egyptian solution was to rely on a solar calendar to govern civil affairs and agriculture; this was put in place around the third millennium B.C. This calendar observed the same new year's day as the older lunar one, which for the Egyptians was the day, about July 3, of the appearance on the horizon just before sunrise of the star

Sirius, the "Dog Star." This event was significant for the Egyptians, for it occurred at nearly the same time the Nile River flooded each year, the key to their agricultural prosperity. The new Egyptian solar calendar also retained the division of days into months, although they were no longer based on lunar cycles. The Egyptian year in the reformed calendar contained 12 months of 30 days, with 5 days added throughout the year, bringing the total number of days to 365. It was only a fraction of a day different from the length of the solar year as determined by modern scientific means.

The Sumerian Calendar

Like the early Egyptian calendar, the ancient Sumerian calendar, developed around the twenty–seventh century B.C., was lunar. To the Sumerians, however, the Moon's cycles were apparently more significant, for they retained lunar months and a 354–day year. They made alignments with the seasons by adding extra days outside the regular calendar. (This process of adding extra days as necessary to reconcile the lunar with the solar year is called intercalation.) The calendar of the sacred city of Nippur, which became the Sumerian standard in the eighteenth century B.C., assigned names to the months, with the intercalary month designated by royal decree.

The Seven–day Week

The ancient Babylonians, a Sumerian people with a highly developed astronomy, are thought to be the first people to observe a seven-day week. The concept was probably based upon the periods between the distinct phases of the moon, which roughly correspond to seven days. The Babylonians also regarded the number seven as sacred, probably because they knew of seven principal heavenly bodies—Sun, Moon, Mars, Mercury, Jupiter, Venus, and Saturn—and saw supernatural significance in their seemingly wild movements against a backdrop of fixed stars. The days of the week were named for these principal heavenly bodies, one assigned to each day according to which governed the first hour of that day.

In addition to their lunar calendar, the Babylonians also devised a solar calendar based upon the points at which the Sun rises in relation to the constellations. This calendar is the basis for the zodiac system, the key to astrology.

From the Babylonians, the ancient Hebrews are believed to have adopted the practices of intercalation and observance of a seven-day week, probably during the time of Jewish captivity in Babylon beginning in 586 B.C. Babylonian influence may also have played a role in their observing every seventh day as special—the Jewish concept of Sabbath. Evidence for an earlier Jewish calendar (from at least the twelfth century B.C.)

does exist, however; thus, the observance of a Sabbath may well have existed before the Babylonian captivity. In any event, it is clear that the tradition of the seven-day week, as well as the retention of the concept of months, has much to do with the Western inheritance of Jewish calendar practices. (See also **The Hebrew Calendar,** below.)

The seven-day week as we know it today was carried into Christian use in the first century A.D. and was officially adopted by the Roman emperor Constantine in the fourth century. Interestingly, the English names for the days still reflect their origin in the names of the seven principal heavenly bodies of the ancient Babylonian astronomy:

- **Sunday:** Old English *Sunnan daeg,* a translation of Latin *dies solis,* "day of the sun."

- **Monday:** Old English *Monan daeg,* a translation of Latin *lunae dies,* "day of the moon"; compare with the French *lundi.*

- **Tuesday:** Old English *Tiwes daeg,* "day of Tiw," an adaptation of Latin *dies Martis,* "day of Mars" (the god Tiw being identified with the Roman Mars); compare with the French *Mardi.*

- **Wednesday:** Old English *Wodnes daeg,* "Woden's Day," an adaptation of Latin *Mercurii dies,* "day of Mercury" (the god Woden being identified with the Roman Mercury); compare with the French *mercredi.*

- **Thursday:** Old English *Thunres daeg,* "Thunor's day" or "Thor's day," an adaptation of the Latin *dies Jovis,* "day of Jove" (the god Thor being identified with the Roman Jove); compare with the French *jeudi.*

- **Friday:** Old English *Frize daeg,* "Freya's Day," an adaptation of the Latin *dies Veneris,* "day of Venus" (the goddess Freya being identified with the Roman Venus); compare with the French *vendredi.*

- **Saturday:** Old English *Saetern(es) daeg,* derived from the Latin *Saturni Dies,* "day of Saturn."

The Hebrew Calendar

Little is known of the Hebrew calendar prior to the Exodus from Egypt (c. 1250 B.C.) except that it appears to have contained four single and four double months called *yereah.* The early Hebrews apparently did not study the heavens and timekeeping as did their Sumerian and Egyptian neighbors. In fact, it was only after the period of Babylonian exile (586–516 B.C.) that a more fully developed method of timekeeping was adopted to modify the ancient practices. After their return from captivity, the Hebrews employed a calendar very similar to that of the Babylonians, intercalating (adding as necessary) months into the lunar calendar so it would correspond with the solar year. Unlike the Babylonians, who marked the beginning of the new year in the spring, the Hebrews retained the custom of recognizing the new year in the autumn, the time of their principal religious festivals of Rosh Hashanah (New Year), Yom Kippur, the Sukkoth, all falling in the month of Tishri (September/October). Still, similarities between the Jewish and Babylonian calendars are clear from a comparison of the names used in each system for the months:

Names of the Months in the Babylonian and Jewish Calendar Systems

Babylonian	Jewish	Equivalent
Nisanu	Nisan	March/April
Aiaru	Iyar	April/May
Simanu	Sivan	May/June
Du'uzu	Tammuz	June/July
Abu	Ab	July/August
Ululu	Elul	August/September
Tashritu	Tishri	September/October
Arahsamnu	Heshvan	October/November
Kislimu	Kislev	November/December
Tebetu	Tebet	December/January
Shabatu	Shebat	January/February
Adaru I	Adar	February/March
Adaru II	Veadar	(intercalary)

Thus, the year in the Jewish (and Babylonian) calendar consists of 12 lunar months, with the addition of the intercalary month as necessary to synchronize with the solar year. The months contain alternately 29 or 30 days; the beginning of each is marked by the appearance of the new moon.

The Hebrew week ends with the observation of the Sabbath, lasting from sunset Friday to sunset Saturday, a day to rest and pay homage to God. The use of weeks and observation of a day of rest are primarily contributions from Jewish tradition to our present–day calendar. (See also **The Seven–day Week,** above.)

The Jewish Era, designated *A.M.* (for Latin *anno mundi,* "year of the world"), begins with the supposed date of Creation, which tradition sets at 3761 B.C. After more than two thousand years, devout Jews still observe essentially the same calendar for religious purposes, although they follow other calendars for their business and social lives. With its roots based in scripture, the Hebrew calendar has remained a primary binding force of tradition and continuity throughout the long and varied history of the Jewish people.

The Early Roman Calendar

Ancient Rome played a significant role in the development of our modern method of reckoning time. The earliest known Roman calendar, created according to legend by the city's founder, Romulus, in the eighth century B.C., had 10 months totaling 304 days: 6 months of 30 days and 4 months of 31 days. The new year began in March, the time when agricultural activities were revived and new military campaigns were initiated, and ended with December, which was followed by a winter gap that was used for intercalation. The Etruscan king Numa Pompilius (reigned 715–673 B.C.) reformed Romulus's primitive calendar, instituting a lunar year of 12 months. The two new months, following December, were named *Januarius* and *Februarius,* and were respectively assigned 29 and 28 days.

While this reform was a clear improvement, it was set aside in Rome during a time of political unrest that began about 510 B.C. Still, its advantages were remembered, and in 153 B.C. Numa Pompilius's calendar was again adopted. At the same time the beginning of the Roman civil year was changed to January 1, which became the day that newly elected consuls assumed office.

Days of the Roman Month

The Romans did not have a method for numbering the days of their months in a series. They did, however, establish three fixed points from which other days could be reckoned. These three designations were: 1) *Kalends,* the first day of the month (ancestor of English *calendar*); 2) *Nones,* the ninth day; and 3) *Ides,* originally the day of the full moon of the lunar month. In months of 31 days (March, May, July, October) the Nones were the seventh day and the Ides the fifteenth, while in the shorter months the Nones fell on the fifth and the Ides on the thirteenth day.

The Romans also recognized a market day, called *nundinae,* which occurred every eighth day. This established a cycle for agriculture in which the farmer worked for seven days in his field and brought his produce to the city on the eighth for sale.

The Julian Calendar

It was not until the mid-first century B.C., by which time the reformed lunar calendar had shifted eight weeks out of phase with the seasons, that emperor Julius Caesar determined that a long-term and scientific reform of the calendar must take place. He enlisted the aid of the Alexandrian astronomer Sosigenes to devise the new calendar. The solar year was reckoned quite accurately at 365.25, and the calendar provided for years of 365 days with an additional day in February every fourth year. In 46 B.C. a total of 90 days were intercalated into the year, bringing the calendar back into phase with the seasons. As a result, what would have been March 1, 45 B.C. was, in the new system, referred to as January 1, 45 B.C. Thus 46 B.C. was a long year, containing 445 days, and was referred to by Romans as *ultimus annus confusionis,* "the last year of the muddled reckoning."

In 10 B.C. it was found that the priests in charge of administering the new Roman calendar had wrongly intercalated the extra day every third year rather than every fourth. In order to rectify the situation, the emperor Augustus declared that no 366–day years should be observed for the next 12 years, and made certain that future intercalation would be properly conducted. With this minor adjustment, the Julian calendar was fully in place, so to remain for the next 1,626 years.

The Gregorian Calendar

Since the Julian calendar year of 365.25 days (averaging in the leap-year day) was slightly longer than the actual length of a solar year, 365.242199 days, over time even this system proved wanting, growing out of phase by about three or four days every four centuries. By the time of Pope Gregory XIII in the late sixteenth century, the difference between the calendar and the seasons had grown to ten days; the vernal equinox of 1582 occurred on March 11. Left without change, the Julian calendar would have resulted in fixed holy days occurring in the "wrong" season, which bewildered church officials. Moreover, certain fixed holy days were also used to determine when to plant and harvest crops.

Pope Gregory's reform, presented in the papal bull of February 24, 1582, consisted of deleting ten days from the year (the day following October 5 was designated as October 15) and declaring that three out of every four "century" years (1700, 1800, etc.) would not be leap years; if a century year, such as 1600, were divisible by 400, it would be a leap year. These modifications established the form of our present calendar.

In spite of its superior accuracy, the Gregorian calendar met with resistance in various parts of the world, and was not used until the eighteenth century in Protestant Europe and the American colonies, and even later still in areas under strong Byzantine influence.

Although the Gregorian calendar measures out a year that is slightly longer than the solar year (differing by about 25 seconds a year, or 3 days in every 10,000 years) its general workability and accuracy have led to its use worldwide for nearly all nonreligious purposes.

Calendar
of Holidays

January

January 1
New Year's Day
Solemnity of Mary the Mother of God

January 1 or 2
St. Basil's Day

January 2
Second New Year

January 5–6
Epiphany Eve and Epiphany
Twelfth Night
Day of the Three Kings/Día de los Tres
Reyes

First Monday after Twelfth Day
Plough Monday

January 6 or 7
Old Christmas

January 7
Gannā
St. Distaff's Day
St. John the Baptist's Day

January 11
St. Brictiva's Day

January 12
Old New Year's Day

January 12–15
Festival of Our Lord Bonfim

January 13
St. Knut's Day
Old Silvester

January 14
Magh Sankranti

January 15
Pilgrimage to the Shrine of the Black
Christ
Adult's Day

January 16
St. Honoratus's Day

January 19 and 20
Timqat (Epiphany) and St. Michael's
Feast

January 20
St. Sebastian's Day
St. Agnes Eve

January 21
St. Sarkis's Day

January 22
St. Dominique's Day (Midwife's Day)
St. Vincent's Day

January 24
Festival of Abundance

January 25
Burns Night

Last Tuesday in January
Up Helly Aa

Fifteenth Day, Shevat (January–February)
Tu Bi-Shevat (Fifteenth Day, Shevat)

Month of Magha (January–February)
Urn Festival

Month of Tagu, Days 1–4
Thingyan

Last Month, Last Day of Lunar Year
New Year's Eve

Moon 1, Days 1–15
New Year

Moon 1, Day 1
Tibetan New Year (Losar)

Moon 1, First Two Weeks (circa February)
Prayer Festival

Moon 1, Day 7
Festival of the Seven Grasses

Moon 1, Day 9
Making Happiness Festival

Moon 1, Days 14–19 (circa February)
Butter Sculpture Offering Festival

Moon 1, Day 15
Great Fifteenth
Burning of the Moon House Festival
Lantern Festival
Birthday of the Great Emperor–Official
of the Heavens

Moon 1, Day 16
Sixteenth Day

Moon 1, Day 19
Rats' Wedding Day

January–February
Rice Festival

Thai/Tai
Thai Poosam

February

Circa February
Tsagan Sara (New Year)

February
Clean Tent Ceremony
Winterlude

February 1
St. Brigid's Day

February 1–3 (circa)
Setsubun

February 2
Candlemas/Candelaria
Feast of the Virgin of the Suyapa
Queen of Waters Festival

February 3, 5
St. Blaise's Day, St. Agatha's Day

February 5
Igbi

February 10
Feast of St. Paul's Shipwreck

February 11
St. Vlasios's Day

February–March (Day 10 of Dhu'l-hija)
Id Al-Kabir (The Great Feast)

Moveable: February–March (Sunday before Lent)
Cheese Sunday

Moveable: February–March
Shrove Monday
Shrove Tuesday/Mardi Gras
Carnival
Ash Wednesday

Moveable: February–March (First Sunday in Lent)
Chalk Sunday

Moveable: February–April
Lent

Calendar of Holidays

February 14
St. Valentine's Day

Circa February 15–17
Igloo Festival

February 22
Boys' Day

February 25
St. George's Day

February 28
Feast of the Spring
Naked Festival

February 29
Leap Year Day/St. Oswald's Day

February (Full Moon)
Maka Buja

February–March (Full Moon)
Kason
Dol Purnima
Holi
Masi Magham

Pjalguna (February–March)
Sivaratri

Moon 2, Day 1 (February–March)
Wind Festival

February or March
Getting Out of the Water Festival (Kuomboko)

Moveable: February–March (Fourteenth Day of Adar)
Purim

March

First Two Weeks in March
Festival of the Water of Youth

March 1
First of March
St. David's Day

March 3
Hina Matsuri (Girls' Day)

Circa March 5
Feast of Excited Insects

March 8
Women's Day

March 9
Feast of the Forty Martyrs

Circa Mid-March, 1 Moons after Dosmoche
Storlog

March 17
St. Patrick's Day

March 19
St. Joseph's Day
Pookhyái

Circa March 20
Ibu Afo Festival
Emume Ala

Circa March 21
Vernal Equinox

Circa March 21 and Thirteen Days Thereafter
New Year

March 25
Day of the Annunciation

Moveable: March–April (Fourth Sunday in Lent)
Mothering Sunday

Moveable: March–April (Fifth Sunday in Lent)
Carlings Sunday

March–April (Saturday before Palm Sunday)
St. Lazarus's Day (Lazarovden)

March–April (Sunday before Easter)
Palm Sunday

Moveable: March 22–April 25
Easter and Holy Week

First Sunday after Easter (Low Sunday)
Domingo de Cuasimodo
St. Thomas's Day

Day after St. Thomas's Day (Low Sunday)
Blajini Day

Second Monday and Tuesday after Easter
Hocktide

Day 25 after Easter
Feast of Rousa

Day 28 after Easter
Ropotine

Moon 3, Day 5
Pure and Bright

Moon 3, Day 23
Birthday of Matsu

March–April
Gajan of Siva
Birthday of the Monkey God
Birthday of the Lord Vardhamana
    Mahavira

March–April (Full Moon)
Panguni Uttiram

Day 9, Bright Fortnight, Chaitra (March–April)
Ramanavami

March–May
Flying Fish Ceremony

April

Circa April
Road Building Festival

April
Awuru Odo
Cherry Blossom Festival
New Year

April 1
April Fools' Day

April 2
13 Farvardin/Sizdeh Bedar

April 4
St. Isidore's Day

April 5 or 6 (105 Days after the Winter Solstice)
Pure Brightness Festival

Circa April (Eight Days Beginning on Day 15 of Nisan)
Pesach/Passover

Last Day of Passover and Day after Passover
Maimona

April 12 or 13
New Year

April 13–15
New Year

April 19–25 (The Thursday in This Period)
First Day of Summer

April 23
St. George's Day

April 25
St. Mark's Day

April 30
May Eve
Walpurgis Night

Moon 4, Day 8
Buddha's Birthday

April (Various Dates)
Planting Festivals
Wangkang Festival

April–May
First of Baisakh/Vaisakh

Full Moon (Purnima) of Vaisakha (April–May)
Buddha Jayanti

May

Circa May (Day 33 of the Omer Period)
Lag Ba-omer

May
Nongkrem Dance

May (Throughout the Month)
Flowers of May

First Sunday in May
Sunday School Day

First Tuesday in May
Fool's Fair

May 1
May Day
St. Joseph's Day

May 1–May 30
Birth of the Buffalo God

May 3
Day of the Holy Cross

May 5
Cinco de Mayo

May 5 (Formerly Moon 5, Day 5)
Boys' Day

Easter to July
Holy Ghost Season

Monday, Tuesday, and Wednesday before Ascension
Rogation Days

Moveable: Forty Days after Easter
Ascension Day

Moveable: Fifty Days after Easter
Whitsun/Pentecost

First Sunday after Whitsunday
Trinity

Moveable: Thursday after Trinity
Corpus Christi/Body of Christ

Seventh Thursday after Easter
Semik

First Thursday after Corpus Christi
Lajkonik

May 11–14
Ice Saints

May 14
Crossmas

May 15
St. Sofia's Day
St. Isidore's Day

May 17
Death of the Ground

May 24
Queen's Bithday (Victoria Day)

May 24–25
Pilgrimage of Sainte Sara

May 25
St. Urban's Day

May 29
Oak-Apple Day (Royal Oak Day)

May 31
Memorial Day (Day of the Dead)

May (Full Moon)
Wesak Day

Moon 5, Day 5 (May–June)
Double Fifth
Tano

Moon 5, Day 14
Gods of the Sea Festival (and Boat Race Day)

Moon 5, Day 15
Gogatsumatsuri

May–June
Sithinakha/Kumar Sasthi
Vata Savitri
Rocket Festival

May–June (Jaistha)
Ganga Dussehra

May–June (Day 6 of Sivan)
Shavuot

May to July (Height of Rainy Season)
Okere Juju

Circa May–July
Days 1–10 of Muharram

Late May or Early June
Star Snow (Qoyllur Rit'i)

June

Early June
Tyas Tuyï

June
Egungun Festival

June 1–2
Gawai Dayak

June 11
Cataclysmos Day

June 13
St. Anthony's Day

June 13–29
Festas Juninas

June 22–August 21
Aobao Gathering

June 24
St. John's Day/Midsumer Day
Day of the Indian

June 25
Festival of the Plow

June 27–July 27
Lesser New Year

June 29
Day of St. Peter and St. Paul

June or July (Rainy Season)
Car Festival (Rath Jatra)

Moon 8, Waning Day–Moon 11, Full Moon (June/July to September/October)
Vossa/Khao Vatsa/Waso

Moon 6, Day 6
Airing the Classics

Moon 6, Day 15
Shampoo Day (Yoodoonal)

Moon 6, Day 24
Birthday of the Lotus
Yi (China) New Year

May to October, Peaking in July
Festa Season

June–July or August–September
Pola and Hadaga

Late June to Early September
Powwow

July

Circa July
Olojo Festival (Ogun Festival)

Early July
Festival of the Ears of Grain

July
Nazareth Baptist Church Festival

July 1–2
Canada Day/Dominion Day

July 2 and August 16
Palio

July 4
Independence Day/Fourth of July

July 6
Feast of San Fermin

July 8
Feast of St. Elizabeth

July 11
Naadam Festival

July 14
Bastille Day

July 15
St. Swithin's Day
Festival of the Virgin of Carmen

July 25
St. James's Day

July 26
St. Anne's Day
Pardon of Ste. Ann d'Auray

July 29
St. Olaf's Wake

Moon 7, Day 7 (July–August)
Birthday of the Seven Old Maids
Star Festival/Double Seventh

Moon 7, Days 13–15 (July–August)
Obon

Moon 7, Day 15 (July–August)
Hungry Ghost Festival

July–August
Procession of Sacred Cows
Ghanta Karna
Kandy Esala Perahera
Marya
Snake Festival
Teej
Tish-Ah Be-Av

July–August (Full Moon)
Sacred Thread Festival

July or August
Maggomboh
Imechi Festival

Late July–First Tuesday of August
Carnival

Late July or Early August
Carnival

Full Moon in Summer
Tea Meetings

August

Early August
Llama Festival

August
Good Year Festival
Panchadaan

August 1
Feast of the Progress of the Precious
and Vivifying Cross
Honey Day
Lammas
Lúghnasa
Parents Day

August 2
Feast Day of Our Lady of the Angeles

August 2–7
Nebuta Festival

August 6
Transfiguration of Christ

August 10
Festival of St. Laurence

August 10–12
Puck's Fair

August 15
Assumption of the Virgin

August 20
St. Stephen's Fete

Circa August 24
Thanksgiving

August 30
La Rose

End of August
Reed Dance

August–September
Prachum Ben
Feast of the Dead
Festival of the Elephant God
Gokarna Aunsi

Plough Festival
Janmashtami
Lord Krishna's Birthday
Khordad-Sal
Paryushana
Agwunsi Festival
Insect-Hearing Festival

Moon 8, Day 15 (August–September)
Mid-Autumn Feast

Moon 8, Day 16 (August–September)
Birthday of the Monkey God

Various Dates
Harvest Festivals

September

Circa September
Okpesi Festival

September
Indra Jatra

September 8
Nativity of the Virgin

First and Second Days of Tishri (September–October)
Rosh Hashana

September 11
Coptic New Year
Enkutatash (New Year)

September 14
Holy Cross Day

September 15
Keiro no Hi (Respect for the Elderly Day)

Tenth Day of Tishri
Yom Kippur

12 Rabi-ul Awal (August–October)
Ma-ulid

Circa September 21–22
Autumnal Equinox
Jūgowa

September 27
Maskal

September 29
St. Michael's Day

Fifth Day of the Fifth Lunar Month (Late September–Early October)
Bon Kate

Moon 9, Day 9 (September–October)
Double Ninth
Chrysanthemum Day
Festival of the Nine Imperial Gods

Month 10 (September–October)
Ho Khao Slak

Days 24 and 25 of Tishri (September–October)
Simhat Torah and Is'ru Chag

September–October
Durga Puja/Dasain/Dussehra/Durgotsava
Oktoberfest
Pitra Visarjana Amavasya

October

Circa October (Wagyut Moon, Day 15)
Ok Pansa/Ok Vatsa/Thadingyut

October
Lord of the Earthquake

First Sunday in October
St. Michael's Day
Water Festival

Second Sunday in October
Lotu-A-Tamaiti

October 5
Han'gul Day

October 7
Festival of the Virgin of Rosario

October 17
Romería of Our Lady of Valme

October 18
St. Luke's Day

October 21
Festival of the Black Christ

October 25
St. Crispin and St. Crispinian's Day

October 26
St. Demetrius's Day

October 28
Thanksgiving
Punkie Night

October 31
All Hallow's Eve/All Saints' Eve

Moon 10, Day 1 (October–November)
Sending the Winter Dress

Moon 10, Day 25 (October–November)
Sang-joe

Kartik (October–November)
Gopashtami ("Cow Eighth") and
Govardhan Puja

October–November
Diwali/Deepavali/Tihar
Karwachoth

**Seven Days, Beginning Fifteenth of Tishri
(October–November)**
Sukkot

**Moveable: October or Later (after Rainy
Season)**
Mother's Day

November

Late Autumn
Keretkun Festival

Circa November
Seal Festival
Loi Krathong

Early November (Near End of Rainy Season)
Sango Festival

November
Tori-no-inchi

November 1
All Saints' Day

November 2
All Souls' Day

Friday before November 3
Creole Day

November 3
St. Hubert's Day

November 5
Guy Fawkes Night

**Twenty-seventh Day of Rajab (November 6
in 1999)**
Night of the Ascension

November 8
St. Michael's Day

November 11
St. Martin's Day
St. Mennas's Day

November 15
Shichi-go-san (Seven-Five-Three)

Circa November 15
Haile Selassie's Coronation Day

November 18
Feast of St. Plato the Martyr

November 19
Settlement Day

November 21
Presentation of the Virgin Mary in the
Temple

November 25
St. Catherine's Day

Fourth Thursday in November
Thanksgiving

November 30
St. Andrew's Day

Moon 8, Day 29 (November)
Seged

Month 12 (November)
Boun Phan Vet

Moveable: Month of Shaban
Shaban

Moveable: November–December
Ramadan (Month of Fasting)

December

Circa December (Tasaungmon Full Moon)
Tawadeintha/Tazaungdaing

Sunday before Advent (Early December)
Stir-Up Sunday

Four Weeks before Christmas, Beginning on a Sunday
Advent Season

Early December (Variable)
Bear Festival

Circa December (Eight Days Beginning on 25 Kislev)
Hanukkah

December 4
St. Barbara's Day

December 6
St. Nicholas's Day

December 7
Burning the Devil

Circa December 7–8
Itul

December 8
Immaculate Conception
Needle Day

Second Sunday before Christmas
Mother's Day

December 12
Our Lady of Guadalupe

December 13
St. Lucy's Day

December 14
St. Spiridion Day

December 16
Braaiveleis

December 16–25
Cock Crow Mass

Sunday before Christmas
Father's Day

Friday before Christmas
Cuci Negeri

December 18
St. Modesto's Day

Circa December 21
Ysyakh

December 21
St. Thomas's Day

Circa December 22
Winter Solstice

December 23
Festival of St. Naum
St. Thorlak's Day
La Noche de Rabanos (Night of the Radishes)

December 25–30 (Variable)
Kushi Festival

December 25
Christmas

December 26
Boxing Day
Kwanzaa
St. Stephen's Day

December 27
St. John's Day

December 28
Holy Innocents' Day

December 31
New Year's Eve
Sylvester Day

Late December
Sing-Sing

Moon 12, Day 8 (December–January)
Rice Cake Festival

Moon 12, Day 20 (December–January)
Day for Sweeping Floors

Moon 12, Day 23 or 24 (December–January)
Kitchen God Visits Heaven

Moon 12, Day 28 (December–January)
King's New Year

December–January
Little Feast

December–August
Odo

Words to Know

A

Absolute monarchy: A form of government in which a king or queen has absolute control over the people, who have no voice in their government.

Act of merit: An act of charity that, in Buddhism, is said to help the doer find favor with Buddha and earn credits toward a good rebirth.

Advent: A Christian holiday. From the Latin *adventus*, "coming," referring to the birth of Jesus. Advent is a four-week period of preparation for Christmas, beginning on the Sunday nearest November 30.

Age of Enlightenment: A philosophical movement during the eighteenth century when European writers, journalists, and philosophers influenced thousands through new ideas about an individual's right to determine his or her own destiny in life, including having a voice in government. The movement emphasized the use of reason to challenge previously accepted church teachings and traditions and thus is sometimes referred to as the Age of Reason.

Aliyah: From the Hebrew for "ascent" or "going up." The waves of Jewish immigrants to Israel in the nineteenth and twentieth centuries.

Allah: The "one God" of Islam.

Ancestors: A person's, tribe's, or cultural group's forefathers or recently deceased relatives.

Asceticism: A way of life marked by severe self-denial as a form of personal and spiritual discipline; for example, depriving the body of food and owning few material goods.

Ash Wednesday: A Christian holiday. Ash Wednesday is the seventh Wednesday before Easter and the first day of Lent, a season of fasting commemorating Jesus Christ's forty days of temptation in the wilderness. The name is derived from the practice of priests placing ashes on the foreheads of worshipers as a remembrance "that you are dust and unto dust you shall return."

B

Bastille: A castle and fortress in Paris, France, built in 1370 and later used as a prison. Bastille Day commemorates the storming of the Bastille by French peasants and workers on July 14, 1789, sparking the French Revolution.

Bee: A large gathering, usually of farm families, to complete a task and celebrate with food and drink, games, and dancing.

Beignet: A square fritter without a hole that is a popular snack during Carnival in France and French-influenced New Orleans, Louisiana. Fried pastries are popular throughout the world during Carnival, a time when people traditionally tried to use up their butter and animal fat before the Christian holiday of Lent.

Black Madonna: Poland's most famous religious icon, a painting of the Virgin Mary holding the infant Jesus, said to have been painted by Saint Luke during the first century A.D.

Blessing baskets: Baskets of Easter foods and pysanky (Easter eggs), covered with hand-embroidered cloths and carried to church to be blessed on Holy Saturday in Ukraine and Poland.

Bodhi tree: The "tree of wisdom." Buddha achieved enlightenment while sitting under a bodhi tree.

Bourgeoisie: In French, the middle social class.

Buddha: Prince Siddhartha Gautama (c. 563–c. 483 B.C.) of India, later given the name Buddha ("the Enlightened One"). His teachings became the foundation of Buddhism.

Buddhism: One of the major religions of Asia and one of the five largest religious systems in the world. Buddhists believe that suffering is an inescapable part of life and that peace can be achieved only by practicing charity, temperance, justice, honesty, and truth. They also believe in a continual cycle of birth, illness, death, and rebirth.

Byzantine Empire: The Eastern Roman Empire, with its capital at Constantinople (present-day Istanbul, Turkey).

C

Cajun: The name given to French Canadians who emigrated from Acadia, a former name for Nova Scotia. The name was eventually shortened from "Acadian" to "Cajun."

Calligraphy: Ornamental handwriting. In Islam, it is the Arabic script in which the Koran is written and which is used inside mosques as an art form.

Calypso: A popular musical style originating in Trinidad and Tobago in which singers create witty lyrics to a particular rhythm.

Carnavalesco: An individual who helps design, plan, and choreograph Carnival parades and shows in Brazil.

Caste system: A social system in which people are divided into classes according to their skin color and ancestry.

Catholic Church: The ancient undivided Christian church or a church claiming historical continuity from it.

Celts: A people who lived in Ireland, Scotland, England, Wales, and northern France before the birth of Christ, more than two thousand years ago. Also refers to modern people of these areas.

Chinese zodiac: A zodiac system based on a twelve-year cycle, with each year named after one of twelve animals. A person's zodiac sign is the animal representing the year in which he or she was born.

Christian Protestantism: Christian church denominations that reject certain aspects of Catholicism and Orthodox Christianity and believe in salvation by faith alone, the Holy Bible as the only source of God's revealed truth, and the "priesthood" of all believers.

Civil disobedience: Nonviolent action, such as protest marches, taken by an individual or group in an attempt to bring about social change.

Civil rights: Rights granted to every member of a society regardless of race, sex, age, creed, or religious beliefs. Specifically, the rights given by certain amendments to the U.S. Constitution.

Collective farm: A large farm, especially in former communist countries, formed by combining many small farms for joint operation under government control.

Colonial rule: A country's rule of a foreign land that has settlers from the ruling country, or colonists, living there.

Commedia dell'arte: Italian comedy of the sixteenth to eighteenth centuries that created some of the most famous characters in Italian costume. Among them are Harlequin, with his multicolored suit, and Punchinello, who later became a famous character in puppet shows.

Communism: A political and economic system in which the government controls and owns the means of production of goods and distributes the goods equally among the population.

Concentration camps: Nazi German military camps where civilians, primarily Jews, were held during World War II (1939–45). Millions were tortured, gassed, or burned to death in these camps.

Constitutional monarchy: A form of government in which a nation is ruled by a king or queen but the people are represented through executive, legislative, and judicial branches.

Continental Congress: Men representing twelve of the thirteen American colonies (all but Georgia) who formed a colonial government in 1774 in Philadelphia, Pennsylvania, and set forth the principles of the American Revolution (1775–83).

Cornucopia: A horn-shaped basket overflowing with vegetables and fruits. The cornucopia is a symbol of a bountiful harvest, often used as a Thanksgiving decoration. Also called "horn of plenty."

Council of Nicaea: In 325, a church governing body led by Roman emperor Constantine (reigned 306–37) met in the city of Nicaea (in what is now Turkey). The council formally established the Feast of Christ's Resurrection (Easter) and decreed that it should be celebrated on the Sunday following the first full moon after the spring equinox.

Coup d'état: A military takeover of an existing government.

Crazy days: In many European countries, the final days of Carnival celebrations, the wildest and most widely celebrated.

Creole: A person descended from or culturally related to early French or sometimes Spanish settlers of the U.S. Gulf Coast; they preserve a characteristic form of French speech and culture.

Crucifixion: A Roman method of execution, in which a person is nailed to a wooden cross to die.

Crusades: Religious wars of the eleventh, twelfth, and thirteenth centuries in which Christians fought to win the Holy Land from the Muslims.

D

Dedication: The setting apart of a temple or church for sacred uses with solemn rites.

Dharma: Laws of nature that were taught by Buddha. The primary symbol of Buddhism is a wheel with eight spokes, called the dharma wheel, which symbolizes life's constant cycles of change and the Eightfold Path to enlightenment.

Diaspora: The breaking up and scattering of a people from their homeland, especially the scattering of the Jewish people from Israel throughout the world.

Divination: Predicting the future through ritual; fortune-telling.

Dragon parade: A Chinese New Year parade featuring long dragon costumes manipulated by many dancers.

Dreidel: A four-sided top, each side marked with a Hebrew letter, all together representing the phrase "A great miracle happened there," referring to the Hanukkah miracle in ancient Jerusalem. The term also refers to the Hanukkah game played by Jewish children with the top.

Druids: An order of Celtic priests.

E

Easter bunny: Originally the Easter hare, called "Oschter Haws" by the Germans; a mythical rabbit who is said to bring colored eggs and candy to children on Easter Sunday.

Easter egg: An egg colored or decorated for Easter.

Easter lily: The white trumpet lily, native to Bermuda but widely cultivated in the United States. It blooms at Easter time and is known as a symbol of purity and of Christ's Resurrection.

Eastern Orthodox Church: A branch of the Christian church with many members in Eastern Europe, Western Asia, and the Mediterranean. The Eastern Orthodox Church began in the Greek city of Constantinople (now Istanbul, Turkey), the seat of

Roman emperor Constantine's (reigned 306–37) Eastern Roman Empire.

Elders: Older family or community members, such as grandparents, who are honored and respected for their experience and wisdom.

Enlightenment: Understanding the truth about human existence; a spiritual state marked by the absence of desire or suffering, upon which Buddhist teaching is based.

Epiphany of Our Lord: A Christian holiday. Traditionally observed on January 6, Epiphany marks the official end of the Christmas season. In Western Christian churches, Epiphany commemorates the visit of the Three Wise Men to see the infant Jesus in Bethlehem; in Eastern Orthodox churches, it is celebrated as the day of Jesus' baptism.

Epitaphion: A carved structure covered with a gold-embroidered cloth and decorated with flowers that is a symbol of Christ's tomb in the Greek Orthodox Church.

Epitaphios: "Feast of Sorrow." A Good Friday ritual in the Greek Orthodox Church, enacted as a funeral procession for Jesus Christ.

Equinox: The first day of spring and the first day of fall of each year, when the length of the day's sunlight is equal to the length of the day's darkness. This occurs on about March 20 or 21 and September 22 or 23.

Essence: The "spirit" of a thing, such as food or burnt offerings, which is believed to be usable by the dead in many cultures.

F

Fantasia: "Fantasy." Brazilian name for Carnival costume.

Fast: To voluntarily go without food or drink, often as part of religious practice, as during Ramadan or Lent.

Feudal system: The predominant economic and social structure in Europe from about the ninth to the fifteenth centuries, in which peasants farmed land for nobles and in turn received a small house and plot of land for themselves.

First fruits: The first harvesting of a crop, considered sacred by many cultures.

Folk holiday: A nonreligious holiday that originates with the common people.

Fool societies: In Germany and other parts of Europe, guilds formed by tradesmen to plan and organize Carnival celebrations.

Four Noble Truths: The four principles that became the core of Buddha's teaching: 1) Suffering is everywhere; 2) The cause of suffering is the attempt to satisfy selfish desires; 3) Suffering can be stopped by overcoming selfish desires; and 4) The way to end craving and suffering is to follow the Eightfold Path, eight steps concerning the right way to think and conduct oneself.

Freedom of the press: The right of people to publish and distribute pamphlets, newspapers, and journals containing their own thoughts and observations without censorship by government or church.

French Quarter: A historical section of New Orleans, Louisiana, where the wildest and most elaborate Mardi Gras celebrations are staged.

G

Gelt: The traditional Jewish name for money given to the poor during Hanukkah. Also refers to any Hanukkah gift and to play money (chocolate coins wrapped in gold foil) used in playing dreidel.

Gilles: A special men's society in Belgium whose members dress in identical costumes and masks and march in Mardi Gras parades.

Golden Stool of the Ashanti: A wooden stool covered with a layer of gold. The stool is sacred to the Ashanti people of Ghana, to whom it is a symbol of their nation and their king.

Good Friday: The Friday before Easter Sunday, a day for mourning Christ's death.

Gregorian calendar: The calendar in general use in much of the world in modern times. It was introduced by Pope Gregory XIII in 1582 as a modification of the Roman Julian calendar.

Griot: A storyteller who passes on the history of a people orally and through music.

Guerrilla: A member of a small military organization that uses unconventional fighting tactics to surprise and ambush their enemies.

Guillotine: A machine for beheading criminals, widely used by French revolutionaries during the late 1700s and for many years afterward in France. It consisted of a wooden frame with a heavy, tapered blade hoisted to the top and then dropped, immediately severing the victim's head.

Guising: An old Scottish custom of dressing in disguise and going from house to house asking for treats; a forerunner of Halloween trick-or-treating.

H

Hanukkiah: A Hanukkah menorah, or candleholder. It has eight main branches and a ninth for the servant candle, used to light the other eight.

Harvest festival: A festival for celebrating the gathering of crops at the end of the growing season.

Harvest moon: The full moon nearest to the time of the fall equinox (about September 23), so called because it occurs at the traditional time of harvest in the Northern Hemisphere. It appears larger and brighter than the usual full moon, and the moon is full for an extra night, giving farmers more hours to harvest crops.

Hegira: The flight of Muhammad and his followers in 622 from Mecca to Yathrib, later known as Medina, where Muhammad was accepted as a prophet. The Hegira marks the beginning of the Islamic calendar.

Hidalgo's bell: A cathedral bell rung by Father Miguel Hidalgo y Costilla in the town of Dolores on September 16, 1810, to call the native people of Mexico together in a revolt against Spanish rule.

Hinduism: The major religion of India and one of the world's oldest religions. It is based on the natural laws of dharma and conforming to one's duty through ritual, social observances, and meditation.

Holocaust: The mass slaughter by the Nazis of some six million Jews and thousands of other European civilians during World War II (1939–45), chiefly by gassing and burning the victims.

Holy Communion: A church rite in which Christians eat and drink blessed bread and wine as memorials of Christ's death. Christ is said to have initiated the rite during the Last Supper.

Holy Grail: A cup or plate that, according to medieval legend, Jesus used at the Last Supper.

Holy Land: Palestine, where Jesus Christ lived, preached, died, and was resurrected, according to the Bible. Major holy sites are Jerusalem and Bethlehem.

Holy Shroud: In the Orthodox Church in Ukraine, a specially woven and embroidered cloth that represents Jesus' burial cloth, used for Holy Week services.

I

Icons: Religious scenes or figures such as Christ and the Virgin Mary, usually very old, painted on wooden panels or on linen or cotton cloth glued to panels. Revered by Christians in the Eastern Orthodox and Catholic Churches, some are believed to have miraculous powers.

Iftar: The nighttime feast served after sunset during Ramadan.

Imam: Person who leads prayer and recites from the Koran during worship services in a mosque.

Immigrants: People who leave their home country and enter another to settle.

Islam: The major religion of the Middle East, northern Africa, parts of Southeast Asia, and some former Soviet Union countries. Islam is the world's second-largest religion. Believers, called Muslims, worship their one god, Allah, and assert that Muhammad (c. 570–632), founder of Islam, is his prophet.

Islamic calendar: The lunar calendar used to determine the date of Islamic holidays. Each of twelve months begins with the first sighting of the new moon. Each lunar month has either twenty-nine or thirty days, and each year has 354 days.

J

Jataka Tales: A collection of more than five-hundred tales said to have been told by Buddha. The tales were passed down orally through generations and finally written down several hundred years after his death. About Buddha's previous lives, the tales concern such issues as responsibility, friendship, honesty, ecology, and respect for elders.

Jesus Christ: The founder of Christianity. Jesus was born in Bethlehem in about 6 B.C. and died in about A.D. 30, when he was crucified. According to Christian tradition,

Jesus was the Son of God, and he came into the world to die for the sins of mankind. His followers believe that as Christ rose from the dead and ascended into heaven, so too will they.

Julian calendar: The calendar introduced in Rome in 46 B.C. and on which the modern-day Gregorian calendar is based.

K

Kitchen God: A Chinese deity honored during the lunar New Year. He is said to reside in the kitchen and report to the Jade Emperor (the highest deity, who resides in heaven) once a year on the actions of each household.

Koran: The Islamic holy book, written in Arabic and containing Scriptures also found in the Jewish Torah and the Christian Bible, as well as rules on all aspects of human living. The Koran is believed to have been revealed to the prophet Muhammad by Allah through the angel Gabriel.

Krewes: Secretive, members-only clubs that organize Mardi Gras parades and activities in New Orleans, Louisiana.

L

Lakshmi: The Hindu goddess of wealth, honored during Diwali, the Hindu New Year.

Last Supper: Also called the Lord's Supper; the last meal Jesus Christ shared with his disciples, believed to have been a Passover

meal and at which Christ is said to have initiated the rite of Holy Communion. Christians observe the Thursday before Easter in memory of the Last Supper.

Legal holiday: A day declared an official holiday by a government, meaning that government offices, schools, and usually banks and other offices are closed so that workers may observe the holiday.

Lent: A Christian holiday. Lent is the traditional six-week period of partial fasting that precedes Easter. It is a time to remember the forty days that Jesus wandered in the desert without food. Many Christians give up a favorite food or activity during Lent.

Lunar New Year: A movable holiday marking the first day of the first lunar month on the Chinese lunar calendar. It begins at sunset on the day of the second new moon following the winter solstice (between late January and the end of February) and ends on the fifteenth day of the first lunar month.

M

Mardi Gras: *See* Shrove Tuesday.

Martyr: One who voluntarily suffers death for proclaiming his or her religious beliefs and refusing to give them up.

Masked ball: A formal dance at which those attending wear costumes and masks that conceal their identity.

Mass: A celebration of the Christian sacrament of the Eucharist (Holy Communion), commemorating the sacrifice of the body and blood of Christ, symbolized by conse-crated bread and wine.

Maundy Thursday: The Thursday before Easter Sunday, said to be the day Christ took the Last Supper, prayed in the Garden of Gethsemane, was betrayed by Judas Iscariot, and was arrested. In many church-es, this is a day for taking Holy Commu-nion in memory of the Last Supper.

Mecca: The holiest city of Islam. It is locat-ed in Saudi Arabia and is the birthplace of the prophet Muhammad. Muslims strive to make a pilgrimage to Mecca at least once during their lifetime and face toward Mecca each time they pray.

Menorah: A seven-pronged candleholder used in Jewish worship ceremonies.

Messiah: The "anointed," the Savior proph-esied in the Bible to save the world from sin. To Christians, the Messiah is Jesus Christ.

Metta: One of Buddha's main teachings, involving the concept of loving kindness. Metta is a way to overcome anger through love, evil through good, and untruth through truth.

Middle Path: A major tenant of Buddhism advocating equilibrium (balance) between extremes in life and avoiding things or ideas produced by selfish desires. Buddhists believe the best way to travel the Middle Path is through meditation, as Buddha did.

Mishnah: The Jewish code of law, passed down orally for centuries before being writ-ten down by rabbis during the second cen-tury.

Missionaries: People sent to other countries to teach their religious beliefs to native peo-ples and carry on humanitarian work.

Monk: A man who is a member of a reli-gious order and usually lives in a monastery or wanders from place to place teaching religious principles.

Monsoon: The name give to a season of heavy rains and wind in India and south-ern Asia.

Mosque: An Islamic temple for prayer and worship, consisting of a large dome and at least one pointed tower, or minaret. Mosques are decorated with calligraphy from the Koran.

Movable holiday: A holiday that falls at a different time each year, depending on the calendar used to determine the celebration. For example, Thanksgiving, Ramadan, and Easter.

Muhammad: Islam's greatest prophet. Muhammad was an Arabian who lived dur-ing the sixth century (c. 570–632). He is considered the founder of Islam.

Mumming: Merrymaking in disguise during festivals.

Muslim: A follower of the Islamic faith.

N

Nativity: The birth of Jesus Christ, as told in the biblical New Testament.

Nazarenos: Honorable men who lead Holy Week processions in Spain, wearing long robes and pointed hoods that cover their faces.

New moon: The thin crescent moon that appears after sunset following nights during the beginning of the new moon phase, when no moon can be seen. The new moon is used to mark the beginning of each month in both the Islamic and Jewish calendars.

Night of Power: The twenty-seventh night of Ramadan, which Muslims believe is the night when the angel Gabriel first began giving the words of the Koran to the prophet Muhammad.

Nirvana: A state of perfect peace and joy; freedom from greed, anger, and sorrow.

Nun: A woman who is a member of a religious order.

O

Ofrenda: Spanish word for an offering made to the dead or to a religious figure.

Oratorio: A long choral music piece for many voices, without action or scenery, usually on a religious theme. For example, Handel's *Messiah.*

P

Pagan: Referring to the worship of many gods, especially to early peoples who worshiped gods of nature.

Palm Sunday: The Sunday before Easter, when Jesus' entry into Jerusalem is com-

memorated with palms, which were used to line his path.

Papier-mâché: A mixture of flour, paper, paste, and water that hardens when dry and is often used to create figures and objects for Carnival parade floats and for many other craft projects.

Parade float: A large platform that is elaborately decorated and carries people and scenery representing a specific parade theme. Floats are usually mounted on a trailer and pulled through the streets by a motor vehicle. Float design and building is often considered an art.

Parol: A traditional Filipino symbol of Christmas, a star-shaped lantern made from bamboo and paper, called the Star of Bethlehem.

Paschal candle: A large candle, sometimes weighing hundreds of pounds, that is lit in some churches on Holy Saturday and used to light many individual candles for congregation members. The Paschal candle represents Christ as the light of the world.

Passion of Jesus Christ: The sufferings that Christ endured between the night of the Last Supper with his disciples and his death by crucifixion, often reenacted by Christians during Holy Week.

Passion play: A dramatic musical play reenacting Christ's Passion and crucifixion.

Passover: An observance of the Jews' deliverance from slavery in Egypt, as told in the Bible. Jewish families were commanded to smear the blood of a sacrificial lamb on their doorways so that the angel of death would pass over their homes. Passover is still a major Jewish observance. Christians also commemorate Passover by taking Holy Communion on Maundy Thursday, the day Christ is said to have eaten a Passover meal with his disciples at the Last Supper.

Patron saint: A saint believed to represent and protect a group of people, church, nation, city or town, animals, or objects. A saint to whom people pray for help in certain circumstances.

Penitents: In Holy Week processions in Spain, the Philippines, and Central and South America, persons who walk in the procession carrying heavy wooden crosses, in chains, or whipping themselves as punishment and repentance for wrongs they have done and to commemorate Christ's suffering as he carried the Cross.

Pilgrimage: A journey, usually to a holy place or shrine.

Pilgrims: Name given to English colonists who arrived at what is now Plymouth, Massachusetts, in 1621 and settled there. This group is credited with celebrating the first Thanksgiving, with members of the Wampanoag Indian tribe.

Pongol: A sweet, boiled rice dish that is prepared to celebrate the rice harvest in parts of India. Pongol is also the name given to this holiday.

Pope: A high-ranking bishop who is head of the Roman Catholic Church and resides in the Vatican in Rome.

Proclamation: An official formal public announcement, usually by a government leader or representative.

Promised Land: According to the biblical book of Genesis, the land of Canaan, promised by God to Abraham, the father of the Jews. The prophet Moses led the Hebrews to the Promised Land after freeing them from slavery in Egypt. Refers to modern-day Israel.

Prophet: One who speaks for God or a deity; a divinely inspired speaker, interpreter, or spokesperson who passes on to the people things revealed to him or her by God.

Proverb: A wise saying or adage, often part of the cultural heritage of a people.

Puritans: Members of a sixteenth- and seventeenth-century religious Protestant group in England and New England that believed in a strict work ethic and opposed ceremony and celebration.

Pysanky: Ukrainian and Polish Easter eggs created by using the wax resist, or batik, method.

R

Rabbi: A Jewish religious teacher and leader.

Reincarnation: A Hindu belief that all life is part of a universal creative force called Brahman and that human and animal souls are reborn into new bodies many times before they return to Brahman.

Resurrection of Jesus Christ: The rising from the dead of Jesus Christ, the central figure of Christianity, worshiped as the son of God. The Resurrection is celebrated at Easter. Christians believe that Christ died to reconcile humans with God and that believers will have eternal life of the spirit.

S

Sabzeh: A dish of sprouts grown by Iranian families in preparation for Nouruz, the New Year celebration. The sprouts are said to absorb bad luck from the past year.

Saint: A person, usually deceased, who has been officially recognized by church officials as holy because of deeds performed during his or her lifetime.

Samba: A fast dance made famous in Rio de Janeiro, Brazil, in which the feet and hips move but the upper body is kept still. The samba is performed by large groups of dancers, called samba schools, who wear elaborate matching costumes in Carnival parades.

Samhain: An annual festival of the Celts that marked the end of the fall harvest and the beginning of winter. It is said to be the forerunner of Halloween and New Year celebrations in parts of Europe.

Sangha: A Buddhist community of monks and nuns.

Secular: Nonreligious.

Seven Principles of Kwanzaa: A set of principles developed for Kwanzaa laying out rules of living for the community of people of African descent: unity, self-determination, collective work and responsibility, cooperative economics, purpose, creativity, and faith.

Shofar: An ancient Jewish traditional trumpet-like instrument made from a ram's or antelope's horn that is blown in the synagogue during Rosh Hashanah and Yom Kippur.

Shrine: A place, either natural or manmade, set aside for worship of a god or saint; a box or structure containing religious relics or images.

Shrove Tuesday: The Tuesday before Ash Wednesday, also called Fat Tuesday (Mardi Gras in French). Shrove Tuesday is the final day of Carnival and the one on which the biggest celebrations are held. Traditionally a time for confessing sins (called "being shriven") and for using up the fresh meat and animal fat, eggs, and butter in the household before the forty-day fast of Lent.

Solstice: The first day of summer and the first day of winter in the northern hemisphere, when daylight hours are the longest and shortest, respectively. The solstices fall about June 22 and December 22 of each year.

Spring couplets: Two-line rhymes written in Chinese calligraphy that are displayed during Chinese New Year as a wish for good luck.

Star of David: A six-pointed star believed to have decorated the shield of King David of Israel, who ruled about 1000 B.C. A widely used symbol of Judaism.

Stations of the Cross: The locations in Jerusalem and the corresponding events leading to the Crucifixion and Resurrection of Christ. A central theme of Christian religious art and sculpture, Holy Week processions, and Passion plays.

Steel drum: A drum created in Trinidad and Tobago, originally by using discarded steel oil barrels. Steel drum bands and music have become popular worldwide.

Suhur: The pre-dawn meal served each morning of Ramadan.

Supernatural: Transcending the laws of nature; referring to ghosts and spirits and the spiritual realm.

Superstition: A belief that something will happen or not happen as a result of performing a specific ritual, for example, eating certain foods to bring good luck.

Swahili: A major African language. Many of the terms relating to Kwanzaa are drawn from Swahili.

Synagogue: A Jewish house of worship.

T

Tableau: A group of people in costume creating a living picture or scene portraying a historical, mythological, musical, or narrative theme.

Taboo: Something forbidden by religious or cultural rules, sometimes because of the fear of punishment by supernatural powers.

Talmud: The authoritative book of Jewish tradition, consisting of the Mishnah and the Gemara, comments of rabbis about the Mishnah.

Tamboradas: Loud, steady drumbeats that sound in many Spanish cities and villages beginning at midnight on Holy Thursday and continuing until late on Holy Saturday night, announcing the Passion and death of Christ.

Throws: Objects such as plastic bead necklaces and coins, flowers, candy, or fruit thrown to the crowd from parade floats or by marching groups, especially in Carnival parades.

Torah: The Jewish holy book, consisting of the five books of Moses (first five books of the biblical Old Testament), also called the Pentateuch.

Trick-or-treating: A widely popular Halloween tradition for children in which they dress in costumes and go from door to door collecting candy and treats. Children once played tricks on those who did not give treats.

V

Vaya: A sprig of bay or myrtle attached to a small cross made from a palm frond, given by Greek Orthodox priests to members of their congregation on Palm Sunday.

Vegetarian: Eating no meat, and sometimes no animal products, such as dairy foods or eggs.

Viceroy: The governor of a country or territory who rules in the name of a king or queen.

Virgin of Guadalupe: The Virgin Mary, mother of Jesus Christ, as she is said to have appeared (with dark skin and Mexican Indian clothing) to an Indian woodcutter in 1531. She is the patron saint of Mexico's poor.

W

Witch: A woman accused of worshiping Satan and casting spells to help him do evil to humans. Witches are often fictitious characters and the subject of Halloween costumes.

Y

Yule log: A large log burned in a fireplace during the Christmas season, a custom that began in early Europe and Scandinavia.

Z

Zakat: Money given by Muslims to help the poor in obedience to the laws of Islam and as a means of worshiping Allah.

Zion: The name of a fortification in the ancient city of Jerusalem, capital of King David's kingdom in about 1000 B.C. For centuries, Zion has been a symbol of the Promised Land (Israel) and of Judaism.

Zionism: A movement to rebuild the Jewish state in Israel; from the word Zion, another name for Jerusalem.

Zoroastrianism: The ancient religion of Persia, developed by the prophet Zoroaster (c. 628–551 B.C.). Believers perform good deeds to help the highest deity, Ahura Mazda, battle the evil spirit Ahriman.

Junior Worldmark Encyclopedia of World Holidays

New Year

Also Known As:
Lunar or Chinese New Year (China)
Diwali (India)
Nouruz (Iran)
Rosh Hashanah (Israel)
Hogmanay (Scotland)

Introduction

New Year celebrations are among the world's oldest and best-loved holidays. Just as spring brings the promise of rebirth in nature, a new year offers the hope of putting the past behind and starting over fresh. It is a time when people resolve to break bad habits during the coming year.

In some countries, people believe that it is a time when good fortune can be attracted to one's home and family by performing certain rituals. As a religious holiday, it is a time to ask forgiveness from God and from man for wrongdoings, and to resolve to live a better life in the coming year.

History

Historians say the New Year has been celebrated in some form for approximately five thousand years. Many New Year celebrations are linked to ancient midwinter festivals that honored the sun for bringing more light each day after the winter solstice. The winter solstice occurs around December 21 or December 22, when the sun rises higher in the sky and the days get longer. One of the oldest New Year celebrations was held in the ancient Middle Eastern city of Babylon in about 2600 B.C. It was a springtime festival in honor of the chief god, Marduk.

The ancient Egyptians marked the beginning of the year with the twenty-four-day Festival of Opet, held when the Nile River overflowed its banks. Scholars say Indian people probably began celebrating New Year, or Diwali (pronounced dih-WAH-lee), about 1500 B.C. They placed torches around their houses and courtyards to purify them and keep away evil spirits.

The first recorded Persian New Year, called Nouruz (pronounced no-ROOZ), celebration was during the time of King Cyrus the Great (585–529 B.C.). Persian king Darius the Great (550–486 B.C.) had the magnificent estate known as Persepolis built to stage his New Year celebrations. The ancient Greeks, who celebrated the New Year at the time of the first new moon after the summer solstice in June, started the custom of honoring the first baby born in each New Year.

Holiday Fact Box: New Year

Themes

New beginnings and resolutions to do better in the coming year; forgiveness, purification, and renewal; driving out evil and bad luck and welcoming good luck and prosperity.

Type of Holiday

Most New Year holidays are secular, or nonreligious. The Jewish New Year, Rosh Hashanah, however, is considered a sacred religious holiday. Other New Year celebrations, such as Diwali, which is a Hindu holiday, and the Iranian Nouruz, also have some religious meaning and rituals.

When Celebrated

The New Year is celebrated at the beginning of a new calendar year. The new year varies from country to country, depending on what calendar is used. For instance, the Chinese New Year is a movable holiday that marks the first day of the first month on the Chinese lunar calendar. It usually falls between late January and the end of February.

Chinese New Year customs were recorded as early as 500 B.C. An early ceremony for driving out evil spirits involved a sorcerer and young people dressed in red and black shooting arrows into the sky.

The celebration of the Scottish New Year, Hogmanay (pronounced HAHG-muh-nay), began with the ancient Celts (pronounced KELTS) in about 300 B.C. It was a ceremony to rejuvenate the sun and drive away evil spirits during the darkest time of year, just before the winter solstice. Celtic priests performed rites such as building bonfires and harvesting sprigs of sacred mistletoe to keep fairies and evil spirits away.

Roman emperor Julius Caesar set the New Year at January 1 during the first century B.C., when he introduced the Julian calendar. January was named for the Roman god Janus, keeper of the gates of heaven and earth. Janus is shown as having two faces: one looking backward to the old year and the other forward to the new.

During the sixth century, officials in the Christian church established the New Year as the Feast of Christ's Circumcision. Jesus Christ (c. 6 B.C.–c. A.D. 30) is the founder of Christianity, and January 1 commemorates the date of his circumcision, which occurred eight days after his birth. January 1 remained the date of the New Year in many countries when Pope Gregory XIII modified the Julian calendar in 1582 and it became the Gregorian calendar. In Europe, a long season of midwinter celebration began in late fall and continued through February.

From about the twelfth century, Great Britain celebrated March 25 as the beginning of the New Year. March 25 is believed to be the day on which the Virgin Mary learned from the angel Gabriel that she would be the mother of Jesus Christ. England and the American colonies did not adopt the Gregorian calendar—with January 1 as New Year's Day—until 1752, although Scotland adopted it in 1600.

Folklore, Legends, Stories

It is very popular during the Chinese Lunar Year to spend evenings telling folktales. Most of these stories are about good fortune: poor people who become rich; the sick who miraculously become well; and the lonely who find love. The legend most associated with the Chinese New Year is that of the Kitchen God, who is said to live in the home of each Chinese family. A few days before New Year, he returns to heaven. While there, he reports on the activities of the family, both good and bad.

The Hindu New Year, Diwali, is associated with India's classic epic poem the *Ramayana*. The *Ramayana* recounts the life of the hero Rama and his wife Sita. Diwali is also a time to read and share some of the thousands of Hindu folktales. The most popular stories are about Lakshmi, the goddess of good fortune, who is said to visit the homes of humans during Diwali.

Nouruz, which is the Persian New Year, is celebrated at the spring equinox, around March 21. An equinox occurs when the length of the day's sunlight is equal to the length of the day's darkness. This happens only twice a year—once in the spring and once in the fall. According to an ancient Persian myth about the spring equinox, a bull balances the Earth on one horn. At the equinox, he tosses his head, shifting it to the other. The New Year is said to arrive at this moment, and the shift is so great that some say it can be felt on the Earth.

Rosh Hashanah (pronounced ROSH huh-SHAH-nuh) is the Jewish New Year. The Hebrew Bible (the sacred book of Judaism) is filled with legends and stories that recount the history of the Jewish people, but two stories are particularly associated with the

Half a million people help ring in the new year in Times Square in New York City, January 1, 1999. People have gathered at the square every year since 1907 to watch the slow descent of the ball signaling the start of the new year. Reproduced by permission of AP/Wide World Photos.

New Year and are traditionally read during this time—the story of Abraham and Isaac and the story of Jonah and the Great Fish. Both stories deal with the themes of faith in God and God's forgiveness.

Customs, Traditions, Ceremonies

The major purpose of celebrating the New Year is to drive out the old year and all bad things attached to it to make way for new beginnings. In ancient Israel, the sins of the people were symbolically placed on a goat, which was then sent away from the village, carrying their sins with it. In Scotland and other countries, rituals are held to "kill" the old year to make way for the new. An old Hogmanay custom is to make a straw dummy representing the passing year and set this "Auld Wife" on fire as bells ring out the old year.

New Year housecleaning

People throughout the world believe that a spotless, thoroughly swept, freshly painted, well-repaired home will ensure a good beginning for the New Year. Hindus believe that the goddess Lakshmi looks into every home to see if it is clean. If it is not, she will not bring good fortune to the family on Diwali. To prepare for Nouruz, Iranians even throw out their old pottery and buy new.

Rituals to bring good luck

On the Wednesday before Nouruz, called Fire Wednesday, many Iranian families jump over small fires, chanting, "Your ruddiness [redness, a sign of good health] to me; my pallor [paleness or sickness] to you." This custom is believed to bring good health in the New Year. Many people in other countries sprinkle one another, drink, or wash with the first water drawn from a well or stream on New Year's Day for extra good fortune.

Another popular Nouruz custom is to grow a container of sprouts from seed, beginning about two weeks before the New Year. This dish of sprouts, called the *sabzeh* (pronounced sob-ZEH), is said to absorb the family's ill luck from the past year. It is

thrown away on the last day of Nouruz. This symbolizes throwing out the bad luck of the old year.

In India, people involved in business and commerce take the New Year very seriously. Business owners close old account books and start new ones. Carpenters, repairmen, farmers, artists, and craftspeople ask Lakshmi, the goddess of good fortune, to bless the tools of their trade and pray that she will grant them success in the coming year.

Hindu girls and women honor and bless their brothers in a special ceremony, and in turn, brothers honor their sisters with gifts. The oldest woman of the household sweeps the house as other family members follow her, shouting and clapping their hands to drive out the goddess of bad luck, Alaksmi. Then doors and windows are opened to let the goddess Lakshmi in to bless the house and family.

An ancient and much-loved custom in Scotland is "first-footing." The Scots believe that the first person to step over their threshold on New Year's Day determines their luck for the year. This person is called the "first-footer," and ideally he should be a tall, handsome, healthy, dark-haired man. Traditional gifts brought by the first-footer are shortbread or cake, a small bottle of whiskey, a small bag of salt, and a lump of coal or a stick of firewood. Scots believe these gifts ensure that the family will have food, whiskey, good health, and warmth in the coming year.

New Year's Eve traditions

On New Year's Eve, the Chinese place a new picture or representation of the Kitchen God, the most honored of the household gods, above the stove. One week

Balloons attached to New Year's resolutions are released in Tokyo, Japan, at the stroke of midnight on January 1, 1996. In spite of good intentions, many people do not keep their resolutions and find themselves making the same ones year after year. Reproduced by permission of AP/Wide World Photos.

before, the family burns their old Kitchen God to send him off to report to the Jade Emperor in heaven. First, however, they feed him sweets and smear his mouth with honey so that he can say only sweet things about the family.

On the eve of Nouruz, a table is spread with a beautiful cloth and set with candles and good-luck objects. Photographs of family and loved ones, brightly colored boiled eggs, and a plate containing new coins to be given as gifts, are also often placed on the table.

On the eve of Rosh Hashanah, the woman of the house lights candles before sunset and says a blessing to thank God for bringing the family together to share another special moment. The blessing is followed by a holiday feast.

New Year's Eve celebrations in cities in Europe and North America are big, noisy street parties. People watch in anticipation until clocks strike twelve, meaning the old year is over and the new has begun. Then they hug and kiss, wishing one another the best in the New Year. Many families see the

New Year in at home, watching these festivities on television.

New Year's Day and beyond

On New Year's Day in China, people attend temple fairs. On the seventh day of the New Year, everyone celebrates a birthday, and each person is said to be one year older.

In India, lighting the Diwali lamps, called *dipas* (pronounced DIH-puhs), is the most beautiful ceremony of the New Year. It is carried out all over the country, so that every city and town glows with millions of lights placed along porches, rooftops, windowsills, and doorways. Thousands of dipas placed on little wooden rafts can be seen floating on the Ganges River. The dipa-lighting ceremony is held at sunset after evening prayers.

Jewish families attend long morning and evening services at the synagogue (pronounced SIN-uh-gog; Jewish house of worship) each day of Rosh Hashanah. The most powerful part of the service is the ceremony of the *shofar,* an ancient trumpet-like instrument made from the horn of a ram or antelope. It is tradition to blow the shofar one hundred times on each day of Rosh Hashanah.

On the thirteenth, and last, day of Nouruz, Iranians pack a picnic lunch and go outside to a park or to the countryside for an all-day outing. This custom is called Thirteenth Day Out. It began as a way to avoid having bad luck find the family at home on the unlucky thirteenth day of the New Year.

Scotland's Hogmanay celebrations include Celtic dance parties called *ceilidhs* (pronounced KAY-leez), street theater, carnivals, fairs, and a gathering of the Scottish clans (traditional family groups).

Making New Year's resolutions or wishes

In Western countries, people often make New Year's resolutions on New Year's Day, promising themselves to do better in school or work, exercise more, eat right, or break an unhealthy habit. Asian people often express these as New Year "wishes." In spite of good intentions, many people do not keep their resolutions and find themselves making the same ones year after year. The Jewish New Year, Rosh Hashanah, is the time when people hope to clear away their sins by asking forgiveness. They can then start fresh, resolving to live closer to God in the coming year.

Giving and receiving gifts

Gift giving at the New Year probably began with the Romans, who gave small gifts called *strenae* to friends and family at midwinter celebrations. During the seventeenth century in Europe, the New Year was known as the Festival of Gifts. Some bought expensive gifts, and others gave small tokens such as cakes and fruits, along with good wishes for a happy New Year. Children in Russia still receive gifts from Grandfather Frost and the Snow Maiden at the New Year instead of at Christmas.

At the Lunar New Year, the Chinese give children red packets called *hong bao* (pronounced hong-pow), containing "lucky money." Adults may give one another "lucky" flowers, fruits or fruit trees, silk clothing, or jewelry.

On the morning of Nouruz, Iranian parents give their children coins, boiled eggs painted with beautiful designs and wrapped as gifts, and candy and sweet cakes. Adults give family and friends flow-

Keystone Cop Mummers clown their way past City Hall in Philadelphia, Pennsylvania, during the
New Year's Day Mummers Parade in 1997. This annual parade began about 1875.
Reproduced by permission of AP/Wide World Photos.

ers, special foods, and new pottery to help replace the old dishes that were broken before Nouruz began. Hindu children receive gifts and candy for Diwali.

During Rosh Hashanah, many Jewish congregations bring bags of food to the synagogue to be distributed to the poor. Jews also help the poor by giving them clothing and money and providing shelter for the homeless.

Visiting and reunions

Reuniting with family for the New Year is a custom in much of the world. Asians believe being together on New Year's Eve will bring good health and success to the family as a whole in the New Year. Visiting family and friends, neighbors, and business associates during the New Year is also considered important and is the way many people spend their days during New Year holidays. Visits often include forgiving old wrongs, settling old quarrels, and starting over fresh with relationships.

Parades and football games

Colorful parades are part of New Year celebrations in nearly every country. In the United States, the city of Pasadena, California, has held its Tournament of Roses Parade each New Year's Day since 1886. Similar parades are held in other American cities, preceding college football games that are widely televised. The annual Philadelphia, Pennsylvania, Mummer's Parade, with King Momus leading clowns, dancers, and musicians, began about 1875.

Chinese New Year parades held in Asia and by large Chinese communities in North America are some of the longest, noisiest, and most colorful parades in the world. San Francisco's Chinatown has the world's largest dragon parade. The Golden Dragon, 160 feet long, is the grand finale of the four-hour parade. The Chinese New Year closes with the Lantern Festival, on the fifteenth day of the new lunar year, when huge parades and fireworks displays are held.

Edinburgh, Scotland, is famous for its long, torchlight processions held December 30, the night before Hogmanay. Some seven thousand marchers wind through the city streets carrying torches to light up the winter's night.

Clothing, Costumes

Buying new clothes, shoes, and jewelry for New Year's is a custom in many countries because people believe it is lucky to have new things to wear to start the new year. In China, New Year clothes are most often in the lucky color red; some people believe it is bad luck to walk on the "new" ground in old shoes. Hindu women buy new jewelry and clothing to wear to attract the goddess Lakshmi, who is said to bring prosperity.

Jewish husbands buy their wives new clothes and jewelry for Rosh Hashanah. In Iran, everyone has at least one new article of clothing to wear for Nouruz. Some Indians take a Diwali bath in perfumed oil, which is believed to be like taking a bath in the sacred Ganges River. First-footers in Scotland wear the traditional Scottish kilt, with all the accessories.

Foods, Recipes

Each culture has its own traditional New Year foods. These special foods are associated with good fortune, good health, and prosperity. The Chinese eat certain foods, such as lettuce or oranges, because their names sound like "lucky" words. Americans, especially in the southern states, believe that eating dishes made with black-eyed peas is a must.

Eating sweet foods is believed to bring sweetness in the New Year. This might explain why sweets are traditional foods and gifts for the New Year, especially pastries or candies made with dried fruits, nuts and seeds, honey, and yogurt. Apples dipped in honey are a traditional food for Rosh Hashanah.

In Mexico, Spain, and Portugal, people eat twelve grapes, raisins, or pomegranate seeds, one for each chime of the clock at midnight on New Year's Eve. Many people enjoy champagne, whiskey, or other alcoholic drinks at New Year's Eve parties, as they drink a toast to the new year at the stroke of midnight.

Arts, Crafts, Games

People all over the world have special ways of decorating their homes or setting their table for New Year's. The Chinese consider red the luckiest color for New Year's, based on the ancient legend about the monster Nian, who feared red. They hang strips of red paper around windows and doorways with good luck wishes and two-line poems called "spring couplets" imprinted on them. New Year prints are hung on the walls, with pictures of good luck symbols and happy scenes. Flower markets are busy selling "lucky" flowers and fruit trees to be used as decorations and gifts.

The millions of lanterns that adorn cities and towns during the Lantern Festival, on the last days of the Chinese New Year, are hung from doorways and storefronts. They can be simple or intricate, with moving parts and entire scenes. Lanterns are made from silk or paper, or even carved from ice.

Iranians set a table for Nouruz with a beautiful tablecloth, candles, mirror, the Koran (the sacred book of Islam), family photos, and trays of coins and other lucky items. Jewish families place candles on the table for Rosh Hashanah, and Hindu families decorate an altar to Lakshmi, the goddess of good fortune, with incense, flowers, and fruit. They also paint designs in colorful patterns on the floor or walkway to welcome visitors and the goddess Lakshmi.

New Year greeting cards are popular in many countries. In India, they may have a picture of Lakshmi or a Diwali lamp. Rosh Hashanah cards may be decorated with the Star of David or a biblical scene. Chinese New Year cards have pictures of lucky trees, flowers, or fruit.

Playing indoor and outdoor games and attending or watching sporting events are common ways to spend time during the New Year. Men in India love to gamble on Diwali, hoping for good luck and extra winnings. Americans watch college and professional football games on television. The Scots attend Highland games, which feature traditional Scottish shows of skill such as tossing the caber (a long, heavy pole). Iranians love to play chess and outdoor games for Thirteenth Day Out picnics.

Symbols

Each culture in every country has special symbols associated with New Year. Some symbols, however, are universally associated with sending off the old year and welcoming the new. These include an old man who represents the tired old year; the baby who stands for new beginnings; light in the form of the sun or fire, that shines through the darkness of winter and the past; fireworks that "scare" off the old and herald in the new; and clocks, the great indicators of time.

Special objects, gods, and goddesses

Every culture has special objects or personalities associated with the New Year. These may be gods or goddesses, such as the Kitchen God of the Chinese and the Hindu goddess of good fortune, Lakshmi. They may be objects such as the red money envelopes given to Chinese children, or the shofar blown for Rosh Hashanah. The Chinese dragon and lion, the colored eggs given as Nouruz gifts, and the mistletoe and green sprouts believed by Scots to ward off bad luck, are all examples of objects associated with the New Year.

The old man and the baby

A baby as a symbol of the new year appeared as early as the fifth century B.C. The ancient Greeks portrayed their god of wine, Dionysus, as an infant during their New Year rites. The ancient Egyptians also used the baby as a symbol of rebirth and renewal. The Romans portrayed the old god Saturn as the passing year and the youthful god Jupiter as the new.

Early southern Europeans worshiped an infant god of the vineyards. Beginning in the fourteenth century, the Germans used a drawing of a baby with a "New Year" banner wrapped around it as a symbol. They also portrayed the old year as an old man with a long white beard. In the 1700s, German immigrants introduced this custom to the American colonies.

Lights and fire

Ancient Egyptians worshiped a sun god and built great temples to honor him. The locations for these temples were carefully chosen to coincide with the position of the sun during the changing seasons. When the seasons began to change, the sun's rays would enter the temples' central shrine.

Fire was used in midwinter celebrations everywhere. The fires were thought to rejuvenate the "weakening" sun as it dropped lower in the sky and shone for fewer hours during the dark, winter days. Bonfires were also built to keep away evil spirits during this gloomy time. The Scots still consider fire an essential element of Hogmanay celebrations.

Torchlight processions, fireworks, bonfires, and laser shows are featured in many New Year celebrations. Indians light millions of Diwali lamps for the New Year, and Iranians jump over fire to bring good health. People of many cultures light candles on New Year's Eve. The Chinese conclude their New Year with the Lantern Festival, in which lanterns in thousands of shapes glow in every city and town.

Noise and fireworks

The Chinese have an ancient legend that an evil monster feared loud noises, lights, and the color red. Since that time, they have been frightening away evil spirits at the New Year with noise, explosion, and red objects. Red artificial fireworks are among the most popular New Year decorations. Real fireworks are often exploded at the feet of dragon and lion dancers who march to the sound of drums and gongs in New Year parades.

Shooting fireworks begins after midnight on New Year's Eve in countries throughout the world. Cities often hold big public fireworks displays. People also fire cannons, bang gongs, ring bells, shoot guns, and blow noisemakers. The sounding

Ayamaran Indians raise their hands to receive blessings from "Father Sun" as they celebrate the Ayamara New Year in Tiawanacu, Bolivia, in June 1998, marking the start of the year 5506 in their culture. Reproduced by permission of AP/Wide World Photos.

of the shofar at the Jewish New Year is haunting and is sometimes said to confuse Satan as he accuses the people of wrongdoing. Hindu families clap their hands and shout to drive out the goddess of bad luck on the eve of Diwali.

Clocks and other indicators of time

The clock striking twelve midnight to usher out the old year and bring in the new is one of the most familiar New Year symbols. In Scotland and other parts of Great Britain, church bells were muffled until midnight on New Year's Eve to ring out the old year. Then the bells were released to ring in the new. Today, many cities in Scotland start fireworks displays after the tolling of the church bells at midnight on Hogmanay.

In the United States, thousands gather at Times Square in New York City to watch a lighted ball drop from a tall building as the clock strikes midnight. This has been a New Year tradition for nearly one hundred years.

In Iran, people watch a leaf floating in a bowl of water or an egg placed on a

Vietnamese women pray in Dinh Bang village during a spring New Year celebration in February 1999. To celebrate the changes of seasons in ancient times, people performed ritual dances wearing masks and primitive costumes to represent spirits believed to wander the earth. Reproduced by permission of AP/Wide World Photos.

mirror for signs that the spring equinox has arrived. The Chinese and the Hindus wait for the new moon of their first calendar month to signal the beginning of the New Year. Rosh Hashanah begins at sunset on the first day of the Jewish calendar. All of these events are celebrated at the moment they occur, making them the high point of New Year holidays.

Music, Dance

To celebrate the changes of seasons in ancient times, people performed ritual dances wearing masks and primitive costumes to represent spirits believed to wander the earth. People also danced to worship the sun, moon, and animals of the hunt. These dances may have evolved into modern-day mumming (dressing in costume), as well as Chinese lion dancing and dragon processions.

Lion dancers perform inside a large, colorful lion costume, with flashing eyes and twitching tail, all controlled by the dancers. Martial arts students in a dragon procession carry the "dragon," which may reach up to 160 feet. They whirl and twist along the streets to make the dragon seem to come alive.

Chinese stilt dancers, Iranian music and dance processions led by the black-faced character "Haji Firouz," and traditional Scottish folk dancing at parties, or ceilidhs, are all a part of New Year celebrations.

"Auld Lang Syne" by Scottish national poet and songwriter, Robert Burns (1759–1796), is one of the world's most popular New Year's Eve songs. People sing it after the stroke of midnight, often joining hands or linking arms as they remember past years and old friends and look forward to the future. Rosh Hashanah services in the synagogues include beautiful hymns that are hundreds of years old.

Special Role of Children, Young Adults

New Year's is the most festive time of year in China, Iran, and India. Children love to receive gifts and candy, go to fairs and amusement parks, and visit friends and relatives. Grandparents often give money to children, and children show their respect by visiting and giving gifts in return.

Many Chinese children dress in costumes for Lunar New Year and Lantern Festival parades. Martial arts students participate in lion dances. Iranian children go on outings with their parents and participate in a form of trick-or-treating on Fire Wednesday. Jewish children often attend synagogue services with their parents, and Scottish children dance at the ceilidhs and help welcome their family's first-footer on Hogmanay.

China

Name of Holiday: Lunar New Year; Chinese New Year

Introduction

The Lunar New Year, or Chinese New Year, is the oldest, longest, most festive, and most important holiday of the year for the Chinese and for many other Asians. It has traditionally been a fifteen-day festival signaling the end of winter and the coming of spring. It is a time to make a fresh start in living, reunite with family, and pay respects to ancestors. It is also a time to seek the blessings of the gods for the new year while driving out evil spirits and bad luck that might be lingering from the old.

The Lunar New Year is a movable holiday marking the first day of the first month on the Chinese lunar calendar. It begins at sunset on the day of the second new moon following the winter solstice, between late January and the end of February. It ends with the Lantern Festival on the fifteenth day of the same month.

History

The Lunar New Year has been celebrated in China for some five thousand years. Its origin is uncertain, but historians say it probably began as a celebration of the new growing season, during which farmers performed rites to bring rain and a successful harvest.

Many of the customs of the Lunar New Year were recorded as early as 500 B.C., and were widely written about during the

Han (pronounced HAHN) dynasty (206 B.C. to A.D. 220). The main festival was the La, or People's New Year, a religious festival that occurred shortly after the winter solstice, between January 16 and 27. On the eve of the La, an ornate ceremony called the Exorcism, or No, was performed to drive out demons, evil, and the spirits of disease from the emperor's palace.

At one point, the ritual performed at the emperor's palace involved more than one hundred boys, ten to twelve years old, who wore red headbands and black tunics. They beat on drums to drive away evil spirits. Other people wore good-luck charms and carried brooms to sweep away evil.

As time went on and the La and No and other festivals grew more entwined, the Lunar New Year evolved into a time for making a fresh start in all matters of living. In preparation for the New Year, people took pots of boiled wheat and milk to Buddhist temples to be distributed to the poor. Every house was cleaned and repainted, and the people drove out demons and bad spirits with loud noises, torches, and the color red, a traditionally lucky color.

The New Year celebration soon became so important that people saved money all year to buy good luck items. Preparation for the New Year lasted the entire month before the holiday, a time known as the Little New Year. In the early 1900s, the New Year celebration lasted fifteen days, from the new moon of the first month until the full moon, when the Lantern Festival began.

When the People's Republic of China was established in 1949, Communist leaders disapproved of what they considered the superstitions, as well as the spending, associated with the New Year celebration. Although the early Communist government permitted the major festivals, the celebrations became quieter and were carried out mostly in the homes. Public New Year celebrations included political gatherings, sporting events, and political dramas.

By the 1980s, some cities in China had revived old New Year traditions of fireworks displays and parades with dragons, lions, clowns, and big lantern displays. Today, many villages and cities throughout China celebrate the old festival, although much of the celebration still goes on in homes rather than in the streets. The "exorcism" ritual survives in the symbolic spring housecleaning in preparation for the New Year.

Folklore, Legends, Stories

On New Year's Eve, families gather to tell Chinese folktales about happiness, prosperity, and good fortune. Such tales help families create an atmosphere that will attract good luck in the New Year. They also enjoy retelling legends that are centuries old.

Legends of the Kitchen God

The Kitchen God, also called the God of the Hearth or the Prince of the Oven, is one of the oldest and most revered of the Chinese gods. He plays an important role in the Chinese New Year celebration in many homes. A few days before the New Year, he is said to return to heaven to report to the Jade Emperor, the most powerful of the gods.

After living in the family's kitchen all year long, the Kitchen God has much to tell about the family, both good and bad.

A main street in the famed Chinatown in Yokohama, Japan, is decorated with colorful flags as the town awaits the Chinese New Year in February 1997. Reproduced by permission of AP/Wide World Photos.

Therefore, the family gives him a big send-off and seals his lips with honey so that he can say only sweet things—or better yet, nothing at all.

In ancient times, the Kitchen God was depicted as a frog on the hearth. Today he is often represented in the home in a colorful picture, with his wife by his side, and perhaps shown with a dog and a rooster. He can also be in the form of a statue or simply a piece of red paper with the Chinese characters for "Kitchen God" written on it.

According to one legend, the Kitchen God was once a man who left his wife for a younger woman. His new wife was careless with money, however, and soon left him; now he was poor and had to beg for food. One day he came to a widow's house, and the kind woman fed him. After he had eaten, he recognized the widow as being his first wife. He felt so guilty for leaving her that he jumped into the oven and burned to death. The gods gave him the honor of being the Kitchen God because he had realized his mistake.

Scaring Nian

An ancient legend tells of a fierce monster called Nian (Year) that terrorized

A Thai woman frees a bird from a cage while praying for good luck during the Chinese New Year celebrations at Hoa Lampong Temple in Bangkok in January 1998. On New Year's Eve, families gather to tell folktales about happiness, prosperity, and good fortune. Reproduced by permission of AP/Wide World Photos.

villages. A god told the people that the monster was afraid of only three things: the color red, loud noises, and bright lights. So the people dressed in red, carried torches, and shouted and banged drums to drive Nian from their land. Since some of its earliest celebrations, the Lunar New Year has been partly devoted to driving out evil spirits or bad luck, and making way for benevolent spirits or good luck.

Lucky words

In the Chinese language, many words have the same pronunciation but different meanings. These "homonyms," along with words that rhyme, create the symbolism of the Chinese New Year celebration. Certain characters, foods, flowers, and colors are said to bring good luck because they sound like or rhyme with other words or phrases meaning good fortune, prosperity, wealth, good health, or happiness.

For example, people eat fish on New Year's Eve, because the word for "fish" is *yu*, which is pronounced the same as the word for "abundance." Oranges are also

Animals and the New Year: The Chinese Zodiac

The Chinese zodiac is based on a twelve-year cycle, with each year named after one of twelve animals. For example, 1984 was the Year of the Rat, and 1999 the Year of the Rabbit. When the cycle is complete, it begins anew, with animals representing each year in the same order. The twelve animals are the rat, ox, tiger, rabbit, dragon, snake, horse, ram (or sheep), monkey, rooster, dog, and pig (or boar). The zodiac animal for the year is a big feature in New Year's parades.

A person's zodiac sign is the animal representing the year in which he or she was born. A person is said to have the traits of that animal. Someone born in the year of the ox is said to be strong, patient, and determined; a person born under the sign of the dragon is energetic, fun, and outgo-ing. Each year is also said to be lucky for business ventures and world events based on the characteristics of its zodiac animal.

In very ancient Chinese civilization, months and days were named for wild animals such as the crocodile, deer, anteater, ape, otter, boa constrictor, leopard, and lizard. Buddhist monks who lived as many as two thousand years ago are said to have developed the Chinese zodiac.

One legend says that the Buddha (c. 563–c. 483 B.C.), the founder of Buddhism, called all the animals to come to him. The twelve animals of the zodiac are the only ones that responded to his call. He rewarded each by naming a year after the animal. The order an animal appears in the cycle indicates the order the animal appeared to the Buddha.

considered very lucky as New Year decorations and gifts, because the word for "orange"—*gam*—is pronounced the same as the word for "gold."

New Year superstitions

Many Chinese take certain New Year "superstitions" very seriously, in hopes that their careful observance will bring good luck and prosperity in the coming year. On New Year's Day it is considered bad luck to use scissors, knives, or needles because they might "cut" the good luck that is said to come with the New Year.

Washing hair on New Year's Day is said to "drown" luck. Many people do not sweep or discard trash for the first three days of the New Year so as not to sweep or throw out good luck. It is also considered bad luck to punish children, because if they cry on New Year's Day, they will cry all year. People say only kind words to one another to set the tone for a pleasant year.

Customs, Traditions, Ceremonies

A big Lunar New Year celebration requires a lot of preparation, and the Chinese believe they can attract prosperity by spending money on decorations, special foods, and gifts. Therefore, the last lunar month of the year is marked by a flurry of shopping, just like the months before Christmas in Western countries. A spotless, thoroughly swept, freshly painted home is also said to invite good luck. Many people use a special New Year calendar to tell them which days are luckiest to carry out each chore.

The Lunar New Year is also a time for paying old debts, so that debt is not carried over into the New Year. Debtors who could not pay once had to hide in temples or leave town to avoid being found by creditors. People also make amends to anyone they have argued with during the old year in order to start the new year without conflict.

Chinese family members who live away from home often spend part of the last lunar month traveling home for the New Year. Family togetherness on New Year's Eve is said to ensure a successful and happy year for the family as a whole. As a result, many airports, train stations, and highways are jammed during the last month of the year.

The color red

Red is considered the luckiest color for the New Year. It is believed to drive out evil and bring joy and good luck. Black is considered very bad luck at New Year's. Long red strips of paper are hung from both sides of the front door, with good luck wishes painted on them. Smaller strips of red paper are hung over the doorway and around windows, each containing a "spring couplet," a two-line rhyme written in Chinese calligraphy. This thousand-year-old custom was once used as a way for families to express their education and wit.

Red candles and flowers are also used to decorate for the New Year, as are strings of red artificial firecrackers, since real ones are banned in most cities today.

Lucky flowers and the money tree

People decorate with peach and plum blossoms, chrysanthemums, daffodils, and fruits for the Chinese New Year. Huge flower markets are busy throughout the season as people buy flowers with names that sound like lucky words. The pink "pineapple flower" is very popular because its name rhymes with the phrase meaning "the flower that brings fortune." Other popular flowers are the peony, a symbol of spring and wealth, and the orchid.

Pine and cypress boughs are placed in a vase and decorated with coins, paper flowers, fruit, and lucky symbols to make a "money tree," symbolizing prosperity.

Greeting cards

New Year greeting cards feature pictures of good luck symbols like dragons, deer, bats, pomegranates, and peaches. Banners hung on front doors sometimes show "the Three Stars," three smiling old men named Fu (Happiness), Lu (Success), and Shou (Long Life). Home altars displaying the family ancestry scrolls are decorated with oranges for wealth, tangerines for good fortune, and apples for peace.

The Kitchen God reports to heaven

The Kitchen God, the most honored of the household gods, has watched the family's activities from his niche above the stove all year long. Just before New Year, on the twenty-fourth day of the twelfth month,

Chinese burn incense in an urn at Beijing's White Cloud Temple on Chinese New Year's Day in 1999. Burning incense is believed to bring good luck. Reproduced by permission of AP/Wide World Photos.

he is sent back to heaven to make his report to the Jade Emperor. The family performs a special ceremony that is an old New Year season tradition, still widely observed.

First, they offer the Kitchen God cakes, fruits, and sweet rice dishes to sweeten his tongue. Then they smear his lips with honey, in hopes that he will say only good things or be unable to speak at all. Then his picture, statue, or the paper representing him is taken down and placed on a miniature chair that family members have made from bamboo stalks and paper. A paper horse is placed at his side to carry him up to heaven. These are taken to the backyard and set on fire, because all things of the spirit are said to travel as smoke.

As the fire burns, straw for the horse and tea for the Kitchen God are thrown in to make the journey more pleasant. Children throw dried beans onto the roof to represent the clatter of the horse's hooves as the Kitchen God rises up to heaven. They shoot off fireworks at the end of the ceremony to frighten away any evil spirits that might detain the god.

The Kitchen God is said to return from heaven one week later, on New Year's Eve. A new statue or picture of him is placed in the kitchen. He and the other household gods are honored with special teas, fruits, cakes, and wine.

New Year's Eve rites

Traditionally, the eve of the Lunar New Year has been a time for making offerings to the gods and seeking their blessings for the coming year. It is also a time for greeting the spirits of the ancestors, which are said to return to be with the family. Because the gods and the ancestors are believed to visit each home on New Year's Eve, everyone dresses their best and the house is in perfect order.

Food, wine, tea, and incense for the ancestors are placed on the family altar. After the offering, the family shares a New Year's Eve dinner, and the home takes on the atmosphere of Christmas Eve in Western countries. After dinner, the head of the house seals the doors with strips of red paper to keep in luck. Visitors stop coming, and the family settles in for the evening. Children play games and everyone sings, tells stories, and shares New Year's wishes, or resolutions. Throughout the evening, family members are careful to use only "lucky" words so they invite only good luck.

In earlier times, children formally bowed to their parents at midnight on New Year's Eve, touching their foreheads to the ground and reciting wishes for a good New Year. Today, greetings are much less formal, but children try to stay awake as long as they can, believing that if they do, it will bring longer life to their parents.

In areas where fireworks are still allowed, the paper seals on the door are broken at midnight and everyone goes out into the streets to shoot firecrackers. The noise and lights go on until just before dawn and then start up again a few hours later, on New Year's Day. Where firecrackers are banned, the head of the house breaks the seals before dawn on New Year's Day, and the family gets up and gets ready for the biggest day of the year.

New Year's Day and customs of the season

The first two days of the Lunar New Year are considered family days, with visiting and feasting at home. When they do go out, people exchange the New Year greeting "Happiness and fortune to you."

People visit temples to honor the gods and attend temple fairs. In Beijing, China, the site of the ancient Temple of the Earth—now Ditan Park—attracts a million people every year to its fair. Children and adults love the magicians, jugglers, comedians, fashion shows, and bird-singing contests, as well as shopping and sampling the many traditional foods.

New Year's Day is considered an especially lucky time for having one's fortune told. Large cities often hold spectacular fireworks displays. Some cities hold big parades on New Year's Day, and others wait until the third day of the New Year, when more people will be out and about.

On the fourth day of the New Year, many people hold open houses and welcome anyone who wants to visit. The God of Wealth is worshiped on the fifth day by hanging a live fish over an offering of food for the god. The fish is then released, as a symbol of long life and plenty.

The seventh day of the Lunar New Year is said to be "Everybody's Birthday." This is also called the "Day of Man." Every-

A Buddhist monk beats a drum during a New Year ceremony at the Lama Temple in Beijing, China, in 1999. In some cultures, beating on drums is thought to drive away evil spirits. Reproduced by permission of AP/Wide World Photos.

one, even newborn babies, turns one year older on this day. Today, many people also observe their birthday on the day they were born. It is considered lucky to eat raw fish and lettuce on Everybody's Birthday, because their names in Chinese sound the same as "fresh life" and "grow."

Good luck gifts

The Lunar New Year is a time for giving gifts, especially money. Children receive red packets with characters meaning "good luck" printed on them. The red packets contain money, always in an even number, because odd numbers are considered unlucky. Children thank those who give them packets, but it is bad manners to open an envelope in front of the giver.

Adults typically give one another "lucky" gifts such as flowers; kumquat, orange, or tangerine trees or their fruit; and a citrus fruit shaped like an old man's fingers, called "Buddha hand." They also give silk clothing and jewelry.

Lions dance and dragons roar

The Lunar New Year is probably most famous for its noisy and colorful parades. Hong Kong's parade lasts two hours and includes dragon processions, lion dancers, live performers, floats, marching bands, and film and recording stars. Stilt dancers in magnificent costumes and the Chinese zodiac animal for the year are big features. Children often dress in scary costumes to frighten away demons.

In the dragon procession, some fifty martial arts students carry a huge, brightly colored dragon made of paper and silk stretched over a bamboo frame. The students twist, twirl, and jump to make the dragon seem to come alive as it glides through the street. Lights flash from its eyes, its long red tongue rolls out, and its ears twitch. As a symbol of the coming spring and as the ruler of water and rain, the dragon follows a big yellow ball representing the sun or a white ball called the Pearl of Fire. Two dragons sometimes play with—or fight over—the ball.

The dragon can be up to 160 feet long and is traditionally depicted with a camel's head, a deer's horns, a snakelike neck, the claws of a hawk, and the scales of a fish. Silver horns, gold and blue eyes, feathers, glitter, and sequins create more fantasy.

Drums beat and cymbals clash as the dragon moves down the street, driving away evil and bad luck. In some areas, parade-goers still practice the old custom of throwing firecrackers at the dragon's feet. This practice was once so common that dragons caught fire and burned before the end of the parade, no matter how careful the dancers were to avoid them.

The Lion Dance is also a very old Chinese New Year ritual. Lion Dancers are featured in New Year's parades, usually on the third day of the celebration and also during the Lantern Festival, when the parades are so colorful they resemble Carnival celebrations in other countries. The Lion Dance is a two-person dance, with one dancer carrying the head of the costume and the other the body.

As in the dragon procession, the dancers are martial arts students who perform physical stunts to make the lion seem alive. For example, the front dancer jumps onto his partner's shoulders to make the lion seem to stand on its hind legs and look more fierce. The lion has a large, colorful head, flashing eyes, and moving ears and mouth, all controlled by the dancers from inside the costume. Drums and cymbals accompany the lion dancers. Children as well as adults can perform the dance; one-person lion dances are called Lion Cub dances.

As the dancers move down the street, people dangle heads of lettuce with red packets of money inside from balconies and storefronts. The lions get to keep all the money they retrieve, and the cash is used to help support the martial arts school. Because the lions are said to drive out evil and bring extra good luck, the dancers are invited to perform in many places during the New Year. Red money envelopes are always given as "food" for the hungry lions.

Lanterns to rival the moon

The Lunar New Year closes with the Lantern Festival. It begins on the fifteenth day of the new lunar year, the night of the first full moon. According to a legend about the origin of the Lantern Festival, a palace maid named Yuan Xiao missed her family so much that she convinced a fellow servant to tell the emperor that the God of Fire

Children performing the dragon dance in Dalian, China. The dancers are often martial arts students who twist, twirl, and jump to make the dragon seem to come alive. Reproduced by permission of Susan D. Rock.

had threatened to burn the city. By lighting lanterns all over the city, perhaps the god could be tricked into thinking the city was already on fire and leave it in peace.

On the night the lanterns were lit to trick the god, Yuan Xiao made delicious dumplings, and the emperor agreed to let her go out and offer them to the god. While she was away from the palace, she spent a precious evening with her family. The festival became an annual custom, and each year Yuan Xiao spent the evening at her home. The Lantern Festival and the dumplings that are so popular during the festival are both also known as Yuan Xiao, named for the palace maid.

The millions of lanterns that light up the three nights of the Lantern Festival are hung from doorways and storefronts. They can be simple or intricate, with moving parts such as running horses powered by air currents, or carved from ice, as in northern China.

Lanterns are made from silk or paper, decorated with beads and sequins, shaped like the animal of the year or like beautiful houses, cars, birds, insects, lucky bats, or famous people. They can even depict a whole scene. The lanterns are said to guide the spirits of the ancestors back to the world of the dead after their New Year's visit with family members.

Everyone turns out to view the lanterns by the light of the full moon; this is one of the most romantic nights of the year for young lovers. During the day, huge parades and fireworks displays are held. Children dress in costumes and perform skits in the streets. Lion dances are even more colorful and exciting than in the New Year's parades. Processions of jugglers, stilt dancers, acrobats, and people in costume make the Lantern Festival like Carnival.

Chinese New Year celebrations in the West

Chinese immigrants to the Western world settled in certain sections of cities including New York; San Francisco; Los Angeles; San Diego, California; Chicago; London; and Vancouver, Canada. These sections have come to be called "Chinatowns." They are filled with shops selling Chinese specialties, foods, gifts, clothing, and other goods that cannot be found elsewhere in the city. Chinese New Year celebrations in these communities are some of the largest and most colorful in the world. Celebrations last the full two weeks, followed by the Lantern Festival.

San Francisco's Chinatown has the world's largest dragon parade, with five dragons, each manipulated by one hundred people. The Golden Dragon is the grand finale of the four-hour parade, at 160 feet long. Lion and stilt dancers, martial arts schools, marching bands, and other entertainers round out the parade, accompanied by the sound of firecrackers, cymbals, drums, and gongs. Shops and street vendors sell spring rolls and rice, with fruit and litchi nuts for dessert.

Clothing, Costumes

Everyone gets new clothing for the New Year or wears their best clothes on New Year's Day. This custom probably originated with the imperial courts nearly two thousand years ago, when officials wore colored robes to welcome each new season. New clothes also served to disguise the wearer from evil spirits. Every family tries to buy new shoes for the New Year, because it is considered unlucky to walk in old shoes.

Because red symbolizes prosperity, joy, and good luck, it is the most popular color for new clothes in the New Year. Women often wear white dresses and pearls to honor the full moon during the Lantern Festival.

In addition to the exotic lion and dragon costumes worn by dancers, children wear costumes to frighten away evil during parades and festivities.

Foods, Recipes

Special foods with names that sound like "good luck" words are traditional at the Lunar New Year. Oranges, tangerines, and kumquats are especially popular. The name for orange is pronounced the same as the words for "gold" and "sweetness." Oranges are served sliced to look like gold coins. The word for tangerine sounds like "lucky," and *gam kat*, Chinese for "kumquat," sounds the same as the words for "golden luck."

Because "lettuce" sounds like "prosperity," red envelopes containing money are hidden inside some of the lettuce heads that hang from store awnings during the New Year's Day parade.

Fish dishes are traditional for the New Year, especially raw fish. An expensive dish called *yu sheng* (long life and abundance) is prepared by slicing raw fish and

Chiao-Tzu (Chinese New Year Dumplings)

Ingredients

1 package (4 dozen) wonton wrappers

1 pound lean ground pork

2 cups finely chopped Chinese cabbage

1 tablespoon grated fresh ginger

¼ cup plus 1 tablespoon soy sauce

½ teaspoon each, salt and pepper

¼ cup rice wine vinegar

2 to 3 drops of sesame oil

Directions

1. Mix together pork, Chinese cabbage, ginger, soy sauce, salt, and pepper.

2. Put 1 teaspoon of filling in the center of each wrapper.

3. Brush water around the edge of the wrapper with your finger, then fold the wrapper in half, pinching edges to make a rippled curve.

4. Place dumplings on a flat surface and cover with a dry towel until all are assembled.

5. Boil 3 quarts of water in a large pot, and gently drop in 6 dumplings. Boil for 15 minutes, turning each dumpling gently with a large spoon after the first 7 minutes.

6. Remove dumplings with a slotted spoon, draining off water; keep them warm until all dumplings are cooked.

7. Serve with a dipping sauce made by combining ¼ cup each of rice wine vinegar and soy sauce with a few drops of sesame oil.

mixing it into a pickled salad made with vegetables, ground roasted peanuts, ginger, sesame seeds, oil and vinegar, soy sauce, and fried noodles. For "New Year greeting fish," a whole fish is fried and then simmered in a sauce. Part is eaten on New Year's Eve and the rest on New Year's Day, as a surplus carried over from the old year to the new.

Mussels in shells, oysters, shrimp, boiled or steamed chicken or pork, meatballs, dried fish, and sausages are other popular meats. Whole chickens are cooked in broth and offered to the ancestors before putting them on the table. In rural areas, some families still slaughter a pig for the New Year feast. Roasted baby birds on a stick and *baodu* (pronounced bow-DOO), a delicacy made from sheeps' stomachs, are traditional snacks served by street vendors at New Year's fairs.

Special cakes and cookies, as well as candied fruits, nuts, and seeds, are eaten for New Year desserts. A Cake of the New Year (*Nian Gao*) is made from rice flour and sugar and is a symbol of family unity and friendship. Almond cookies dotted with lucky red food coloring and rolled cookies called "love letters" are other popular desserts.

Soup of the Eighth Day

To expel evil and give thanks for the coming New Year, the Chinese prepare a special thick soup on the eighth day of the twelfth month. This soup is called the Soup of the Eighth Day, or *labazhou,* and is named for the ancient La festival. It is a porridge-like soup made from grains such as sticky rice, millet, barley, and corn, along with red beans and dried fruits, nuts, and seeds. A number of legends surround this hearty soup, including one that says it was the food of the Buddha as he sought enlightenment.

No knives or chipped plates

All food is prepared before New Year's Day, because using knives or other sharp instruments is believed to "cut" good luck. Food is served reheated or at room temperature. New dishes or ones in very good condition are used—broken or chipped dishes will bring ill fortune. An eight-sided tray is used to serve "lucky" snacks like candied ginger, plums, lotus root, and melon seeds to guests, because eight is a good-luck number.

Arts, Crafts, Games

The Lunar New Year is filled with arts and crafts, from spring couplets written in Chinese calligraphy to the extravagant dragons featured in parades, followed by ice-carved lanterns for the Lantern Festival. Paper and silk are used for many decorations and costumes. Lanterns can be almost any shape or size and are made from a wide variety of materials.

Music, Dance

Apart from the drums and gongs that accompany the New Year dragon processions and lion dancers, bands of musicians stroll through the streets in villages and towns during the Lunar New Year entertaining families, who give them red packets of money in return. Musicians and dancers also entertain in the cities, adding to the festive atmosphere. A Chinese folk dance and play called *yang ge* (rice-sprout songs) is popular during the Lantern Festival. These songs originated with farmers, who sang as they planted rice shoots in the fields.

One form of traditional Chinese New Year dancing is the "Dry Boat" performance, in which a boy and a girl pretend to be on a romantic outing in a rowboat. Wearing costumes, they walk about the stage with a "boat" covering their legs, so they seem to be rowing on water. The performance often includes a picnic and an afternoon of courtship, in which the boy plucks lotus flowers from the water's surface and hands them to the girl.

Special Role of Children, Young Adults

In anticipation of the New Year, children help clean house, decorate, and prepare food. They participate in sending the Kitchen God off to heaven and share in offerings made to the gods and the ancestors at family altars. On New Year's Eve, children do their best to stay awake so that their parents might have a long life.

Although most children no longer *kow tow* (kneel and bow with their foreheads touching the floor) to their parents on New Year's Eve, children are always expected to show respect for their parents and elders. Today, children often bring their parents a cup of tea on New Year's morning and give them gifts of a pair of Mandarin oranges, with a wish for long life, good health, and good luck.

Children who are learning the martial arts may participate in the Lion Dance in New Year's parades. Others dress up in scary costumes, doing their part to frighten away evil spirits. In areas where firecrackers are still allowed, children set them off throughout the season, beginning at midnight on New Year's Eve.

For More Information

Cheong, Colin. *China.* Milwaukee, Wis.: Gareth Stevens, 1997.

Stepanchuk, Carol. *Red Eggs and Dragon Boats: Celebrating Chinese Festivals.* Berkeley, Calif.: Pacific View Press, 1994.

Waters, Kate, and Madeline Slovenz-Low. *Lion Dancer: Ernie Wan's Chinese New Year.* New York: Scholastic, 1990.

Web sites
"Dancing with the Dragon." [Online] http://www.festivals.com/newyear (accessed on February 15, 2000).

"Lunar New Year's Traditions." [Online] http://www.insidechina.com/culture/festival/newyear/luntrad.php3 (accessed on February 15, 2000).

India

Name of Holiday: Diwali

Introduction

Diwali (pronounced dih-WAH-lee) is a major holiday of the Hindu religion. Hinduism (pronounced HIN-doo-IZ-uhm) is one of the oldest religions, with roots dating back to 3,000 B.C. Diwali is celebrated by approximately 600 million Hindus all over the world. In addition to India, Diwali is celebrated in countries that have large Hindu populations, including Myanmar, Malaysia, Sri Lanka, Singapore, Fiji, the United States, and Great Britain.

Depending on where it is celebrated, Diwali lasts from one to five days. Small oil lamps, candles, or electric lights are placed along rooftops, doorways, and windows. For this reason, it is called the Hindu Festival of Lights. Diwali is a movable holiday, falling at the time of the new moon in the Hindu lunar month of Kartika (pronounced kar-TEE-kuh), which usually occurs in October or November. In some parts of India, the new year is celebrated in mid-April, at the time of the spring planting.

History

The majority of the world's approximately 600 million Hindus live in India. The people who first settled India, about six thousand years ago, called their religion Sanatana Dharma, "the Eternal Religion." They worshiped a mother goddess and a horned god, as well as certain trees and animals. In about 1500 B.C., a northern people called the Aryans settled in India. They worshiped gods of natural forces, such as wind, thunder, sky, and sun. The two faiths came together and grew into the religion called Hinduism.

Hindus believe that all life is part of a universal creative force called Brahman and that human and animal souls are reborn into new bodies, or "reincarnated," many times before they return to Brahman.

They also believe that how a person acts in this life affects their next life. So, if a person behaves badly in this life, they will be punished in the next. This is called "karma."

It is uncertain when the first Diwali celebration was held, but scholars say it probably began very early in the development of Hinduism, about 3,500 years ago, and evolved into the festival it is today. The name *Diwali* comes from the Sanskrit (the ancient language of the Hindu religious books) word *deepavali,* which means "row of lights."

Hindus traditionally placed little oil lamps called *dipas* (pronounced DIH-puhs) on window ledges and rooftops and around courtyards as a way of purifying their house and garden and to keep away evil spirits. This was done on a night of the new moon, with winter approaching. It was the time of year for planting winter crops, and the people prayed to the gods for a good growing season that would bring a bountiful harvest in early spring.

Setting out lights on Diwali eventually came to symbolize lighting the way for the god Rama (pronounced RAH-muh), a hero in the epic poem the *Ramayana* (pronounced rah-muh-YAH-nuh), as he returned from exile after overcoming evil forces. The lights were also said to attract the goddess of good fortune and prosperity, Lakshmi (pronounced LUKSH-mee), to each home in hopes that she would bless the family and the village with good fortune in the coming year.

Today, Diwali is a joyful celebration of the victory of light, which represents good and knowledge, over darkness, which represents evil and ignorance. It is a time for new beginnings; many Hindus wait until Diwali to start a new business or open a school. Existing businesses close old account books, settle their debts, and open new books. Owners pray to Lakshmi for prosperity in the new year. People clean and repaint their houses and buy new clothes. With its bright lights, sweets, gifts, and greeting cards, Diwali is often compared with the Christian holiday of Christmas.

Folklore, Legends, Stories

Diwali is associated with one of India's two classic epic poems, the *Ramayana.* Families read this poem and other books on the evening of Diwali. It is also a time for telling some of the many Hindu folktales that have been passed down for hundreds of years.

The story of Rama

In the *Ramayana,* Lord Vishnu, one of the three primary gods of Hinduism, wishes to overcome the powerful but evil Ravana (pronounced ruh-VAH-nuh). To do this, he must take human form. He is born as Rama, the eldest of four sons of the king of Ayodhya.

As Rama is about to inherit the throne from his father, one of the king's three wives insists that *her* son become king instead and that Rama be sent into exile in the forest for fourteen years. Because the king had granted this wife two wishes, he must do as she asks. So Rama, his faithful brother Lakshman (pronounced LUKSH-mun), and Rama's bride, the beautiful Sita (pronounced SEE-tah), leave the kingdom and wander in the forest.

Far to the south, the evil Ravana hears of Sita's beauty and sends his demons to kidnap her. An old vulture sees the demons take

A Hindu religious leader tosses red flower petals in the air as he prays at the walled Aditya Jaya Temple in Jakarta, Indonesia, in celebration of Diwali in 1999. Reproduced by permission of AP/Wide World Photos.

Sita. As she is being carried away, Sita drops her jewelry from the sky, and it lands in the hands of the clever flying monkey Hanuman (pronounced HAH-noo-muhn).

Rama and Lakshman return to find Sita missing, and the old vulture tells them that she has been kidnaped. They set out to find her, and they soon meet Hanuman, who shows them the jewels Sita dropped from the sky. After sending out search parties of animal helpers, Rama learns that Sita has been taken to Ravana's kingdom on the island of Lanka. Hanuman magically leaps across the ocean to Ravana's kingdom and sees Sita sitting in a grove.

Rama's army of animals attacks the city, but Ravana's demons fight back fiercely and the animals are injured. Hanuman flies to the Himalayas to bring back a mountainful of healing herbs. The animals regain their strength and the fight begins anew. Rama and Lakshman defeat Ravana's brother and his son. Then, with bows and arrows and whirling disks, they manage to kill Ravana and save Sita.

The fourteen years of exile are over, and Lord Vishnu has defeated Ravana as he set out to do in the incarnation as Rama. The people of the kingdom of Ayodhya light rows of candles in small clay pots to welcome Rama, Sita, and Lakshman home.

Lakshmi, the goddess of good fortune

Many Hindus light the lamps of Diwali to guide Lakshmi, the goddess of good fortune and prosperity, to their homes in hopes that she will bless the family with a prosperous new year. (Hindus believe that a wealthy person is being rewarded for good deeds in a past life.) Lakshmi is depicted as a beautiful woman wearing gold jewelry. She is usually seated on the petals of a lotus flower or on a richly adorned elephant or tiger.

Hindu paintings often show Lakshmi with water lilies in her hand or in the background. Worshipers put water lilies or flower garlands—which she is said to love—around her statue. Her picture is on Diwali greeting cards, and many Hindus have a statue of her on their home altar.

On Diwali, Lakshmi is said to walk to the city from her summer home in the country, or to come down to villages on the plains each fall after a summer in the hills. She is sometimes said to fly on the back of a swan or to have been freed from captivity in the netherworld. Because it is night when Lakshmi comes, she needs lights to show her the way. So she blesses each household that places dipas to guide her and passes by any that do not.

An old Indian folktale, "Lakshmi and the Clever Washerwoman," tells of a poor washerwoman who finds the queen's pearl necklace. The only reward she asks is that her home be the only one in the kingdom allowed to light dipas on Diwali. Her wish is granted. Because Lakshmi blesses only those houses that display dipas to light her way, the washerwoman's house is the only one Lakshmi visits.

Lakshmi knocks at the door, tired and cold from stumbling in the darkness. The old woman agrees to let her in if she will promise to stay with her family for seven generations. Lakshmi promises to do so. Meanwhile, the washerwoman's longtime companion, Poverty, begs to be let out the back door. The washerwoman agrees to let him out if he will promise to stay away for seven generations. So, for seven generations the washerwoman and her family are freed from poverty and blessed with prosperity.

Customs, Traditions, Ceremonies

Because India's many cultural and religious groups have their own beliefs and practices, Diwali celebrations vary throughout the nation, although all feature thousands of little lights. Diwali is a happy, festive occasion of new beginnings. People wake up early and go to bed late so they can enjoy Diwali fireworks and the fantastic light display.

In northern India, many people worship Rama and Lakshmi. In some parts of India, Hindus worship the goddess Kali on Diwali; others remember an ancient king, Bali; still others remember a great hero, Mahavira. In Bengal, Hindus light lamps to guide the souls of the dead, who are believed to return, and a religious group called the Sikhs (pronounced SEEKS) celebrate the freeing of a great guru (religious teacher) by an Asian emperor.

In some parts of India, people pray to the elephant-headed god Ganesha (pronounced guh-NEH-shuh), the god of wis-

Celebrants douse each other with water and powder during a New Year festival in Bangkok, Thailand, in 1999. Many consider the first water of the New Year lucky, and some splash themselves and their loved ones for a happy and healthy year. Reproduced by permission of AP/Wide World Photos.

dom and good luck. In keeping with the "out with the old, in with the new" theme of Diwali, they put their old statue of the god out to sea or drop it into the river and buy a new one for their altar. Hindus in Western countries celebrate Diwali for only one day, whereas groups in India celebrate for up to five days.

Cleaning, painting, and making a new start

To prepare for Diwali, Hindus clean their homes thoroughly and apply fresh paint or whitewash. In villages, they may replaster mud walls. Hindus believe that Lakshmi looks into every home to see if it is clean. If it is not, she will not bring good fortune to the family.

Morning bath and new clothes

On the morning of the main Diwali celebration, every family member takes a ceremonial bath scented with perfumed oil and puts on new or freshly washed best clothes. Then they remove their shoes and pray, either at the family's altar at home or at a local temple.

Sisters often bathe their very young brothers or prepare their older brothers' bath, because Diwali, like other Hindu holidays, is a special occasion for brothers and sisters to show love and respect for one another.

Puja for Lakshmi

On the morning of Diwali, many families perform a prayer ceremony, or *puja* (pronounced POO-jah), in honor of Lakshmi. This is often done at home, before the family's altar and its own statue of the goddess. The altar has already been decorated with items like fruit, flower garlands, puffed rice, and silver coins as offerings to Lakshmi. In front of her statue, the family places a dipa filled with an oil called *ghee,* which is made by separating butter until the oil rises to the top and then pouring it off into a container. Ghee is also widely used in Indian cooking.

During the ceremony, the mother places a dipa or a lighted candle in the center of a large silver tray. Around the light she places objects that are associated with Lakshmi, such as more coins, puffed rice, fruits, cheeses, nuts, a pretty mirror, or a scroll that symbolizes the coming year. She turns the tray in circles before the altar, so that Lakshmi might "see" the items she is being offered. While she is presenting the offerings to the goddess, the mother prays for success and prosperity in the new year for her family. She then sings a sacred song to Lakshmi.

After this ritual, the father may read from one of the four most ancient Hindu holy books, the Vedas (pronounced VAY-duhs), and say a prayer. When the ceremo-

ny is completed, everyone hugs and wishes one another a happy new year.

The night that sets India aglow

Lighting the Diwali lamps is the most beautiful ceremony of the year. It is done throughout India, so that every city and town glows with millions of lights. Many Hindus still decorate their homes with the traditional dipas. They are made from clay, often by the children, and filled with a small amount of mustard oil or ghee. The mother and children twist small pieces of cotton into wicks for the dipa. A few inches of wick is placed in each lamp and covered with oil, except for the end to be lit. It takes dozens of dipas to line porches, rooftops, windowsills, and doorways.

Before the lighting ceremony, the lamps have all been set in place and filled with oil. Hindus believe that ceremonial prayers and lighting many lights on Diwali will bring them blessings during the coming year. The family leaves one dipa burning all night at Lakshmi's altar to welcome her to their home. Today, candles or strings of white or colored electric lights are often used, especially in India's cities. These lights are reminiscent of the Christmas lights used to decorate homes in many other countries.

In the dipa-lighting ceremony, held at sunset after evening prayers, a grandfather or other elder lights the first dipa, then other family members light the rest of the dipas from the first lamp. People sometimes place glasses of colored water in front of the lights to multiply their effect.

After the lights are all glowing, many parents give their children candy, gifts, money, and new clothes for Diwali.

Then the family goes outside to enjoy the millions of lights. They also may set off fireworks or watch a town fireworks display.

Many people visit the cities of Bombay or Amritsar on Diwali to see spectacular lighting displays. Thousands of lights line the steps of a reflecting pool at the Golden Temple, a magnificent Sikh shrine in Amritsar, where the lights are mirrored by the surface of the water.

In cities and towns located near a river, women and girls sometimes make little bamboo or wooden rafts and set dipas on each one to float them on the river. It is considered a sign of good luck if the dipa floats all the way across. Thousands of dipas can be seen floating on the Ganges River on Diwali.

Some villages build Diwali bonfires from scrap wood and branches that children have collected. Everyone comes dressed in new clothes to meet friends and neighbors around the bonfire.

Dancing monkeys and victory fireworks

During the day of Diwali, after the morning bath, a prayer ceremony, and a big breakfast, most communities hold a parade and a street fair, with street musicians and dancers, dancing monkeys, and other entertainers. A beautifully adorned statue of Lakshmi is carried through town in a procession.

Children are usually given a little money to buy firecrackers, toys, and candy at the fair. Cities and towns hold a big fireworks display on Diwali night. Hindus believe that fireworks can keep away evil, so the bigger and noisier they are, the better. Many fireworks have pictures of Lakshmi on them. Displays might include rockets that shoot up in the shape of flowers and rainbows, or fireworks arranged to tell a story about the victory of good over evil, such as the classic tale of the god Rama's defeat of the demon Ravana.

Blessing the tools and account books

Diwali is considered the new year for business and commerce in India. Everyone tries to pay off their debts and make a fresh start financially. Business owners close old account books and start new ones. They clean stores and offices, bring in fresh flowers, and put new merchandise on the shelves. Employers give their workers gifts of appreciation.

Businesses decorate with Diwali lights, and owners go to the temple to pray for a successful business year to come. New account books are blessed in a special ceremony in which the Sanskrit word *sri* (a title of honor) is written in a pattern on the books. The new books are placed as offerings before Lakshmi, and owners pray to the goddess for more customers and profits during the coming year.

All types of work are honored and blessed at Diwali, as are the tools and materials used to do the work. Carpenters, repairmen, and craftspeople polish their tools and lay them before Lakshmi to ask her blessing on them for the coming year. Artists and writers give thanks to their brushes, pens, pencils, and ink and seek Lakshmi's blessing for continued creativity. Farmers ask for blessings on their tools and animals as they plant winter wheat and rice at the beginning of the new growing season. Hindus everywhere give thanks for blessings of the previous year.

Brother and Sister Day

Diwali is also a time for sisters and brothers to give special attention to one another. This is done on one of the final days of Diwali. Married women come home for the ceremony, and girls and women of all ages honor their brothers by drawing a design around them on the floor. Each sister then performs a ritual that includes drawing a line on her brother's forehead with a red powder or a paste made from saffron and rice, tossing grains of rice onto his head, and praying for his safety, prosperity, and good health in the coming year. She then brings food to him on a silver tray.

In return, each brother places a gift on his sister's serving tray, such as jewelry, clothes, or money. If a woman's brother lives far away and cannot come home, she might perform the ceremony in his absence, and he might send her a gift. If there are only boys in the family, the mother invites a niece or the daughter of a friend to be her sons' "sister."

Driving out the goddess of ill fortune

The opposite of Lakshmi, the goddess of wealth and prosperity, is the goddess of ill fortune and poverty, Alaksmi. One of the last ceremonies to be performed on Diwali is driving out this bad-luck goddess. It is traditional for the oldest woman of the house to sweep the entire house, while other family members move from room to room, yelling and clapping their hands to drive out Alaksmi. Then, doors and windows are opened to let Lakshmi in to bless the house and family.

Clothing, Costumes

An important Diwali custom is to make or buy new clothes for each member of the family. If this is too expensive, each person wears his or her best outfit on the holiday. All clothes are washed as part of the thorough housecleaning done to prepare for Lakshmi's visit on Diwali.

Women may wear flowers and bangle bracelets, with a long, colorful skirt called a *ghagra* and a blouse. In southern India, children wear flower crowns and bells around their ankles on Diwali.

Many Indians today wear Western clothing, but the traditional dress for Hindu women is the sārī (pronounced SAH-ree), a long, flowing cloth wrapped around the waist, with one end draped over the right shoulder. A special sārī for Diwali might include extra decorations like embroidery, beads, or sequins.

Gold jewelry like that worn by the goddess Lakshmi is also very popular during Diwali. Pictures show her wearing gold wrist and ankle bracelets, large gold earrings, many gold rings, necklaces, a gold belt, and a gold headdress. Indians buy as much gold jewelry as they can afford for Diwali and offer it to Lakshmi during the prayer ceremony before putting it on.

Foods, Recipes

On the first day of Diwali, after prayers are said, families eat a special breakfast of as many as fourteen different foods. This is the main meal of the holiday. It is a family feast similar to Christmas or Thanksgiving dinner, but with all vegetarian foods, because most Hindus do not eat meat. They believe in the sacredness of all living creatures.

The food is served on large, round metal trays called *thālīs* (pronounced THAH-leez), which are often decorated with fresh flowers. Each dish is placed on the tray in a separate little bowl called a *katorī* (pronounced kuh-TOR-ee).

Some favorite Diwali foods are orange *dāhl* (cooked lentils), because orange is considered the color of prosperity; roasted eggplant mixed with tomatoes and spices; pickles and chutney; flat breads called *chapatis, paratha,* or *rotī*; rice; and puffed breads called *poori*. Curry dishes are also popular. They are made with a gravy and spices, including chili peppers, for a fiery hot taste.

Dishes made with yogurt are also eaten with the meal, and a multitude of sweets are served throughout the holiday. Most Hindu holiday feasts include "the five nectars of the gods"—honey, sugar, milk, yogurt, and ghee, a kind of butter.

A pyramid of sweets

A colorful array of sweets fills bakery windows during Diwali, sometimes stacked in pyramids up to fifteen feet high. Indian people love sweets and believe that they soothe the body and the soul. Each region of India has its specialties, but most are either dry and cut into squares or shaped into balls. Others are semi-liquid and soft, like puddings. Sweets and fruit baskets are given as gifts during Diwali.

A favorite Diwali treat is *khil,* or puffed rice. It is offered to Lakshmi on her altar, and children love to munch on it. Sugar candies in various shapes, coconut and spice-filled pastries, and candy made from boiled milk, grain, nuts, butter, and sugar are favorites. Cheese-filled pastries and cheese balls dipped in syrup are also popular.

Good Luck Lentils

Ingredients

2 tablespoons ghee or vegetable oil

2 cups orange lentils

4 cups water

1 can stewed tomatoes

1 large chopped onion

4 cloves garlic, chopped

1½ teaspoons ground cumin

1 teaspoon turmeric

1 large bell pepper, finely chopped

1 tablespoon sugar

salt and pepper to taste

Directions

1. Wash lentils in 2 or 3 changes of water.

2. Heat ghee or oil over medium heat in a large, heavy saucepan. Add onion, garlic, bell pepper, ground cumin, and turmeric, stirring and frying for about 3 minutes.

3. Add lentils, water, sugar, salt and pepper, and stewed tomatoes. Bring to a boil, then reduce heat and cook until lentils are soft, about 45 minutes.

4. Add more salt and pepper to taste, if necessary. Serve over rice as a main dish or alone as a side dish.

Making a Dipa

You can make a Diwali lamp, or *dipa,* with a piece of self-hardening clay. Begin by forming the clay into a ball about the size of a small orange. Then press the ball on a table to form a disk about 1½ inches high. Use your thumbs and forefingers to press a bowl into the center of the disk while shaping the edge to make a round lamp.

Using a pencil or chopstick, press a spout-like lip into one part of the lamp's rim. The lip should extend out about ½ inch so that the end of the wick can rest on the lip as it burns. Use regular candlewick from a craft store for the dipa wick. Coil about 4 inches of the wick in the bottom of the lamp, leaving one end resting on the lip of the dipa. This end will be lit. Pour vegetable oil into the lamp until the bottom portion of the wick is covered.

Arts, Crafts, Games

To prepare for Diwali, women and children make colorful patterns on the floor in front of household shrines or in front of the home to welcome both visitors and the goddess Lakshmi. These designs are called *rangoli* or *kolam.* The designs are drawn with water-based paint and colored rice flour and sometimes also say "Welcome" or "Happy New Year."

Throughout India, homes and shops are decorated with marigolds, hibis-cus, and other flowers for Diwali, because the goddess Lakshmi is said to love them. Some people also decorate home altars with paper symbols of prosperity, like cars, houses, and money, similar to offerings made to spirits of the dead during the Chinese Hungry Ghosts Festival and Ching Ming. In some areas, boys make fancy castles and forts out of mud, hoping to attract a bit of prosperity to their "kingdoms."

Painted clay or papier-mâché figurines and animals are offered for sale at stalls during Diwali street fairs; these attract children who are looking for something to buy with their holiday gift money. People may also have their hands painted with traditional Indian designs called *mehandi* during the fair.

Diwali greeting cards with colorful pictures of the goddess Lakshmi or god Ganesha are very popular today. Families send them to friends, neighbors, and business associates or customers.

Games

Because it is believed to be a time of good luck, playing games of chance involving dice is popular among Indian men on Diwali. The goddess Parvati is said to bless those who gamble on this day with prosperity throughout the year.

Music, Dance

Singing and folk dancing play a part in the celebration of Diwali, and special programs and plays feature music and dancing. When families worship Lakshmi, they sing songs to her, thanking her for blessings of the past year and for bringing them to a new year. Musicians and dancers perform in the cities on weekends before and after Diwali.

The most well-known Indian instruments are stringed instruments called the *sitar* (pronounced sih-TAR) and the *sarod* (pronounced suh-RODE) and a pair of drums called a *tabla* (pronounced TAH-bluh). Indian dancers wear rows of bells on their ankles and beautiful costumes. Men and women dancers reenact stories about Hindu heroes, gods, and goddesses.

Special Role of Children, Young Adults

Like Christmas in the West, Diwali is often considered a children's holiday. Parents and grandparents give children money or gifts. Children love the sweets they receive on Diwali, as well as the fireworks and the fairs, where they can buy toys and more candy. Children participate in the prayer ceremonies for Lakshmi and perform in plays about Rama, Krishna, Lakshmi, Ganesha, and other gods and goddesses during Diwali. They help make dipas and set them out along rooftops and porches. Older children help light the dipas.

For More Information

Jaffrey, Madhur. *Seasons of Splendor: Tales, Myths and Legends of India.* New York: Atheneum, 1985.

MacMillan, Dianne M. *Diwali: Hindu Festival of Lights.* Springfield, N.J.: Enslow, 1997.

McNair, Sylvia. *India: Enchantment of the World.* Chicago, Ill.: Children's Press, 1999.

Web sites

"Diwali." [Online] http://www.indiancultureonline. com/Festival/i_hindu.htm (accessed on February 16, 2000).

"Festival of Lights." [Online] http://www.diwalimela. com/festivaloflights/index.html (accessed on February 16, 2000).

Iran

Name of Holiday: Nouruz

Introduction

Nouruz (pronounced no-ROOZ), or "New Day," is Iran's oldest, longest, and best-loved festival. It is a time for measuring the old year's successes and failures, letting go of hard feelings toward others, and deciding how to be a better person in the coming year. Nouruz is called "a celebration of life," because it is such a joyous holiday. Schools and businesses close during the thirteen days of Nouruz, and families and friends spend most of the holiday together.

Nouruz is celebrated at the time of the vernal equinox (the first day of spring), which usually falls on March 21. On the Iranian solar calendar, this is the first day of the month of Farvardin and marks the beginning of the year.

History

According to historians, Nouruz has been celebrated in Iran, which was called Persia until 1935, for about three thousand years. The earliest celebrations heralded the sun's return in spring, which brought new life after a long, dark winter. In ancient times, light was said to represent the forces of good, and darkness was said to belong to the forces of evil.

It is believed that the spring equinox was celebrated in similar ways throughout the Middle East—in ancient Mesopotamia, Sumeria, Babylonia, and Persia. The first recorded Persian celebration, however, was during the time of King Cyrus the Great (585–529 B.C.).

Persian king Darius the Great (550–486 B.C.) built the magnificent estate called the Throne of Jamshid, known in the Western world by its Greek name, Persepolis, to stage his New Year celebrations. His subjects came to the beautiful palace from all over the Persian Empire, which took in neighboring lands and covered some two million square miles. Stone carvings at the ruins of Persepolis show King Darius receiving lambs and goats, grain, and other gifts from visitors who traveled from Egypt, India, and Ethiopia.

Historians say that people prayed and performed religious rituals in the morning, then feasted and celebrated with the king during the evening. Throughout Persian history, various rulers held magnificent Nouruz celebrations at their courts, keeping the ancient traditions alive.

Before the Islamic religion was introduced into Persia some 1,400 years ago, the dominant faith was Zoroastrianism (pronounced zore-uh-WAS-tree-uh-nih-zuhm), named for the religious leader Zoroaster (c. 628–551 B.C.). Islam is a religion founded by the prophet Muhammed (c. 570–632). The followers of Islam are called Muslims. Today in Iran, approximately 98 percent of the population are Muslim.

In Zoroastrianism, Nouruz was the last of seven annual festivals celebrating "the seven creations" of the world and the spirits associated with them. Nouruz was held in honor of Zoroastrianism's highest deity, Ahura Mazda. People believed their guardian angels came down to Earth at this time, and they welcomed them by lighting bonfires on rooftops and celebrating and feasting. The sixth day of Nouruz was celebrated as Zoroaster's birthday. This day was called Great Nouruz.

The Greek-Syrian conqueror Alexander the Great (356–323 B.C.) tried to ban the celebration of Nouruz, as did the Arab conquerors who introduced Islam to Persia during the seventh century A.D. The Persian people so loved this holiday, however, that they refused to give it up.

During the Middle Ages (about 500–1500), the holiday spread throughout the Muslim world, even as far as Spain. The week-long celebration featured acrobats and jugglers, bonfires, and games. People exchanged gifts, candy, and colored eggs. Colleges were closed, and if students saw a professor in town, they made him pay them a fine. An Iraqi ruler celebrating Nouruz once had five million silver coins made for the holiday. He then had them painted in bright colors. When his officials were gathered in the square, the ruler threw the five million colorful coins into the air for them to catch.

The Nouruz customs of ancient kings continued in Persia through the twentieth century, when the Iranian rulers known as "shahs" received diplomatic visitors who brought greetings and goodwill wishes when visiting Iran during Nouruz. Today, the celebration of Nouruz remains as important as ever, existing alongside Muslim religious holidays such as Ramadan and Id al-Fitr.

Folklore, Legends, Stories

An ancient Persian myth about the spring equinox says that a bull balances the Earth on one horn. On the first day of spring, he tosses his mighty head and the Earth shifts from one horn to the other. The New Year arrives at the moment the Earth is in the air, balanced, before landing on the other horn. This shift can supposedly be felt on the Earth and is used to determine the exact time of the spring equinox. Iranians mark this moment in their homes by placing a leaf in a bowl of water or an egg on a mirror. According to legend, when the egg rolls or the leaf turns in the water, the bull has tossed the Earth and the New Year has begun.

Nouruz beliefs and superstitions

As in Scotland and some Asian countries, the first water of the New Year was considered lucky in Persia. On the morning of Nouruz, everyone drew water from a stream or well and splashed themselves and their loved ones for a happy and healthy year.

Just as girls did on Halloween and at New Year celebrations in many lands, young Iranian women once practiced a kind of divination, or fortune-telling, to determine their future husband or the time when they would have a child. On the last Wednesday night of the year, they hid in a dark place and listened to the conversations of those passing by in the street. The young women would predict their fate for the coming year based on the words they overheard. This practice was called *falgoosh,* or "fortune hearing." Men also practiced falgoosh, usually for business purposes, but sometimes to determine their future spouse.

Nouruz Customs on Film

The 1996 movie *The White Balloon,* by Iranian filmmaker Jafar Panahi, tells the story of a seven-year-old Iranian girl whose mother gives her money to buy a special goldfish for the Nouruz celebration. Goldfish in a bowl of water are traditionally placed on the table during Nouruz. When the fish flips over, it signals the return of spring. The girl goes out into the city alone to buy her goldfish. As she tries to complete her mission, she meets people from many different cultures. The movie depicts the differences and similarities of people all over the world.

Iranians believe the "firsts" to enter their home at the turning of the New Year determine the kind of year the family will have. To ensure that Islam will play an important part in their lives, a family member often carries the Koran, the sacred book of Islam, outside the door and then steps right back in, so that Allah (God) will remain with the family in the New Year. Afterward, many people go to the mosque (pronounced MOSK; Muslim temple of worship) to pray; others pray at home.

As with the Scots on Hogmanay, Iranians believe the first person to cross the threshold on Nouruz will bring either good or bad luck to the home during the coming year. They often send a family member outside to knock on the door so they can be the first to enter. The first color to enter the house is said to determine the family's mood for the year, so no black clothing or objects are allowed—the sunnier the color, the better.

Customs, Traditions, Ceremonies

Preparations for Nouruz begin at least fifteen days before the holiday, when families start a dish of wheat, barley, or lentil sprouts in a container on the windowsill. This dish of sprouts is called the *sabzeh* (pronounced sob-ZEH), and it plays an important role in the Nouruz celebration. It represents the growth of new vegetation in the spring but also is said to absorb the family's ill luck from the past year. For this reason, it is thrown away on the last day of Nouruz. People avoid touching someone else's sabzeh, believing bad luck can be transferred from the sprouts through the fingertips.

Iranians thoroughly clean their houses before Nouruz, making needed repairs and often repainting for the New Year. They throw out all old pottery and buy new, if they can afford it. Everyone gets at least one new article of clothing for Nouruz. Businessmen give their employees gifts or bonuses, hoping to bring good luck to the business in the coming year. People who are in mourning mourn for only half the day. If they can, Iranians travel home to be with their families for Nouruz.

Fire Wednesday

Chahar Shambe Soori (pronounced chah-HARR sham-BEH soo-REE), or Fire Wednesday, is a Nouruz tradition that began with the ancient Zoroastrians, who lit fires to welcome the angels at the spring equinox. Many Iranians still perform the ancient custom of jumping over fires on the last Wednesday before Nouruz. This Fire Wednesday ceremony is believed to purify the person and the air and to bring good health in the coming year.

During the day, each family gathers enough wood and brush to build at least three small fires in their courtyard or in the neighborhood street. As darkness falls, they light the fires and every family member runs and jumps over each fire, chanting, "Your ruddiness [redness, a sign of good health] to me; my pallor [paleness or sickness] to you." Afterward, some Iranians observe the old tradition of throwing clay pots filled with water from the rooftops, shouting, "Pain and unhappiness!" as they symbolically throw these unwanted feelings away.

Fire Wednesday is also the night when some Iranian women and children go out for a kind of trick-or-treating. Wearing traditional veils and robes that conceal their identity, they go from door to door, banging a spoon against a metal bowl until the homeowner comes out and gives them a treat. Some say this custom began when women who had a sick family member went from door to door on Fire Wednesday collecting ingredients for a health-restoring soup.

Sharing with the poor to honor the spirits

Many Iranians believe that the spirits of deceased family members return during Nouruz to be with the living for a while. To gain the favor and protection of these spirits, families take money, food, new clothes, candy, and other gifts to cemeteries, where they give them to the living poor. In this way, they honor the dead and also help the living, so that everyone may enjoy Nouruz in an equal way.

Setting the Nouruz table

On the eve of Nouruz, a table spread with a beautiful Nouruz cloth is made ready for the holiday. The table is set with candles, one for each member of the family. Candles are also burned in each room of the house and are allowed to burn down on their own, for good luck. Also placed on the table are a mirror, a copy of the Koran, photographs of family members and other loved ones, a bowl of goldfish, brightly colored boiled eggs, and sometimes a plate containing new coins to be given as gifts.

A number of other items may also be placed on the table, but tradition calls for the addition of the *Haft Sin* (pronounced hoft-SEEN), or "Seven S's." These are seven items that begin with the letter *S* (*sin*) in the Persian language, called Farsi. They are said to represent God's seven archangels and the seven virtues of right living that the angels stand for. The letter *S* is also the first letter of the Farsi words for green (*sabz*) and white (*safid*), which are the colors of spring and purity.

The most common items used for the Seven S's are *samanu* (pronounced sah-muh-NOO), a candy made from flour, sugar, and walnuts; *sumac* (pronounced SHU-mahk), powdered leaves of the sumac shrub; *sabzeh* (pronounced sob-ZEH), green sprouts; *sonbol* (pronounced son-BOL), hyacinth flowers; *seer,* garlic; *senjed* (pronounced sen-JED), olives; and *serkeh* (pronounced ser-KEH), vinegar.

An Iranian boy living in Sydney, Australia, practices the ancient custom of jumping over fires on the last Wednesday before Nouruz, a ceremony believed to bring good health in the coming year, in 1995. Reproduced by permission of Corbis Corporation (Bellevue).

The New Year arrives

Iranians believe a small tremor or turning of the Earth can be felt at the moment the spring equinox arrives, bringing the New Year with it. The Earth is said to be in perfect equilibrium at this time, so that an egg can be balanced on its wide end for several minutes. To "see" the arrival of the New Year, Iranians try different experiments. An egg placed on a mirror is said to rotate at the moment the equinox comes, and a leaf floating in a bowl of water is said to turn.

A goldfish in a bowl will supposedly roll over when Nouruz arrives. Children, especially, watch anxiously for the moment, staying up late at night if necessary. In cities and towns, cannons or gongs sound when Nouruz arrives, and fireworks are set off, representing the victory of light over darkness and spring over winter. Families and friends hug and kiss, telling one another, "May you live for one hundred years." When they go out during the next thirteen days, they will wish everyone they meet, "Nouruz be prosperous!"

Giving gifts and renewing relationships

On the morning of Nouruz, parents give their children coins, boiled eggs painted with beautiful designs and wrapped as gifts, candy, and sweet cakes. Grandparents give their grandchildren money and other presents, called *eidi.* Adults visit family and friends throughout the holiday, taking them flowers, special foods, and new pottery to help replace the old dishes that were broken before Nouruz began.

Visits often include forgiving old wrongs, settling old quarrels, and starting over fresh with relationships. Families usually have some vacation time to spend together and may go to amusement parks, museums, or historical sites.

Thirteenth Day Out

Because the number thirteen is considered unlucky, Iranians have traditionally spent the last day of Nouruz away from home to keep evil from finding their house. This old superstition has evolved into a wonderful springtime custom called Sizdah-Bedar (pronounced seez-DAH-bee-DAR), or "Thirteenth Day Out." On this day, Iranians pack a big picnic lunch and go outside to a park or to the countryside for an all-day outing. There they spread a picnic blanket, share delicious traditional foods, play outdoor games, and visit with friends.

At the end of the day comes the custom of tossing away the *sabzeh,* or green sprouts grown for Nouruz. People walk to a stream or river and throw their sprouts into the running water, symbolically tossing out the bad luck, bad feelings, and poor health of the old year. If there is no water nearby, people just throw the sprouts as far as they can. Young women sometimes tie their bundles of sprouts together and make a wish as they throw it away: "Next year, in my husband's house, with a baby in arms!"

The largest Sizdah-Bedar celebration held outside of Iran is in Irvine, California, where thousands of members of the large Iranian American community gather at William R. Mason Regional Park for the final day of Nouruz.

Clothing, Costumes

For centuries, Persians have bought or made new clothes to wear for Nouruz. The head of the household often sacrificed other needs to buy every family member new clothes the week before the New Year. Buying new outfits for Nouruz is still a custom in modern-day Iran. People wear their brightly colored new clothes on the first day of Nouruz, especially to go visiting.

Traditional dress for Muslim women and girls when they go out in public is the *chador* (pronounced CHUH-duhr), a long veil that covers their head and their entire body, down to their feet. They wear long pants underneath it, and a head scarf called a *hejab* to cover their hair. The chador is most often black, but it can also be in color-

Iranian Rice Cakes

Ingredients

2 cups aromatic rice

2½ cups water

1 cup milk

1 teaspoon salt

2 tablespoons butter

Directions

1. Bring water and milk to a boil in a large saucepan. Stir in rice and salt.
2. Simmer over low heat, covered, for 20 minutes, then remove from heat and let stand for 10 more minutes.
3. Melt butter in a 10-inch skillet and add the cooked rice, pressing down with a spatula to form a flat cake the size of the skillet.
4. Cover and cook over low heat for 1 hour, flattening with the spatula every 15 minutes. The cake is done when it is golden brown on the bottom and the top edges are lightly browned.
5. Remove skillet from heat and let the cake cool until it is just warm to the touch.
6. Turn the skillet upside down over a platter, holding the top of the cake with your other hand. Let the cake slide out gently onto the platter.
7. The rice cake may be eaten warm or cold. Cut it into pie-shaped wedges to serve.

ful prints. Iranian women often wear Western-style clothing at home. Men and boys usually wear traditional baggy trousers with a short-sleeved shirt and wear a turban (head wrap) or the round, black hat typical of central Asian dress.

Foods, Recipes

Rice dishes and sweets, including candies and pastries, are served every day during the Nouruz holiday. A traditional Nouruz meal might include *sabzi polo,* a rice dish flavored with herbs and often served with fish or lamb. Chickpeas may be served as a side dish. Yogurt is included with many meals. Tea is Iran's national drink. Iranians like sweet tea without milk or lemon. They often put sugar cubes in their mouth and sip tea through them. Islam forbids the drinking of alcoholic drinks such as wine and beer.

Sweets served during Nouruz are rice cookies flavored with rose water; raisins and dates; fresh fruits such as apples, oranges, peaches, pomegranates, melons, and grapes; pastries made with nuts and dried fruits; nut mixes with lots of pistachio nuts; and candies made with ground nuts, seeds, and dried fruits sweetened with honey.

A favorite dish served for the Thirteenth Day Out picnic is *ash-e reshteh* (pronounced OSH-eh resh-TEH), a bean and

Grow Your Own Green Sprouts

When Iranians make their container of *sabzeh,* or green sprouts, for Nouruz, they sometimes simply scatter the seeds over a plate and keep them moistened with water as they sprout and grow. Or they may fill a porous clay pot or jar with water and attach the seeds to the outside of the jar with strips of cloth until they stick to the moist surface. Then the strips are removed, and the sprouts grow upward in sunlight, green and full.

You can make a sabzeh by filling a bowl or other container with potting mix from a plant nursery, and scattering lentils or grains of barley or wheat thickly across the surface of the potting mix. Water the mix until it is evenly moist throughout. Then cover the bowl loosely with plastic wrap to hold in the moisture and let it sit on a sunny windowsill. Be sure to sprinkle the seeds with water once or twice a day to keep them moist.

After two or three days, remove the plastic wrap. The seeds should begin to sprout after three or four days and will continue to grow taller each day. When they are a few inches tall, tie them into a bunch with a pretty ribbon, or snip them with scissors and put them in a salad.

noodle soup flavored with garlic, vinegar, and mint. Rice dishes served with sauces are also popular. At 5 P.M., the custom is to eat lettuce leaves dipped in a honey and vinegar dressing. Tea is taken along on the picnic in a copper urn called a *samovar,* which is used to serve tea at home.

Arts, Crafts, Games

The colored eggs that are traditionally given as gifts for Nouruz were once colored using natural plant dyes. The eggs were boiled with onion peel, walnut shells, or straw to make a yellow, brown, or green color. Today they may be colored with commercial dyes or painted by hand.

City streets are decorated with strings of colored lights during Nouruz, similar to Western Christmas decorations. Artists and craftspeople set up booths in the streets, selling jewelry, blankets, and other crafts. Iranian metalworkers make beautiful ornamental containers, and artists create colorful mosaics, tiles, and pottery using Islamic designs and calligraphy. Persian carpets are particularly sought after. They are known for their quality and beauty and are considered works of art.

Iranian artists are famous for their miniatures—paintings of tiny scenes on glass, animal hide, or paper; they were once painted on bone. Islam forbids portraying people or animals in artwork because they are said to distract individuals from concentrating on the Koran and worshiping Allah. But the people and animals in miniatures are so small that they cannot be considered lifelike, so they are accepted.

Music, Dance

About two weeks before Nouruz, a funny character dressed in baggy red trousers, with his face painted black, does a whirling dance through the city streets in

Iran. He has come to announce that the New Year will soon arrive. He sings a funny song and beats his drum, often leading a procession of dancers and musicians playing pipes, drums, and tambourines. The leader calls himself *Haji Firouz,* and he is a well-known symbol of Nouruz. As the musicians build excitement for the coming holiday, they pass a cap to collect coins from passersby.

On the Thirteenth Day Out, strolling folksingers and dancers, clowns, and actors performing short plays entertain the crowds gathered for picnics at the parks. Kettledrums and string instruments such as the *sitar* (pronounced sih-TAR), *santur,* and the *oud,* as well as wind instruments similar to the oboe are used in traditional Iranian music.

Special Role of Children, Young Adults

Nouruz is a happy time for children, who have a two-week vacation from school. They play games as their parents visit with adults, and sometimes perform plays or give concerts during the holiday. Their parents and grandparents give them gifts and money for the New Year, and they enjoy picnics, trips to amusement parks, or tours of interesting historical places typical of the Nouruz holiday.

For More Information

Fox, Mary Virginia. *Iran.* Chicago, Ill.: Children's Press, 1991.

Rajendra, Vijeya, and Gisela Kaplan. *Iran: Cultures of the World.* New York: Marshall Cavendish, 1995.

Web sites

"Nowrooz: A Celebration of Life." [Online] http://www.persianoutpost.com/htdocs/nowrooz.html (accessed on February 16, 2000).

"Persian Culture." [Online] http://persia.net/culture/noruz.htm (accessed on February 16, 2000).

Israel

Name of Holiday: Rosh Hashanah

Introduction

Rosh Hashanah (pronounced ROSH huh-SHAH-nuh; Beginning of the Year) signals the start of the Jewish New Year and is celebrated by Jewish people throughout the world. Unlike the secular, or nonreligious, New Year's Day, it is a solemn occasion that marks the beginning of the Ten Days of Penitence. These ten days, also known as the High Holy Days, are a time of prayer, fasting, and penitence in preparation for the most solemn day of the year, the Day of Atonement, or Yom Kippur (pronounced YOME kih-PUR).

During these ten days, Jews believe the Book of Life, which is the heavenly record of those who are good, remains open. People can be forgiven of their sins and have their names written in the book for the coming year. At the end of Yom Kippur, the book is closed and sealed.

Rosh Hashanah is a movable holiday celebrated according to the Jewish calendar, a lunar calendar that is more than five thousand years old. It is celebrated on the first two days of the seventh month, known as Tishri (pronounced TISH-ree), which falls in September or October.

History

The ancient Hebrews were farmers and herders who lived near present-day Israel. They celebrated the new year according to the harvest. They actually celebrated two new years: one at the new moon nearest the grain harvest in spring; the other at the new moon nearest the gathering of fruits in autumn. The first day of each new year was originally a day to also remember the dead, because the Hebrews believed that spirits of the dead rejoined the living for a short time.

A day for blowing the horn

Most of the rituals and customs of the Hebrew people are found in the Torah, the Old Testament books of the Bible. In the Torah books of Leviticus (23:23–25) and Numbers (29:1–6), God instructs the people of Israel how to celebrate the new year. They are told to rest, blow a horn, and make burnt offerings to God. The horn referred to is the *shofar* (pronounced sho-FAR), a ram's horn hollowed out to make a trumpet-like instrument. Its wild notes were used as a call to battle in ancient Israel.

Early accounts of Rosh Hashanah

Early names for Rosh Hashanah were Yom ha-Zikaron (Day of Remembrance) and Yom ha-Din (Day of Judgment). According to the Zohar, a book of Jewish mysticism, the first of Tishri is the day on which God created Adam, the first man. The Hebrews proclaimed God as the only king, and the first of Tishri as a renewal of his rule. It became known as "the birthday of the world."

The first mention of Rosh Hashanah as the "Beginning of the Year" is found in the *Mishnah*, the Jewish code of law. The Mishnah was passed down for generations by word of mouth and written down by rabbis (Jewish teachers of religion) during the second century A.D.

The rabbis who recorded the law designated Rosh Hashanah as the New Year and proclaimed it the time when God judged each person's thoughts and deeds and determined his or her destiny for the coming year. God was also said to judge nations and decide whether they would have abundance or famine, peace or war. These rabbis established the order of the ceremony for blowing the shofar, which is still carefully observed today.

The three books of God

From about A.D. 100 to 500, rabbis wrote down their comments about the rules established in the Mishnah. These comments were collected in a book called the Talmud. It was through these writings that the connection between Rosh Hashanah and Yom Kippur was established. They state that a person is judged on Rosh Hashanah and his fate is sealed on Yom Kippur. They also include ways to make amends for wrongdoing: a person should give to the poor, pray, ask forgiveness from man as well as from God, and live a good life.

The Talmud introduced the three books said to be opened by God on Rosh Hashanah—the Book of Life, the Book of Death, and the book for those who are in between, neither totally good nor totally wicked. Persons in this last book, which includes most people, are given the ten days until Yom Kippur to repent and return to God so that their name will be written in the Book of Life for the coming year.

According to the Talmud, the shofar is blown during Rosh Hashanah to con-

A Jewish man blows the shofar during a special dawn prayer ceremony at the Wailing Wall in Jerusalem in preparation for Yom Kippur in 1997. The shofar's wild notes were used as a call to battle in ancient Israel. Reproduced by permission of AP/Wide World Photos.

fuse Satan, who accuses people and tries to influence God's judgment against them. The great Jewish philosopher Maimonides (mih-MAH-nuh-deez), who lived during the twelfth century, said the main purpose of the shofar is to awaken people and call them to repent.

Rabbis soon declared the month of Elul, which comes before Tishri, as a time for Jewish people to thoroughly examine their lives over the past year and determine which moral laws they had broken so they could begin seeking God's forgiveness. Rosh Hashanah represents judgment but also hope and faith in God's forgiveness. The Talmud says, "And God will say to Israel, even to all mankind: 'My children, today, on Rosh Hashanah, I look upon all of you as if you had been created for the first time.'"

Folklore, Legends, Stories

Stories from the Torah are read in the synagogue (Jewish house of worship) at Rosh Hashanah. The High Holy Days are also filled with beautiful poems, prayers, meditations, and hymns, as well as stories

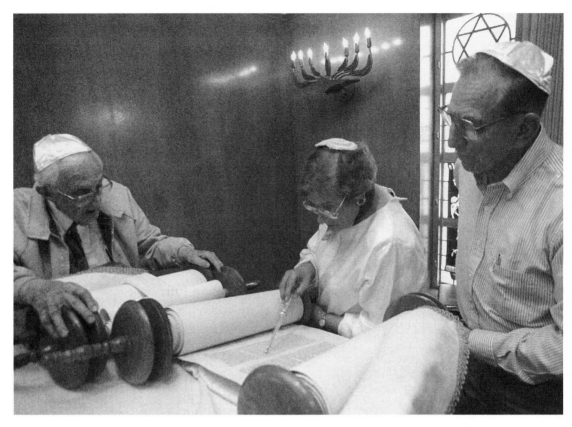

A student rabbi is given some assistance in finding the right passage in the Torah, the Old Testament books of the Bible, for the first service of Rosh Hashanah in October 1997. Reproduced by permission of AP/Wide World Photos.

about Jewish martyrs, rabbis, and the Jewish people, both ancient and modern.

Abraham and Isaac

The story of Abraham and Isaac, found in the Torah in the Book of Genesis (Chapters 18, 21, and 22) is always read on Rosh Hashanah. Some say the story is read to show that only God controls life and death. Others say recalling the story is a way of asking God to grant forgiveness to the Jewish people because of the faith of their ancestor Abraham.

According to the Torah, Abraham was a wealthy, kind, and generous man who was a leader of a Hebrew clan. Abraham's faith in God was very strong. God spoke to Abraham and told him that he and his wife Sarah would have a son. One day, three strangers visited Abraham and Sarah, who was then ninety years old. One stranger told Sarah that she would have a son within a year. Abraham recognized the voice of God in the stranger's words. Sarah laughed in disbelief, telling the man she was too old to bear a child. Yet, by a miracle, Sarah gave birth to a son, and he was named Isaac.

When Isaac was about eleven years old, God spoke to Abraham, instructing him to take his son to a mountain and make an offering of the child. Although Abraham was sad and frightened, he did as God told him. At the last moment before the sacrifice, when Isaac was lying bound on a stone and Abraham had raised the knife to kill him, God again spoke. This time he told Abraham not to harm Isaac. Abraham had proved his faith in God by doing as he was told without question. He was willing to give up his beloved son because God had asked him to.

When God spoke, Abraham quickly untied Isaac and looked around for an animal to sacrifice in his place. He saw a ram caught by its horns in a thicket, and the ram became the sacrifice to God. God spoke to Abraham and said he and his children for generations to come would multiply and be blessed on the earth.

Ancient tradition says one horn of this ram became the shofar blown by God on Mount Sinai when he gave the Hebrew leader Moses the Ten Commandments. The Ten Commandments are the basic laws about how people should treat each other and what their duties are to God. The other ram's horn will be blown to announce the coming of the Messiah, or Savior of the world.

Jonah and the great fish

On the afternoon of Yom Kippur, the story of the Hebrew prophet Jonah (Book of Jonah, Chapters 1–4) is read in the synagogue as an example of God's love for all people and his willingness to forgive sin.

One day, God told Jonah to go to the city of Nineveh and warn the wicked people there that he would destroy their city in forty days if they did not change

their ways. Jonah did not want to go to Nineveh, so he boarded a ship setting sail for a faraway port, thinking he could hide from God and avoid his duty. That night, a terrible storm struck, battering the ship until the captain thought it would be destroyed. Every man drew straws to see who had so angered God that he caused the storm; it was determined it was Jonah.

Jonah admitted that he had disobeyed God. The sailors tossed him overboard and he was swallowed by a great fish. Inside the fish's stomach, Jonah prayed to God to save him. After three days the fish vomited him onto land.

Jonah hurried to Nineveh to warn the people. They repented for forty days, and God forgave them and saved the city. This angered Jonah because he thought the people deserved to be punished, so he sat outside the city, hoping God would change his mind. One day, God made a beautiful gourd plant grow up over Jonah to shelter him from the sun. The next day, however, God made a worm to destroy it.

Jonah felt sorry for the plant and asked God why it had to die. God answered that if Jonah could have compassion for the plant, which he did not grow and had enjoyed for only one day, he should consider how much more pity God had for the thousands of people of Nineveh, whom he had created. God had mercy on them because they had not been able to tell right from wrong. Jonah then understood that God loves all people and is willing to forgive them when they repent.

Powerful words

An important part of each Rosh Hashanah service is the beautiful meditative poems called *piyyutim.* Over the centuries, they were added to synagogue services to increase emotion. They are usually written so that the first letter of each line or stanza spells the poet's name or follows the Hebrew alphabet.

One of the most powerful of these poems is the *Unetaneh Tokef,* said to have been written by Rabbi Kalonymos ben Meshullam of Mainz, Germany, during the eleventh century. The *Unetaneh Tokef* is recited in the synagogue on the first day of Rosh Hashanah services. One version of the second verse is as follows:

> The great Shofar is sounded. A muted small voice is heard. The angels too are frightened, fear and trembling seize them, and they declare: "This is the day of judgment, of mustering the host on high! . . ." You determine the latter end of every creature and record their ultimate verdict. On Rosh Hashanah it is written down for them, on Yom Kippur it is sealed: How many shall leave and how many shall be born, who shall live and who shall die, who shall attain his full span of life and who shall not, who shall perish by fire, and who by water, who by the sword and who by wild beasts, who by hunger and who by thirst, who by storm and who by plague, who shall have rest and who shall be restless,... who shall be free from sorrow and who shall be tormented,... who shall be poor and who shall be rich. But Teshuvah, Prayer, and Good Deeds can avert the severity of the decree....

Customs, Traditions, Ceremonies

Rosh Hashanah is very different from most other New Year celebrations. Although it is hopeful and joyful in many ways, it is primarily a religious holiday, and most observances take place in the synagogue. Noisy and colorful parades, gift giv-

ing, parties, and superstitions are not a part of the High Holy Days, although New Year themes of starting life anew and making positive changes are essential to the holiday.

To prepare for Rosh Hashanah, Jewish people clean house, buy new clothes, get haircuts, send special greeting cards, and cook holiday foods. Husbands buy new clothes or jewelry for their wives, and children get treats, making the celebration something like the Hindu New Year, Diwali. Observance of all Jewish holidays, including the Sabbath (Saturday), begins at sunset on the evening before the holiday and ends when three bright stars come out on the last day of the holiday.

On the eve of Rosh Hashanah, called Erev (pronounced EH-rev) Rosh Hashanah, the woman of the house lights festival candles before sunset on the first day and one-half hour after sunset on the second day of Rosh Hashanah. She pronounces a blessing called *Sheheheyanu* (pronounced shuh-heh-huh-YAH-noo): "Blessed are You, Lord our God, You are He who has kept us in life, has sustained us, and has permitted us to reach this moment."

The Rosh Hashanah greetings

On Erev Rosh Hashanah, people greet one another with the wish "May you be inscribed [in the Book of Life] for a good year." After the eve of Rosh Hashanah, the greeting changes to "As God puts His final seal on you, may it be for good!"

These greetings are said to have originated in Germany during medieval times (500–1500). The greetings were always spoken until the 1500s, when Jews began to send cards and letters to friends and family. Today, Rosh Hashanah greeting

Persons of the Jewish faith gather at a lake in New York City's Central Park to cast bread upon the water, an ancient custom representing the casting off of sins, on the first day of the Jewish New Year in September 1995. Reproduced by permission of AP/Wide World Photos.

cards bear a New Year wish that can apply to anyone: "Ketivah ve-hatimah tovah" ("May the decision to be inscribed and sealed be good").

Rosh Hashanah in the synagogue

Each day of Rosh Hashanah, Jewish families attend long morning and evening services at the synagogue. The story of Abraham and Isaac is read from the Book of Genesis, along with other passages from the Torah. Prayers, poems, hymns, and a sermon by the rabbi are also included in the services. People often become emotional and cry or wail during the reading of the *Unetaneh Tokef* and at other particularly moving points.

The most powerful part of the service is the ceremony of the shofar, introduced with a reading of Psalm 37, which begins: "Fret not thyself because of evildoers, neither be thou envious against the workers of iniquity." The reading is repeated seven times, and then all is quiet as the people stand.

The "master of blowing," the person chosen to blow the shofar, says the blessing: "Blessed are You, O Lord our God, You are He who has commanded us to hear the voice of the shofar." Then the haunting sounds come from the ram's horn, just as they did in the time of Moses. It is tradition to blow the shofar one hundred times on each day of Rosh Hashanah.

The shofar is difficult to blow because it has no mouthpiece. It takes hours of practice to learn the shofar ceremony, which was set forth in the Mishnah some eighteen hundred years ago. The notes and the order in which they are blown are not to be changed. The shofar has three separate sounds: *shevarim,* three broken blasts that sound like sobbing; *teruah,* nine short notes that sound like wailing; and *tekiah,* a long, unbroken blast of alarm. The *tekiah gedolah* is an extra-long blast at the close of the service.

The shofar has traditionally been made from a ram's horn, but a long, curved antelope horn is popular today. It may have designs or Hebrew letters carved into it.

Casting sins into the sea

On the afternoon of the first day of Rosh Hashanah, or the second day if the first falls on a Sabbath, many Jewish families perform an old ritual called the *Tashlich* (pronounced tash-LICK). Taschlich is Hebrew for "You will cast." It is based on a verse from the Book of Micah (7:19): "He will turn again, he will have compassion upon us; he will subdue our iniquities; and thou wilt cast all their sins into the depths of the sea."

Jews walk to the bank of a stream or river or to the seashore and recite a prayer. Then they empty their pockets of lint or throw breadcrumbs into the water to sym-bolize shaking their sins into the sea. Some Jews shake the hems of their clothing, and others actually jump into the water. If there is no body of living water (containing marine life, like fish) nearby, the ceremony can be performed while facing in the direction of such a body of water.

The Days of Awe

Rosh Hashanah and Yom Kippur and the days in between are called *Yamim Noraim,* the Days of Awe. From Rosh Hashanah to Yom Kippur, Jews have the opportunity to repent and make amends for the sins they have committed over the past year. During this time, the Book of Life is said to remain open to give everyone a chance to return to God and be inscribed and sealed in the book for the year to come.

Many people attend synagogue for each of the ten days, where psalms and prayers are recited each day. An extra line, "Remember us for life, O King who delightest in life; inscribe us in the Book of Life for Thy sake, O living God," is added to one prayer during the Days of Awe.

Some Jews fast until noon of each day, except for the Sabbath (known as the Sabbath of Return) and the day before Yom Kippur, when Jews are commanded to feast to prepare for the fast of the following day. People spend the Days of Awe searching their souls for wrongs done to God or man and asking forgiveness for both. One way to obtain forgiveness is by giving to charity and helping people in need. Jews say to one another, "May you end this day with a good signature."

As the final day to seek forgiveness for sin before the Book of Life is closed for

An Orthodox Jewish man swings a live chicken over his head while reciting prayers asking God's mercy in Jerusalem in preparation for Yom Kippur in October 1997. From Rosh Hashanah to Yom Kippur, Jews have the opportunity to repent and make amends for the sins they have committed over the past year. Reproduced by permission of AP/Wide World Photos.

another year, Yom Kippur is an anxious but hopeful time. Jews promise to follow God's *mitzvoth* (pronounced mits-VOTE), or commandments for living, in the coming year.

At sunset on the day of Yom Kippur, the *Neilah* (pronounced NEE-luh), "closing" or "locking," service is held, symbolizing the closing of the Book of Life.

A baker prepares the traditional holiday desert teiglach at a New York City bakery in September 1999. Teiglach, a mound of baked dough balls mixed with candied cherries and drenched with honey and sugar, is eaten during the Jewish High Holy Days. Reproduced by permission of AP/Wide World Photos.

The final prayer is the *Shema* (pronounced shuh-MAH), meaning "hear," the holiest Jewish prayer: "Hear, O Israel, the Lord our God, the Lord is One." Then the shofar sounds its longest and loudest blast, the *tekiah gedolah,* announcing the closing of the Book of Life.

Clothing, Costumes

White is the color for Rosh Hashanah and the High Holy Days. It sym-bolizes hope, the purity of angels, and faith in God's mercy. People dress their best on Rosh Hashanah, often in new clothes. In the synagogue, rabbis and cantors, as well as married men of the congregation, wear long, white robes called *kittel.* The kittel is a symbol of the linen robe worn by the high priest in the ancient Temple of Jerusalem.

Foods, Recipes

Families share feasts on the eve of Rosh Hashanah, on the second day of Rosh Hashanah, and on the day before Yom Kippur. During Rosh Hashanah, they also share a festive but light lunch after synagogue services each day. Food is prepared ahead of time to keep God's commandment to do no work on the High Holy Days.

For the evening feasts on Rosh Hashanah, the table is set with the family's best linen and china, and a basket of autumn fruit is used for a centerpiece. Candles are lit before the family sits down to eat. A prayer called *kiddush* (pronounced KIH-dush) is said over a glass of wine and a loaf of freshly baked bread called *challah* (pronounced KAH-luh).

Challah is an egg bread that is round to resemble a crown, representing God's kingship and the "head" of the year. It also resembles a wheel, representing the cycle of the year. Challah can also be braided and is sometimes shaped like a ladder, on which a person can go up with good deeds or down with bad.

Fish is served on Rosh Hashanah as a symbol of plenty. An old Jewish tradition is to serve the head of the family the head of the fish, while saying, "May you be the

Honey Cake for a Sweet Year

Ingredients

1 cup sugar

4 eggs

¾ cup strong brewed coffee

1 cup honey

½ teaspoon almond extract

½ cup melted butter

4 cups plain flour

3 teaspoons baking powder

1½ teaspoons baking soda

¼ teaspoon each of ground cloves and nutmeg

1 teaspoon each of ground cinnamon and ginger

¼ cup seedless raisins

¼ cup chopped walnuts

whipping cream or non-dairy topping

Directions

1. Cream together eggs and sugar in a large mixing bowl until fluffy.
2. Combine honey and coffee in a small bowl. Add to egg mixture, along with melted butter and almond extract.
3. Combine flour, baking powder, baking soda, cloves, nutmeg, cinnamon, and ginger, mixing well.
4. Add raisins and nuts to flour mixture, then combine egg and flour mixtures, beating until smooth.
5. Pour batter into greased 10 x 10 square or 10 x 14 oblong baking pan. Bake for 1 hour at 350 degrees. Cut cake into squares.
6. Whip cream, sprinkling in a little sugar and cinnamon if desired. Serve pieces of cake with whipped cream or non-dairy topping.

head and not the tail!" This expresses the hope that the person will be a leader among his or her people. Pomegranates represent a wish for fertility. Black-eyed peas represent the many good deeds of the Jewish people.

Just like the Chinese New Year, many foods are eaten at Rosh Hashanah because their names suggest good things for the new year. For example, beets represent beating down enemies, leeks represent hard feelings leaking away, and caraway seeds represent the carrying away of sin.

Newly ripened fall fruits, such as grapes and apples, are put on the table. Fruits such as figs, dates, and raisins are often served stewed or baked in breads and desserts, along with chopped nuts. Fruit, carrot, or sweet potato stews are also popular.

As do Hindus at Diwali, Jews eat sweet foods at Rosh Hashanah as a symbol of a good and pleasant year. They avoid sour or bitter foods. Honey is used in many dishes, and a jar of honey is set on the table as a token of a sweet year. Family members spread honey on the first slices of challah, while saying the blessing "May it be Thy will, O Lord our God, to renew us a happy and pleasant year." Apple slices dipped in honey are a traditional food for Rosh Hashanah. A popular honey pastry is called *teiglach.*

Arts, Crafts, Games

Rosh Hashanah greeting cards may include a number of different designs and can be made from many different materials. Typical artwork includes the shofar, apples, or the Star of David, the six-pointed star that is a symbol of Judaism. In Israel, booths along the streets sell Rosh Hashanah cards with pictures of comic strip characters, political figures, and even war scenes during times of conflict in the Middle East. Typical greetings include *"Leshanah tovah tikatevu vetechatemu,"* "May you be inscribed and sealed for a good year," or simply *"Shanah Tovah,"* "May your year be good and sweet."

Music, Dance

Beautiful hymns, many composed centuries ago, are sung during Rosh Hashanah services in the synagogue. One of the most moving is the *Kol Nidrei.* The melody was composed during the sixteenth century in southern Germany, but it is so inspiring that it has been performed and recorded by singers and musicians throughout the world. It is said to symbolize the suffering of the Jewish people and their love for God, and the notes recall the days of the religious wars, or Crusades, in medieval times.

Special Role of Children, Young Adults

Before going to synagogue services on Rosh Hashanah, parents lay their hands upon their children and bless them. The blessing usually takes the form of a hug. A common blessing is "May God bless you and guard you. May the light of God shine upon you, and may God be gracious to you. May the presence of God be with you and give you peace."

Children may make Rosh Hashanah greeting cards. They visit friends during the Days of Awe and tell them—and brothers and sisters—they are sorry for any wrong they have done to them during the year. They may also help bring food and clothing to the synagogue to give to the poor.

For More Information

Berger, Gilda. *Celebrate! Stories of the Jewish Holidays.* New York: Scholastic Press, 1998.

Drucker, Malka. *The Family Treasury of Jewish Holidays.* Boston: Little, Brown, 1994.

Yolen, Jane. *Milk and Honey: A Year of Jewish Holidays.* New York: G. P. Putnam's Sons, 1996.

Web sites

"Elul and Rosh Hashanah." [Online] http://www.torah.org/learning/yomtov/elulrosh (accessed on February 17, 2000).

"Rosh Hashanah." [Online] http://www.Jewishholidays.com (accessed on February 17, 2000).

"Rosh Hashanah." [Online] http://www.joi.org/celebrate/rosh (accessed on February 17, 2000).

"Rosh Hashanah and Yom Kippur." [Online] http://www.ohr.org.il/special/roshhash (accessed on February 17, 2000).

Scotland

Name of Holiday: Hogmanay

Introduction

Hogmanay (pronounced HAHG-muh-nay) is celebrated primarily in Scotland, although London and some towns in northern England also hold Hogmanay celebrations. In Scotland, Hogmanay is a two-day public holiday, December 31 and January 1. It is Scotland's oldest holiday and largest festival. Hogmanay in Scotland is considered the largest New Year's celebration in Europe.

History

The celebration of Hogmanay began with ancient Europeans called the Celts (pronounced KELTS), who first settled in Scotland in about 300 B.C. The Celts held special ceremonies to ward off evil spirits and to strengthen the sun when it became weak during the darkest time of year, the winter solstice. The ceremonies began with the season called Samhain (pronounced SOW-en), meaning "summer's end," when the fall harvest ended and farmers stored food for the long winter.

The Celts considered Samhain to be the beginning of the new year. During this time, fairies and spirits of the dead were believed to walk the earth. Celtic priests, called Druids, performed rites to keep them from harming the living. The rituals included building bonfires and hanging mistletoe, considered a sacred plant.

Hog *what?*

No one is certain about the origin of the word *hogmanay,* but there are several theories about it. Some say it comes from an old Scottish song that began *oge maidne,* "new morning." Others believe it derives from the phrase *haleg monath,* "holy month."

Christmas comes to Scotland

The Romans invaded Scotland in A.D. 81 and conquered the Celts. The tribes of Scotland eventually adopted the Roman calendar, with its New Year on January 1.

The Romans left Scotland in about 400, and the first Irish Celtic immigrants arrived soon after. In about 560, an Irish Christian named Columba introduced Christianity to Scotland. With Christianity came the celebration of Christmas. During the Middle Ages (about 500–1500), the Catholic Church encouraged a big, two-week Christmas celebration, beginning on December 25 and continuing through Epiphany, January 6.

During the Scottish Reformation in the mid-1500s, religious leader John Knox (1513–1572) and others founded the Church of Scotland. The Church of Scotland became Scotland's official religion in 1690. Church officials frowned on the Roman Catholic Christmas celebrations and even abolished them during the 1640s. Hogmanay, the New Year celebration, became a much bigger holiday than Christmas and remained so until about 1962.

Clacking hooves and thumping hides

From about the mid-1600s to the mid-1900s, Hogmanay was the most important celebration of the year. In some parts of

Scotland, older boys went from house to house on Hogmanay and performed a noisy ritual designed to drive away evil spirits.

The leader of each group wore a dried cowhide over his back with horns and hooves still attached. The boys climbed onto the thatched roof of each house and ran clockwise in circles. The leader clacked the horns and hooves together and the other boys beat at the cowhide with sticks. They all recited ancient chants. Then they climbed down and beat the sides of the house with clubs.

When invited in, the boys circled clockwise three times and chanted or said a prayer. Then they singed a strip of sheepskin in the fire and held the smoldering, foul-smelling skin under each person's nose. This was believed to purify the house and bring good health in the new year. Each boy carried a sack. Before they moved on to the next house, the woman of the family gave the boys cakes to put into their sacks. This custom is still carried out in much the same way on the Scottish island of Lewis.

Men and boys also fired guns at midnight, a custom still popular in rural areas. Scots who immigrated to America during the 1700s and 1800s brought this custom with them. In parts of the southern United States, firing guns became a regular part of Christmas Eve and New Year's Eve celebrations.

New Year, Christmas, or Halloween?

Hogmanay celebrations as they are known today became big events during the late 1800s. Children draped themselves with old sheets folded to make a pocket in front. They went from house to house in an activity similar to Halloween trick-or-treating, collecting treats and a few pennies. They hung up their stockings on Hogmanay instead of Christmas Eve.

As the old year came to a close, people crowded into the streets before midnight and toasted one another with drinks of whiskey as they waited for the town clock to strike twelve. After many hugs and kisses were exchanged, people partied throughout the night. Although many people put up a Christmas tree on Christmas, Santa Claus arrived on New Year's Day with presents for the children.

The popularity of Christmas grew in Scotland during the mid-twentieth century, and it was declared a public holiday in 1967. Within about twenty-five years, a majority of Scots had come to consider Christmas more important than Hogmanay.

Revival of Hogmanay

In 1993, the city fathers of Edinburgh, Scotland's capital, decided to hold a big street party for Hogmanay and revive the old traditions. The party has grown larger each year, and Edinburgh's Hogmanay festivities are now considered Europe's largest New Year celebration. The event has become so popular that officials have to issue passes to some events in order to limit the number of people who can attend. The limit is usually 180,000. Celebrations have also been revived in other cities throughout Scotland.

Folklore, Legends, Stories

Because it shares some of the same origins as Halloween, Hogmanay has been surrounded by superstitions and folklore for centuries. Like New Year celebrations in other parts of the world, Hogmanay was a time to drive out bad spirits of the old year and welcome good luck in the new by performing

Fireworks explode over Edinburgh, Scotland, during the city's Hogmanay street party, where revelers welcomed in the New Year of 1998. Reproduced by permission of AP/Wide World Photos.

certain rituals, often involving fire. Scots kept fires and candles burning all night on Hogmanay to bar evil from the household.

Taking a drink from the first bucket of well water drawn after midnight on New Year's Day was considered essential for a good year. The head of the household drew this water, called the "Cream of the Well" or "Flower of the Well," and shared it with other family members. Scots believed the water could bring luck in love, good health, or a good year of dairy farming. They sprinkled it around the house, sipped it for good health, and used a little to clean objects in the house and barn, especially dairy pails.

At midnight on Hogmanay, families opened the back door wide in a gesture of letting the old year out and then opened the front door to let the new year in. It was considered good luck to wear new clothes or start a new project on New Year's Day, and fishermen tried to make a catch on New Year's Day to bring fishing luck in the year to follow. Scots believed it was bad luck to meet an undertaker, a beggar, or a person who carried nothing on New Year's Day, but it was lucky to meet a wealthy man or someone with their arms full.

People also practiced divination, or fortune-telling, on Hogmanay, just as they did on Halloween. An old rhyme from the Scottish Highlands tells how to predict the weather from the way the wind blows on Hogmanay:

> Wind from the West
> brings fish and bread;
> Wind from the North,
> cold and lashing;
> Wind from the East
> brings snow on the hills;
> Wind from the South,
> fruit on trees.

Hogmanay chants and New Year odes

Some of the most ancient Hogmanay rhymes are the Gaelic chants recited by the "Hogmanay Lads," who climbed onto rooftops and beat a dried cowhide to drive evil from the house. Here is one rhyme translated into English:

> Hogmanay of the sack,
> Strike of the hide,
> Hogmanay of the sack,
> Beat the skin,
> Down with it, Up with it,
> Strike the hide,
> Hogmanay of the sack,
> Hogmanay of the sack.

Modern rhymes tell funny stories about local people. Dressing in costume and performing simple skits from house to house in exchange for food and drink, called "mumming," has also long been popular at Hogmanay. Hogmanay mummers recited rhymes such as this one:

> Rise up, goodwife, and shake your
>   feathers;
> Do not think that we are beggars;
> We're only bairns [children] come to
>   play;
> Rise up and give us our Hogmanay.

Scotland's national poet and songwriter, Robert Burns (1759–1796), wrote a poem called *New Year's Day* (1791), which includes the following lines:

> This day Time winds th' exhausted
>   chain,
> To run the twelve month's length
>   again....

Customs, Traditions, Ceremonies

Like the New Year in many other parts of the world, Hogmanay calls for a thorough housecleaning, making repairs, and mending clothes. Scots repay debts and return items that were borrowed. They make New Year's resolutions and say good riddance to the old year. Families get together for a reunion to start the New Year complete.

First foot brings the year's luck

Scottish people believe that the first person to step over their threshold on New Year's Day determines their luck for the year. (Many Asian people have the same belief.) This person is called the "first-footer," and "first-footing" has been a Hogmanay custom in Scotland for centuries. To make sure they are the first visitor, first-footers begin their rounds just after midnight on Hogmanay, in the wee hours of New Year's Day.

According to tradition, a first-footer should be a tall, handsome, dark-haired man who is not a family member. He should be in good health, he should not have flat feet, and his eyebrows should not be so bushy that they meet in the middle. He should not be dressed in black and should never carry a weapon. He should be kind and free with his money, and he should be carrying certain gifts for the household.

A red-haired person, a woman, or a person who cannot see well or has a physical deformity is considered unlucky. Scots often invite someone who fits the description of a lucky first-footer to be their guest just after midnight or very early on New Year's Day.

The first-footer should take gifts, called *hogmanay,* for the family. Traditional gifts are shortbread or cake, a small bottle of whiskey, a small bag of salt, and a lump of coal or a stick of firewood. Scots believe these gifts ensure that the family will have food, whiskey, good health, and warmth in the coming year.

Many first-footers tie up their gifts with pretty ribbons and pack them in a basket for the family. On entering the house, they put the coal or wood on the fire, place the cake on the table, and pour a glass of whiskey for the head of the household. No one speaks during this time except the first-footer, and only after he has wished everyone in the house a "Happy New Year" can the conversation begin. He might also sing a traditional song:

> I wish you a Happy New Year,
> A bag full of money and a cellar full
>   of beer,
> A nice fat pig to last you all the year,
> So give me a gift for the New Year.

The gift the first-footer is singing about is Scottish shortbread or a black bun, a fruit-filled cake wrapped in a pastry crust. The family always has food and drink prepared for their first-footer. By the end of the evening, popular first-footers—who should always leave by the back door to keep from taking the family's luck out the front with them—can be tipsy after all the Scotch whiskey they have been offered. Many go to parties after first-footing, however, and continue the revelry for up to twenty-four hours after midnight on Hogmanay.

First-footing probably started as Hogmanay mumming, when young men dressed in costumes and strolled from house to house performing skits and songs for food and drink. Young men who had sweethearts tried to be the "first foot" through the young lady's door, to seal the romance for the coming year.

When the clock strikes twelve

People who are not first-footing on Hogmanay might begin the celebration by meeting friends at a pub for drinks. As midnight nears, everyone walks out to the street to see the old year out and the new year in when the clock chimes twelve. Others go home to be with their families. Wherever they are when the New Year is born, Scots hug and kiss one another, wishing one another the best in the New Year. Then they all link arms and sing "Auld Lang Syne," the Western world's most popular New Year song, written by their own national poet, Robert Burns.

An old Hogmanay custom in the Scottish Highlands was to make a straw dummy representing the passing year. They called her the "Auld (Old) Wife" and set her on fire as the clock rang out the old year.

In Scotland and other parts of Great Britain, church bells were muffled to mark the sadness of the old year until midnight, when they were allowed to ring loudly and clearly, to ring in the new. Today, many cities launch impressive fireworks displays after the tolling of the church bells at midnight on Ne'er's Eve ("New Year's Eve" in Scottish dialect), or Hogmanay.

New Year by torchlight and bonfire

Recalling the days of the ancient Celts, the Scots consider fire an essential element of Hogmanay celebrations. Scotland is famous for its long torchlight processions held December 30, the night before Hogmanay. The processions wind through city streets to light up and warm up the cold winter night.

In Stonehaven, marchers swing balls of fire attached to handles with wires. The torchlight procession in Edinburgh, with some seven thousand marchers, is a highlight of the Hogmanay celebrations. Marchers purchase their torches, and the money goes to charity. When the marchers reach their destination, a huge bonfire is lit as revelers watch street theater, dance to Celtic music, and party throughout the night. In Edinburgh, which hosts the biggest New Year celebration in Europe, the party has been held on Calton Hill for hundreds of years.

Biggest New Year in Europe

The huge Hogmanay celebration in Edinburgh lasts for five days. In addition to the torchlight processions and bonfires, the festival includes concerts of all types of music, Celtic dance parties called *ceilidhs* (pronounced KAY-leez; visits), street theater, carnivals, fairs, a gathering of the Scottish clans (traditional family groups), laser shows, sporting events, a big fireworks display after the clock strikes midnight on New Year's Eve, and a huge Hogmanay street party.

Other Scottish cities and towns that hold big Hogmanay celebrations are Glasgow, Inverness, Newtonmore, Fort William, Aberdeen, and Stirling. Visitors come from all over the United Kingdom and Europe to celebrate Hogmanay in Scotland.

Clothing, Costumes

Hogmanay first-footers often wear the traditional Scottish kilt, a pleated wool, skirt-like wrap in one of many plaid patterns called "tartans." The tartan usually represents the wearer's clan, or family. The traditional uniform of Scottish warriors and soldiers, the kilt is worn about knee length, belted at the side, with the lower flap fastened in front with a large, silver pin.

The Scot wears a decorative pouch called a "sporran" over the kilt. The sporran hangs from a chain around his waist down to his lap. For evening dress with the kilt, he wears a ruffled shirt and a velvet or velour jacket of green, blue, or black with silver buttons; wool stockings and black shoes with big silver buckles; a tartan "plaid" (long shawl) draped over one shoulder and pinned with a silver brooch; and a Scottish "tam," a type of hat.

Women and girls wear kilted skirts and white blouses, with a tartan plaid and brooch, high wool stockings and black shoes, and tams. Scottish Highland dancers and those participating in Highland games wear the traditional kilt and accessories.

Foods, Recipes

Foods served to the first-footer on Hogmanay include shortbread—a cookie-like pastry made with flour, sugar, and lots of butter. Also popular are black buns, rich, dark fruitcakes made with raisins, apples, almonds, and currants and baked in a pastry shell.

Scotch whiskey and drinks made with it are the most popular Hogmanay refreshment for adults. In Gaelic, whiskey is called *uisge beatha* (water of life). Popular New Year's drinks made with whiskey are Hogmanay punch—a blend of apple cider and Scotch whisky—and *athole brose,* whiskey mixed with cream, oatmeal, and honey.

Many families offer the first-footer and other guests a full table of Scottish foods, including cold meats such as roast mutton, Scotch broth (soup made with mutton or beef broth and barley), smoked fish, oatcakes, pancakes, scones (a type of biscuit), cheese, dumplings, puddings, and trifles (cake dessert made with fruit, custard, brandy, and jam).

Ode to a sausage

The national food of Scotland is *haggis,* a type of sausage that has been prepared for centuries. Many legends and jokes have been told about haggis; it is often said to be a horned monster that roams the Scottish Highlands. The Scottish national poet and songwriter, Robert Burns, wrote the poem "Address to a Haggis" about this famous treat often served during holidays and festivals. Tradition calls for the haggis to be brought to the table on a large platter, accompanied by a flute player. The guest speaker at the celebration addresses the haggis as if it were a person.

Haggis is made from minced meats (often ground beef or sheep's liver, heart, and kidneys) mixed with spices, fat, onions, and oatmeal, then traditionally boiled in a sheep's stomach to make a large sausage. Today, haggis is stuffed into a plastic or cloth bag before it is boiled. The dish is served with mashed rutabagas and potatoes.

Music, Dance

Scots love music and dancing, and Hogmanay celebrations would be incomplete without lots of both. Since its beginning, the New Year holiday has been accompanied by rhymes sung or chanted when first-footers came to call. One traditional first-footing song goes like this:

> A good New Year to one and all,
> And many may you see.
> And during all the years to come,
> Oh, happy may you be.

Hogmanay Black Buns

Ingredients

1 cup all-purpose flour

½ cup dark brown sugar

½ teaspoon baking powder

1 teaspoon ground ginger

1 teaspoon ground cloves

½ teaspoon cinnamon

2 cups raisins, soaked in warm water for 30 minutes, then drained

½ cup dried cranberries, soaked and drained

2 peeled, finely chopped cooking apples

½ cup chopped almonds or walnuts

½ cup milk

2 beaten eggs

1 teaspoon almond extract

2 nine-inch pie crusts

1 beaten egg white mixed with 1 table-spoon water for glazing

Directions

1. Mix together flour, brown sugar, baking powder, cinnamon, cloves, and ginger. Add eggs, milk, raisins, cranberries, apples, nuts, and almond extract. Stir well until all ingredients are blended.
2. Place 1 pie crust in a pie pan and prick with a fork in several places.
3. Pour mixture into crust, then lay second crust over top, pinching edges together to seal.
4. Dip pastry brush into egg white mixture and brush over top crust to glaze.
5. Cut 4- to 6½-inch slits, evenly spaced, in top crust to vent steam.
6. Bake at 350 degrees for about 2 hours, until golden brown.
7. Let sit overnight at room temperature, then cut into wedges and serve. Wrap and refrigerate to keep after cutting.

"Auld Lang Syne": A New Year's tradition

The most famous New Year song throughout western Europe and North America is "Auld Lang Syne" ("The Days of Long Ago"), by Scotland's own Robert Burns. People have sung this song at midnight on New Year's Eve for some two hundred years, and it has been translated into dozens of languages. Burns originally wrote different music for the song, but his publisher changed it to the now familiar tune. Scottish tradition is to link arms together or hold hands as the clock strikes midnight on Hogmanay and sing:

Should auld acquaintance be forgot
And never brought to mind?
Should auld acquaintance be forgot,
And days of auld lang syne?

For auld lang syne, my dear,
For auld lang syne,
We'll take a cup o' kindness yet,
For auld lang syne.

Bagpipers and dance parties

Scotland is known for music played on bagpipes and drums, and the old Scottish dances, including the Highland Fling, the Sailor's Hornpipe, and the sword dance. Such music and dance, along with ancient Celtic music and dancing are a part of Hogmanay festivities all over Scotland.

Celtic music and dance parties, called ceilidhs, are held everywhere—in town halls, hotels, and fairgrounds, on Calton Hill in Edinburgh, and even in barns in rural areas. The dances are for everyone, from small children to grandparents. They generally last all night, and many even serve breakfast before the participants go home in the morning.

A holiday of music

Hogmanay festivities in Edinburgh and other cities also feature just about every other type of music: Celtic reggae, classical and choral, acoustic, folk, pop, rock, techno, and oldies from the 1960s, 1970s, and 1980s. During Hogmanay week, concerts are featured in gardens throughout Princes Street, Edinburgh's main thoroughfare. Disco and other popular dances are held as well. Hundreds of bagpipers play on Hogmanay to usher in the New Year.

Arts, Crafts, Games

Any number of Scottish arts and crafts, including beautifully woven Scottish wools, silver jewelry, and pottery with a Celtic motif, can be found at the fairs and shops during Hogmanay. No particular art or craft is associated with the holiday.

A bagpiper in Edinburgh, Scotland. Hundreds of bagpipers play on Hogmanay to usher in the New Year. Reproduced by permission of Susan D. Rock.

Sports and games, including such traditional Highland games as tossing the caber (a long, heavy pole), putting the stone (a heavy, flat disc), and wrestling are also held during the Hogmanay celebrations. New Year's Day has always been a big day for playing sports, especially shinty, a game similar to hockey. It was traditionally played in an open area like a park or beach between teams representing neighboring towns.

A New Year's Day triathlon is held in Edinburgh, and golf tournaments as well as sports and games for children are held on

January 2. New Year's Day walks—and, in one area of Scotland, New Year's Eve temperance (non-drinking) walks—are held. Curling, a game played by moving large pucks around the ice, is a popular game today. It was once played outdoors on frozen lakes and ponds, using a flat, heavy stone.

Special Role of Children, Young Adults

For many years, until about the 1950s, Hogmanay was like Christmas for Scottish children, who hung up their stockings in the evening and received presents from Santa Claus on New Year's Day. Groups of children often went first-footing to their grandparents' or other relatives' homes and received treats and a little money.

Poor children went from door to door singing rhymes and receiving coins, treats, and bread and cheese, much like the Halloween custom of trick-or-treating. They stored their goodies in the folds of their costumes, made from old sheets. Children may still visit their neighbors, demanding "hogmanay," or treats, on December 31.

Today, the fairs, processions, sports and games, and music and dances keep Scottish children very busy during Hogmanay. They enjoy the bonfires, fireworks, and laser shows and eagerly await the first-footer, who will arrive with gifts and join the family for a bounteous Hogmanay feast.

For More Information

Griffiths, Jonathan. *Scotland: Festivals of the World.* Milwaukee, Wis.: Gareth Stevens, 1999.

Livingstone, Sheila. *Scottish Festivals.* Chester Spring, Penn.: Dufour Editions, 1998.

Young, Ella, and Maude Gonne. *Celtic Wonder Tales.* Mineola, N.Y.: Dover Publications, 1996

Web sites

"Hogmanay Celebrations in Scotland." [Online] http://www.hogmanay.net/SCOTLAND/Scotland.htm (accessed on February 17, 2000).

Sources

Arlidge, John. "Hogmanay? That's a Hoot Strictly for Sassenachs These Days. *Independent* (London), December 31, 1994, p. 6.

Bateman, Michael. "Food & Drink: A Short Story for Hogmanay." *Independent* (London), December 29, 1999, p. 35.

Dresser, Norine. *Multicultural Manners: New Rules of Etiquette for a Changing Society.* New York: John Wiley & Sons, 1996, pp. 171–79.

Green, Marian. *A Calendar of Festivals: Traditional Celebrations, Songs, Seasonal Recipes & Things to Make.* Rockport, Mass.: Element Books, 1991, pp. 144–45.

Jaffrey, Madhur. *Seasons of Splendor: Tales, Myths and Legends of India.* New York: Atheneum, 1985, pp. 48–69, 80–84.

Keay, John, and Julia Keay, eds. *Collins Encyclopaedia of Scotland.* New York: HarperCollins, 1994, p. 519.

Matthews, John, and Caitlín Matthews. *The Winter Solstice: The Sacred Traditions of Christmas.* Wheaton, Ill.: Quest Books, 1998, pp. 12–23, 188–91, 196–97.

Mitter, Partha, and Swasti Mitter. *Hindus and Hinduism.* East Sussex, England: Wayland, 1982, pp. 6–14, 20, 24–26, 47.

Rosen, Mike. *Winter Festivals.* New York: Bookwright Press, 1990, pp. 18–23.

Spencer, William. *Iran: Land of the Peacock Throne.* New York: Marshall Cavendish, 1997, pp. 30, 38–39, 49–52, 57.

Tan Huay Peng. *Fun with Chinese Festivals.* Union City, Calif.: Heian International, 1991, pp. 2–43.

Waskow, Arthur I. *Seasons of Our Joy: A Handbook of Jewish Festivals.* New York: Summit Books, 1982, pp. 1–45.

Webb, Lois Sinaiko. *Holidays of the World Cookbook for Students.* Phoenix, Ariz.: Oryx Press, 1995, pp. 109, 151–54, 159–61, 270.

Wylen, Stephen M. *The Book of the Jewish Year.* New York: UAHC Press, 1996, pp. 18, 23–42.

Web sites

Birodkar, Sudheer. "Popular Hindu Festivals: Diwali, Dassera and Holi." [Online] http://members.tripod.com/~sudheerb/festivals1.html (accessed on February 17, 2000).

"The Laws of Rosh Hashanah." [Online] http://www.ohr.org.il/special/roshhash/rhlaws.htm (accessed on February 17, 2000).

Massoume. "No Ruz Is a Celebration of Life." [Online] http://www.payvand.com/ny/massoume.html (accessed on February 18, 2000).

O'Sullivan, Jacqueline. "Rosh Hashanah: Joy and Judgement." [Online] http://www.new-year.co.uk/jewish/history.htm (accessed on February 19, 2000).

Powell, J. Madoc. "Mini-unit: Diwali—Hindu New Year." [Online] http://teacherlink.ed.usu.edu/TLresources/longterm/LessonPlans/Byrnes/DIWALI.html (accessed on February 20, 2000).

"Yom Kippur: A Fist to the Heart." [Online] http://www.joi.org/celebrate/yomkipp/afist.htm (accessed on February 17, 2000).

Ramadan and Id al-Fitr

Introduction

Islam is one of the major religions of the world, with over one billion followers, who are called Muslims. There are Muslims in countries all over the world, although the largest concentrations are in countries in the Middle East and Southeast Asia, such as Pakistan, Iran, Iraq, Egypt, and Bangladesh, where more than 90 percent of the population are Muslim.

Islam was founded by the prophet Muhammad (c. 570–632). Ramadan (pronounced RAH-muh-don), the holiest and most important time of year in the Islamic religion, commemorates an event in the life of Muhammed: when the holy book of Islam, the Koran, was revealed to him by the angel Gabriel.

Observing the fast of Ramadan is a major rule of Islam. For the month of Ramadan, Muslims go without food or drink from sunup to sundown each day. They do this because it helps them to remember Allah (Arabic for "God") in a special way during a sacred time of the year, just as daily prayers help them remember Allah each day.

Because it is a time of fasting and prayer, seeking forgiveness, and giving to charity, Ramadan is sometimes compared with the Jewish Yom Kippur. The festive period that follows Ramadan, Id al-Fitr (pronounced EED uhl-FIH-ter), is often compared to Thanksgiving and Christmas.

History

The prophet Muhammad was born in Mecca, a city in Arabia (now in the country of Saudi Arabia), in A.D. 570. In the year 610, during the month of Ramadan, when Muhammad was forty years old, he had a vision of the angel Gabriel, who told him he brought the word of Allah, or God. The angel spoke many times to Muhammad, who memorized his words and repeated them to his followers, who then wrote them down. Most sources say that Muhammad could not read or write.

For the next twelve years, Muhammad preached that there was only one God. This angered the leaders of Mecca because many people who came to Mecca to trade believed in numerous gods and worshiped them at the Kaaba (pronounced KAH-buh;

Holiday Fact Box: Ramadan and Id al-Fitr

Themes

Ramadan commemorates a special event for Muslims—when the holy book of Islam, the Koran, was revealed to the prophet Muhammad. Muslims observe Ramadan by praying, giving to charity, and fasting, or going without food. Ramadan is followed by a period of feasting and celebration called Id al-Fitr.

Type of Holiday

Ramadan is a sacred holiday of the Islamic religion. For Muslims, it is the most important and holy time of the year. It is marked by a month of fasting, from sunup until sundown, during which Muslims refrain from food and drink during the daylight hours.

When Celebrated

Ramadan is a movable holiday based on the Islamic calendar. Ramadan begins on the full moon of the ninth month of the Muslim lunar year. The word *Ramadan* refers to both the holiday and the month in which it falls. Id al-Fitr begins on the new moon of the tenth month of the Muslim lunar year, Shawwal. In most Muslim countries, it is a national holiday that lasts three days.

In 622, Muhammad and his followers were forced to leave Mecca. They fled to the Arabian town of Yathrib, located two hundred miles north of Mecca. This escape is known as the Hegira, or Hejira (pronounced HEH-juh-ruh), meaning "migration," and the year 622 became the first year of the Islamic calendar. Muhammad was accepted in Yathrib as a prophet. The town was renamed Madinat an-Nabi, the City of the Prophet. It was later called Medina, its present name.

In his new city, Muhammad formed an army of ten thousand men, and in the year 630, Muhammad's army marched on Mecca. In awe of the powerful army, the people of Mecca opened the city to Muhammad and accepted the new religion of Islam. When Muhammad reached the Kaaba, he destroyed the shrines to the many gods, but he kissed the black stone. The Kaaba became a holy place for all Muslims.

Arab Muslims believe the Kaaba was built by one of their ancestors, Abraham, many centuries before Muhammad was born. Abraham is featured in the book of Genesis, which is part of the Old Testament of the Hebrew and Christian Bible. He is considered one of the first fathers of Christianity, Judaism, and Islam. Muhammad said he was a descendant of Abraham.

As part of their religious obligations, all Muslims try to travel to Mecca at least once in their lives. This is called the *haj*, or pilgrimage to Mecca. An important part of fulfilling the pilgrimage is to circle the Kaaba seven times counterclockwise while reciting special prayers. The circling begins at the black stone embedded in the western wall of the Kaaba and ends when the pilgrim prays at the Station of Abraham

cube), an ancient building shaped like a cube, with a black stone, probably a meteorite, built into one wall.

A Senegalese man reading the Koran. The Koran forms the foundation for daily life in all Muslim countries. While fasting during Ramadan, Muslims pray and read the Koran as often as possible. Reproduced by permission of David Johnson.

beside the stone. When Muslims throughout the world pray, no matter where they are, they face toward Mecca and the Kaaba.

Muhammad died two years after his army marched on Mecca, at the age of sixty-two. Within one hundred years, Islam had spread throughout the Middle East and western Asia. Because Muhammad himself had fasted during the month of Ramadan, all those who became Muslims continued this practice. Fasting during Ramadan is also said to commemorate the Hegira, Muhammad's journey to Medina.

Folklore, Legends, Stories

A number of superstitions and legends are associated with Ramadan. Muslims believe that during the month of Ramadan, the gates of heaven are open and angels come down to earth to bless the faithful. They also believe that during this time, the gates of hell are closed and the devil is kept in chains.

The life of Muhammad

The story of the life of the prophet Muhammad and his followers and the history of the rise of Islam make up the most familiar lore related to Ramadan and Id al-Fitr. Most of the history about the Prophet and the origin of Islam was written down by Muhammad's followers after his death.

The most important story is how Allah revealed the words of the Koran to the Prophet during the month of Ramadan as he sat in the Cave of Hira, in the mountains of Arabia, near Mecca. The angel Gabriel commanded Muhammad, in the name of Allah, to read. Muhammad replied that he could not read. But again the angel commanded him, and suddenly Muhammad saw a silk scroll with words written in flames. By a miracle, Muhammad read the words on the scroll.

Many legends are told about the Cave of Hira. Some say a spider wove its web across the entrance, others that branches sprouted and covered it completely, and still another that pigeons nested in the surrounding trees to distract Muhammad from his task of receiving the word of Allah.

Some say Muhammad had the power to work miracles, although he never claimed to have divine powers. He called himself nothing more than a messenger of Allah. Various legends say he could control the movement of the planets, that he lived completely without sin, and that he can ask Allah for mercy on behalf of sinners on the last day of judgment.

A collection of stories about an uncle of the prophet Muhammad is popular throughout the Muslim world, especially in Southeast Asia. The collection is called the *Chronicles of Amir Hamza,* and contains stories about how Muhammad's uncle Amir Hamza defended him in many battles.

Middle Eastern lore

One of the most famous literary works by Muslim writers of the Middle East is the book of four-line poems *The Rubáiyát.* It was written by Omar Khayyám, a Persian poet, mathematician, and astronomer who lived during the late eleventh and early twelfth centuries. Another is the book of adventure tales about Ali Baba and the Forty Thieves, Aladdin, and Sinbad the Sailor, called *A Thousand and One Nights,* or *The Arabian Nights.* The earliest stories in the collection are from Baghdad, Iraq, and were written during the late 700s.

One of many Iraqi folktales is called "Five Threads." It is about a pair of sparrows who fasted during Ramadan. At the end of Ramadan, when the feast of Id al-Fitr begins, Papa Sparrow brings home seven grains of wheat for the Id feast. Mama Sparrow arranges them on the table and waits for sundown and for Papa to come home. The sun sets and the moon comes up and Papa has not returned. Mama Sparrow, thinking he has stopped off to eat with his friends, eats one grain of wheat. Then two, then three—until all the wheat is gone.

When Papa finally returns with friends to eat the grains of wheat and finds them gone, he is angry and sends Mama back home to her father. But he soon misses her and tries to win her back. She refuses to come home with him. So he buys her five beautiful colored threads as a present. She is so pleased that she returns home and decorates her nest with the five threads. Papa gets seven more grains of wheat and brings his friends home for a big feast.

Customs, Traditions, Ceremonies

The most important elements of worship in Islam are the Five Pillars of Islam. They must be followed by all Muslims as part of their obligation to Allah. The first, and most basic pillar, is called *sha-hadah*, or confession of faith. Muslims say, "There is no God but the one God, and Muhammed is His prophet," as a declaration of Islamic faith many times throughout the day. The fourth pillar is *sawm*, or the fast of Ramadan.

Breakfast earlier than usual

During Ramadan, each morning before dawn Muslims eat a meal called *suhur* (pronounced soo-HER). They must rise very early and completely finish the suhur meal before dawn arrives and the time for fasting begins. Dawn is said to have arrived when there is enough light outside to see the difference between a black thread and a white thread. In Middle Eastern countries, a *muezzin* (pronounced moo-EH-zin), or caller, shouts "Allah Akbar!" ("Allah is the Greatest!") when it is time for suhur and morning prayers.

Depending on the season when Ramadan falls, suhur can be a large meal or a fairly light meal. In summer, when they must fast for as many as sixteen hours, Muslims eat more for suhur than in winter, when there are only about ten hours of fasting.

The daily fast of Ramadan

The Ramadan fast from sunup to sundown is at the heart of the observance of Ramadan. No food or water may be ingested from the time the sun rises until it has set. A Muslim should not even lick a

"Ramadan"

The moon that once was full, ripe and
  golden,
Wasted away, thin as the rind of a melon,
Like those poor whom sudden ill fortune
Has wasted away like a waning moon.

Like the generous who leave behind
All that was selfish and unkind,
The moon comes out of the tent of the
  night
And finds its way with a lamp of light.

The lamp of the moon is relit
And the hungry and thirsty
In the desert or the city
Make a feast to welcome it.

—*Stanley Cook*

Source: Let's Celebrate, compiled by John Foster. Oxford: Oxford University Press, 1989, p. 47.

postage stamp, chew gum, smoke, take medicines or injections, or wear perfume. Cooks may taste foods, and people who are buying foods may taste them, but the foods must not be swallowed. Some very religious Muslims will not swallow their own saliva, take deep breaths of fresh air, or enjoy the scent of a flower.

Muslims believe that Allah has commanded them to fast and that fasting makes them stronger in their faith and allows them forgiveness for their sins. Fasting also helps Muslims to know how it feels to be poor and hungry so they might better understand and help people who are in need.

Even though they may feel irritable, tired, and hungry as they fast during Ramadan, Muslims must always be polite and kind to others. They must not break promises, gossip, or quarrel, for any of these things will negate the day's fast, which means the day of fasting will not count. Ramadan can be a difficult month, but it is also a rewarding month and a time to grow closer to family, friends, and the Muslim community. Fortunately, in modern times, many offices and businesses shorten work hours during Ramadan so that fasting Muslims are able to get enough rest each day.

There are many guidelines about fasting. Elderly people, children under age twelve, people who are ill, pregnant or nursing mothers, women who are menstruating, soldiers on active duty, and people who are traveling are not required to fast because they need the energy that food and drink gives them. Except for the elderly and children, when the condition that prevented an individual from fasting passes, he or she is expected to make up the days by fasting at another time of year.

People who cannot fast are asked to feed a poor person for each day they do not fast. If a person chooses to fast under difficult circumstances and the fasting causes death, the person is said to have died with honor and to be blessed by Allah. Children under age twelve are asked to fast for one or two days several times during the month of Ramadan. This short period of fasting will help them prepare for the month-long fast in the future.

Breaking the fast with a feast

Muslims break the daytime fast of Ramadan each evening after sundown—as soon as it is too dark to tell the difference between a white thread and a black—with a big meal called *iftar* (pronounced if-TAHR). They first eat some dates and drink water, because this was the way Muhammad and his followers broke the Ramadan fast more than a thousand years ago. Then they wash and perform their evening prayers. After prayers, the family sits down to delicious foods and refreshing fruity drinks, tea, and coffee. Families often invite guests to join the iftar.

After dinner, families go to the mosque (pronounced MOSK; Islamic temple for prayer and worship) for *Taraweeh* (Night Prayers). Those who can bring food for the poor, who might have had little or nothing to eat during the evening. The traditional Ramadan greeting in Arabic is "Assalamu Alaikum! Ramadan Mubarak!" (pronounced muh-BAHR-ak), which means "Peace be upon you. Have a happy and blessed Ramadan."

Nighttime is a time for festivities during Ramadan, especially in the cities, where people go out to restaurants, cafés, and hotels for food and drink, visiting, and entertainment. In Muslim countries, the streets are often decorated during Ramadan, and shops stay open late so that people may purchase gifts for Id al-Fitr.

The Night of Power

Muslims believe that the twenty-seventh night of Ramadan is the night when the angel Gabriel first began giving the words of the Koran to Muhammad. This night is called Lailat al-Qadr, "the Night of Power." Some Muslims pray and read the Koran all night during the last ten nights of Ramadan, and they believe the

Thousands of Muslims congregate at the Jama Masjid (mosque) in New Delhi, India, for prayers on the first day of Id al-Fitr in 1999. Muslims face in the direction of Mecca when praying. Reproduced by permission of AP/Wide World Photos.

last ten odd-numbered nights are especially holy. It is said that angels visit the Earth on these nights and bestow blessings on everyone. Muslims also believe that Allah determines the events of the coming year on the last nights of Ramadan.

Praying to Allah and reading the Koran

Salat, or saying daily prayers is the second pillar of Islam. These prayers are especially important and comforting during Ramadan. Muslims pray five times a day—at sunrise, at noon, at mid-afternoon, at sunset, and before going to bed. They face in the direction of Mecca and the Kaaba when praying.

Before praying, whether at home or in a mosque, Muslims wash their hands, face, forearms up to the elbows, and feet up to the ankles. They remove their shoes before entering a mosque or praying anywhere, because shoes are believed to be unclean.

During prayers, a Muslim has four postures, which are performed while reciting from the Koran. The first is to stand

Mosques

Muslims worship in sacred buildings called mosques (pronounced MOSKS). Mosques throughout the world are built with at least one huge domed roof and at least one minaret, or high tower. Inside the mosque is a large, open room, often with archways and a high ceiling formed by the dome. There are no furnishings, but the floors are usually covered with beautiful carpets. People also bring their own prayer mats to place on the floor of the mosque.

There are no pictures of people or animals to distract Muslims from thoughts of Allah. Instead, the walls and ceiling are decorated with beautifully written verses from the Koran. Colorful geometric designs are also painted on tiles that cover the walls, and many mosques have stained glass windows.

Each mosque has a small nook called the mihrab (pronounced MEE-ruhb), which faces the direction of Mecca. The person who leads the prayers and recites from the Koran, always in Arabic, is called the imam (ih-MAHM).

upright to show upright, good behavior toward Allah. The second is to bow down from the waist to show respect and reverence for Allah. The third is to kneel upright, with hands on knees, and the fourth is to bow face down to the floor, with knees, feet, hands, and face touching the prayer mat or carpet in the mosque to show complete submission to Allah.

If possible, only the hands and face should show during prayer. White prayer robes, head coverings, and socks should be worn over regular clothes. In many Muslim countries, however, workers and businessmen pray on the streets during the day, kneeling on prayer mats in their business suits.

Most Muslim women pray at home, but they are encouraged to go to the mosque to pray on special days, such as the first day of Id al-Fitr. Women and girls enter the mosque through a different door from the men and boys and pray in a special, enclosed room or balcony, or in rows apart from and behind the men and boys.

Many Muslims read from the Koran after suhur, after breaking the fast in the evening, and whenever possible throughout the day during Ramadan. Adults try to read the entire Koran at least once during the month-long observance. Through prayer, reading the Koran, and fasting, Muslims try to grow closer to Allah.

Helping the poor as a way of worship

Muslims believe that helping those in need is part of what Allah has commanded them to do, and they give to the poor and to charity throughout the year. At the end of Ramadan, they pay an additional portion of their earnings to help children and adults around the world, especially in poorer Muslim countries. This giving is called "paying zakat" and is part of the third pillar of Islam. Some of the money also goes to help keep mosques clean and in good repair.

Zakat means "purify," and paying zakat is considered a way of worshiping Allah. Muslims believe that there would be no wealth without Allah's help and that all riches really belong to Allah. In many communities, the zakat is paid a few days before Id al-Fitr so that poorer families can afford to buy food and small gifts for the holiday.

The little feast that is a big holiday

As the fast of Ramadan draws to a close, Muslim families begin watching for the crescent moon that is a sure sign that the tenth month, Shawwal, has begun. This means the long fast of Ramadan has come to an end and the festival of Id al-Fitr, also known as the Feast of Fast Breaking, or the Lesser Feast, can begin.

Id al-Fitr is a joyous occasion of feasting and merriment. Muslims celebrate another year of successful fasting during Ramadan and give thanks to Allah for providing them with the Koran through the prophet Muhammad.

In Muslim countries, Id al-Fitr is a national holiday that lasts for three days. Government offices and most businesses close during Id so that workers can be with their families. Work actually slows down for a week before and after Id as well. Family members living in other parts of the world travel home for Id, which is considered the most important holiday of the year in many Muslim countries.

Flowers, food, and family

People begin preparing for Id during the last week of Ramadan. They clean their houses and decorate both homes and mosques with colorful, fragrant flowers. When shops are open during the last several nights of Ramadan, parents buy toys, candy, and other gifts for their children and gifts for family members, friends, and neighbors, to be given during Id.

On the first morning of Id al-Fitr, everyone rises early, bathes, and dresses in their best clothing. Many Muslims, having denied themselves the pleasures of sweet scents during Ramadan, put on perfume or scented oils. Then they share a big breakfast, during which family members express thanks to Allah for another Ramadan. They also ask forgiveness from one another for any wrongs they may have done.

After breakfast, everyone in the community gathers at a park or large meeting ground for Id prayers. Even the women and girls, who usually stay at home to pray, come to the special gathering on the morning of Id al-Fitr.

The people thank Allah for helping them to fast through Ramadan and for giving them the Koran. They ask Allah to keep them well so that they might fast again next year. The imam gives a special prayer and reading from the Koran. Muslims greet one another with hugs and say, "Id Mubarak!" (pronounced EED moo-BAH-rahk), which means "Happy and Blessed Id!" Friends and neighbors ask one another for forgiveness for wrongs they have done during the past year.

After the prayer gathering, many families go to cemeteries and visit the graves of relatives to pray for their souls. Then they return home for the big Id al-Fitr feast, which includes a bounty of favorite foods.

The sweetest day of the year

Id is a time for visiting relatives, friends, and neighbors. Each home may receive many guests during the days of Id, and each family will visit every home they can. Trays of different kinds of candies, cakes, and pastries are offered to guests, and coffee and tea are served.

Neighbors try to give presents not only to their own children, but to one another's children as well. Each family will buy many gifts to give away during the holiday. In Turkey, Id is called Seker Bayram, the Candy (or Sugar) Holiday. On this sweet holiday, children are given candy wrapped in colorful handkerchiefs.

Clothing, Costumes

The prophet Muhammad is said to have had new clothes made for him during Ramadan and to have put them on for the celebration of Id al-Fitr. Therefore, the Muslim custom of getting new clothes and wearing them on the morning of Id has been a part of the celebration for centuries. Children often receive gifts of new clothing for Id.

Foods, Recipes

Nighttime and pre-dawn meals during Ramadan are big occasions for Muslim families. Many Muslims still break the Ramadan fast each evening as the prophet Muhammad and his followers did, with a few dates and a glass of water, a little salt, or some milk and honey.

After evening prayers comes the big meal called iftar. No one or two special foods are traditional for these meals; families eat their favorite foods, depending on their nationality. In the United States this might be Turkish or Saudi Arabian, Indian or Southeast Asian, or a mixture of many different Middle Eastern and Asian foods. Iftar may also include traditional American holiday foods like turkey and dressing.

Drinking alcoholic beverages is forbidden in Islam. Instead, Muslims serve refreshing fruit drinks. A drink made from raisins, dates, and tamarind is often served for iftar. In Saudi Arabia, a sweet drink is made from apricots.

During the daylight hours of Ramadan, restaurants in Muslim countries are closed, but they reopen at sunset and are filled with people enjoying delicious foods and various forms of entertainment. In large cities, like Cairo, Egypt, hotels and catering companies set up food and entertainment tents for the nighttime crowd during Ramadan. Markets are open during the day, and people are allowed to taste foods they want to buy for iftar, but they must not swallow the food or the day's fast does not count.

The Id feast

In Saudi Arabia and other Muslim countries, the table is set for the Id feast with large platters of different kinds of food. The family uses its most elegant silverware and dishes, and bowls of fruit are placed on the table.

Eating pork is forbidden to Muslims, but other meats such as beef, lamb, and fish are popular. Meat and rice dishes cooked with spices are special favorites for the Id al-Fitr feast. And, because a wide variety of delicious vegetables is grown in the Middle East, vegetables are always an important part of the meal.

Some dishes that are commonly served for the Id feast in Middle Eastern countries include *yalanchi,* a sweet, crunchy, and spicy rice stuffing for eggplant, grape leaves, bell peppers, or other vegetables; fried pastries filled with meat and cheeses; yogurt and bean dishes; shish kabob (meats and vegetables grilled on a skewer); and salads like *tabouli,* which is made with bulgur wheat, tomatoes, parsley, olive oil, and lemon juice; and *baba ghanouj,* made with chopped eggplant, lemon juice, and sesame paste.

Pastries and sweets of all kinds are served throughout the Id holiday. In Egypt, Muslims enjoy a special bread called *kahk.* In Jordan, small cookies called *ma'moul* are made for Id al-Fitr. The dough is made from semolina, dates, and pistachio nuts. It is then pressed in a small wooden mold to give the cookies a special design. Cakes and halvah, a candy made from crushed sesame seeds and honey, are traditional favorites. Also popular is *labaneh,* dried yogurt rolled into balls.

Baklava, made from a light, flaky pastry with honey and nut filling, is a well-known Middle Eastern treat that is very popular in Turkey. People in Turkey also enjoy Turkish Delight, colorful candy made from gelatin formed into cubes and coated with sugar. Muslims in India, Pakistan, and Bangladesh serve a milky pudding made with noodles, nuts, and cardamom for Id.

Muslim women select dried dates for dinner dessert on the first day of Ramadan in Kuala Lumpur, Malaysia, in 1999. During Ramadan people are allowed to taste foods they want to buy for iftar, but they must not swallow the food. Reproduced by permission of AP/Wide World Photos.

Arts, Crafts, Games

During Ramadan in Egypt and other Muslim countries, brightly colored and intricately designed lanterns hang along the city streets. When they are lit at nightfall, everyone knows it is time for eating, drinking, shopping, visiting, and having fun before the fasting begins anew at dawn.

Muslim communities everywhere set up small carnivals and amusement parks for Ramadan and Id al-Fitr. Children love to

Yalanchi (Stuffed Peppers)

Ingredients

1 cup cooked rice

1 medium onion, minced

½ cup seedless raisins, soaked in warm water for 12 minutes, then drained

½ cup pine nuts, finely chopped

1 tablespoon finely chopped fresh parsley

juice of 1 lemon

2½ tablespoons olive oil

½ teaspoon ground cinnamon

½ teaspoon ground allspice

1 tablespoon sugar

salt and pepper to taste

6 large bell peppers

Directions

1. Slice the tops off the bell peppers and pull out the seeds and pulp. Rinse inside to remove loose seeds. Turn the peppers upside down on paper towels to drain.

2. Heat the olive oil in a large skillet and add onion, stirring to fry for about 3 minutes.

3. Add the chopped pine nuts, raisins, spices, sugar, parsley, and lemon juice and stir for about 2 more minutes, adding a little more oil if foods start to stick.

4. Add the rice, and salt and pepper to taste. Stir to heat rice and mix all ingredients, about 3 more minutes.

5. Lightly oil the skins of the peppers with olive oil, and stuff each one with the rice mixture.

6. Place stuffed peppers in a baking pan, spooning any leftover stuffing between the peppers. Bake for about 30 minutes at 350 degrees, until peppers are tender.

Serves 4

go on the rides and play games like coin toss, shooting cap guns for prizes, and egg jousting. Among Muslims in the Philippines, Id al-Fitr is a time for watching sports like horse and boat racing and participating in games of skill and strength.

Symbols

By far, the most important symbol of Ramadan, and the most important symbol of Islam, is the Koran, the holy book of Islam. Muslims believe it contains the exact words that Allah spoke to the prophet Muhammad through the angel Gabriel. The Koran is kept covered with a special cloth when it is not being read; it should not get soiled or touch the ground. When it is being read, the Koran often rests on a folding wooden stand.

According to legend, Muhammad's followers wrote the sacred words on any material they could find, even stones and tree bark. Muhammad's secretary, Zaid, gathered all these writings together and recopied them into the first Koran in the year 650, eighteen years after Muhammad's death.

Koran means "that which is revealed." The Koran was originally written in Arabic, which has its own alphabet and is read from right to left. Today, copies of the Koran are written in Arabic, often with a translation on the facing page. Although the Koran has been translated into many other languages, Muslims prefer to learn Arabic so they can read the Koran in its original language. They believe the words are most beautiful and powerful when read in Arabic.

The Koran forms the foundation for daily life in all Muslim countries. Two hundred of the six thousand verses in the Koran are laws governing a Muslim's relationship to neighbors and community and to Allah. It also contains rules about government, family, economics, and war and peace. In addition, the Koran has many of same stories about Adam, Noah and the Ark, Abraham and his family, Moses, and Jesus that are found in the Jewish Torah and the Christian Bible.

The Koran contains 114 chapters, called *suras* (pronounced SUH-ruhs), arranged according to length, from longest to shortest. Muslims try to memorize the suras. A Muslim who memorizes the entire Koran is called a *hafiz* (pronounced HAH-fiz). The first sura in the Koran has been called the Lord's Prayer of Islam and is said to be the "essence" of the Koran:

> In the name of Allah, the Beneficent,
>   the Merciful!
> Praise be to Allah, Lord of the Worlds,
> the Beneficent, the Merciful,

> Ruler of the Day of Judgment,
> Thee alone we worship; Thee alone
>   we ask for help.
> Show us the straight path,
> The path of those whom Thou hast
>   favored;
> Not of those who have earned Thine
>   anger
> nor of those who go astray.

Children often attend an Islamic school located near a mosque, where they learn about the Islamic religion, learn to read the Koran, and study other subjects. Children who do not attend an Islamic school usually attend classes on Saturday to learn Arabic so they can read the Koran. While they are fasting during Ramadan, Muslims pray and read the Koran as often as possible. Most adults try to read the Koran all the way through at least once during Ramadan.

Islamic religious writings also include the Hadith, six books written during the ninth century that are said to represent Muhammad's daily teachings about life. Only the Koran, however, is accepted as the word of Allah.

In Muslim countries, competitions are held to see who can read the Koran with the best Arabic pronunciation and reading style. Qirah is the art of reading from the Koran, and a person who reads the Koran aloud in the mosque is called a Qari.

A large Koran-reading competition is held in Kuala Lumpur, the capital of Malaysia, during the month of Ramadan, and is attended by Muslims from all over the world. It is a major event in Malaysia, where Islam is the state religion. The competition goes on for six nights. The winner receives a gold trophy, and runners-up receive silver and cash awards.

The new moon

The new moon is the thin crescent moon that first appears following nights when no moon can be seen in the sky. In Islam, and many other religions, the new moon, or crescent moon, symbolizes hope and renewal after a time of darkness. The crescent moon with a single star has been a symbol of Islam since the fifteenth century, when it was introduced by the Turks. Many Muslim countries have this symbol on their flags.

The sighting of the new moon is very important in the observance of both Ramadan and Id al-Fitr. The month of fasting begins when at least two people sight the new moon that begins the month of Ramadan. Id al-Fitr begins with the sighting of the new moon marking the beginning of the month of Shawwal, immediately following Ramadan.

In the earlier days of Islam, a judge or important community figure would walk in a procession to the top of a mountain or hill to try and see the new moon. A green flag was flown from the top of a mosque and a cannon or gun was fired to announce the sighting of the new moon. Today, Islamic officials watch for the new moon from an observatory. When the new moon is sighted, word is spread through radio, television, and newspapers.

In non-Muslim countries such as the United States, Muslims may call their local mosque for information about the sighting of the new moon. If the new moon cannot be seen for several nights because of cloudy weather, the new month begins no later than thirty days after the previous month began.

In Muslim countries, some people still like to go out to the hills or desert or climb onto their rooftops to look for the new moon that indicates the beginning of Ramadan. Seeing the new moon is a joyful and exciting occasion for Muslims, because it marks the beginning of the most important and holy time of year. After exchanging good wishes, people hurry home to pray and to begin preparations for a pre-dawn meal that will keep away hunger for a few hours on the first day of Ramadan fasting.

Dates

The Middle Eastern fruit of the date palm tree has been a symbol of breaking the daily fast of Ramadan since the time of Muhammad. It is said that the Prophet himself, along with his followers, broke the daily fast during the month of Ramadan by eating a few dates and drinking some water. This tradition is still followed today, when Muslims eat dates and drink water at sundown and before the evening prayers each night of Ramadan. Afterward, they sit down to a nighttime feast called iftar.

Muslims eat an odd number of dates—such as three or five—when breaking their fast, because they believe that Allah loves odd numbers. Muslims point to many signs that add credence to this belief. One explanation is that Allah is the one God and one is an odd number; another is that Allah's name appears in the Koran ninety-nine times, also an odd number.

Music, Dance

Like the foods served during Ramadan, music and dance vary from country to country throughout the Muslim

Iraqi girls play on makeshift swings in a Baghdad neighborhood on the second day of Id al-Fitr in 1999. At the many carnivals set up during Ramadan, children swing, take a spin on rides, and play games like coin toss. Reproduced by permission of AP/Wide World Photos.

world. Although music and dancing are not a part of the observance of Ramadan fasting, people may enjoy musical entertainment during the nighttime hours when they are not fasting. In Turkey, people love traditional music and folk dancing, and performances are often held during Id al-Fitr. In Jordan, the men perform a dance accompanied by drumming during Id.

Among Muslims in western Africa, a festival similar to Carnival in other countries is held during the two days before Ramadan. This is a time for singing and dancing in the streets. In Malaya, there is folk dancing during Id, and in the Philippines, musical programs and readings from the Koran make up a special evening program during Id al-Fitr.

Special Role of Children, Young Adults

Children participate in every religious aspect of Ramadan and other Muslim holidays. Although children under twelve either do not fast at all or fast for only a few

Young Pakistani women in Lahore in 1999 shop for clothes in which to celebrate Id al-Fitr.
During Id al-Fitr, children are treated to gifts of clothing, money, shoes, games, and toys.
Reproduced by permission of AP/Wide World Photos.

days during the month of Ramadan, they observe and prepare for the time they will join in the month-long observance. They also enjoy the devotion and family togetherness that accompany this holy month.

Boys attend services at the mosque with their fathers, and girls pray at home with their mothers. The entire family also prays together at home and reads from the Koran daily. During Ramadan, children often visit with friends and family members. They show respect for the elder members of the family, greeting parents—and especially grandparents—by kissing their hands. In many Muslim countries, everyone rises when an elder enters the room.

After Ramadan comes Id al-Fitr, a holiday during which children are treated to gifts of clothing, money, shoes, games, and toys. They also receive lots of candy and other sweets. In Turkey, a sugary gelatin candy comes wrapped in colorful handkerchiefs as part of the children's Id gifts. In the Sudan, children receive candy dolls holding lovely paper fans that are collected as keepsakes over the years. Muslim children look forward to Id al-Fitr the way Christian children anticipate Christmas.

Children enjoy the carnivals during Id, which feature rides, music, and games. Shadow-puppet shows—in which the actors are shadows of cutout figures moved behind a lighted screen—are especially popular with Muslim children in Southeast Asia.

For More Information

Dunn, John. *The Spread of Islam.* San Diego: Lucent Books, 1996.

Ghazi, Suhaib Hamid. *Ramadan.* New York: Holiday House, 1996.

Husain, Sharukh. *What Do We Know About Islam?* New York: Peter Bedrick Books, 1995.

Web sites

"Islamia." [Online] http://www.islamia.com (accessed on February 21, 2000).

"Islamic Holidays and Observances: Ramadan." [Online] http://www.colostate.edu/Orgs/MSA/events/Ramadan.html (accessed on February 21, 2000).

"Ramadan on the Net." [Online] http://www.holidays.net/ramadan (accessed on February 21, 2000).

Sources

Berg, Elizabeth. *Egypt.* Milwaukee: Gareth Stevens, 1997, pp. 8–15.

Ellwood, Robert S. Jr. *Words of the World's Religions: An Anthology.* Engelwood Cliffs, N.J.: Prentice-Hall, 1977, pp. 401–03.

Hassig, Susan M. *Iraq.* New York: Marshall Cavendish, 1994, pp. 67–72, 85–89, 115–20.

Leeming, David Adams. *The World of Myth: An Anthology.* New York: Oxford University Press, 1990, pp. 345–47.

MacDonald, Margaret Read. *Celebrate the World: Twenty Tellable Folktales for Multicultural Festivals.* New York: H. W. Wilson, 1994, pp. 43–51.

MacMillan, Dianne M. *Ramadan and Id al-Fitr.* Hillside, N.J.: Enslow, 1994.

Monroe, Charles R. *World Religions: An Introduction.* Amherst, N.Y.: Prometheus Books, 1995, pp. 211–19.

Pateman, Robert. *Egypt.* In *Cultures of the World* series. New York: Marshall Cavendish, 1995, pp. 72–74, 105–07, 113–20.

Richards, Chris, general ed. *The Illustrated Encyclopedia of World Religions.* Rockport, Mass.: Element Books, 1997, pp. 169, 177.

Schneider, Howard. "Ramadan Changing with Times." *Houston Chronicle.* January 16, 1999, p. 26A.

Thompson, Sue Ellen. *Holiday Symbols 1998.* Detroit, Mich.: Omnigraphics, 1998, pp. 196–98, 386–90.

Webb, Lois Sinaiko. *Holidays of the World Cookbook for Students.* Phoenix, Ariz.: Oryx Press, 1995, pp. 57, 59, 64, 66.

Thanksgiving and Harvest Festivals

Also Known As:
Obzinky (Czech Republic and Slovakia)
Pongol (India)
New Yam Festival (Nigeria)
Incwala (Swaziland)
Thanksgiving (United States)

Introduction

Celebrating and giving thanks for a bountiful harvest is one of the world's oldest holiday customs. People in countries throughout the world continue to set aside certain times of year to give thanks. These harvest holidays coincide with when the harvest occurs in a particular country. For instance, India's rice harvest festival, Pongol (pronounced PONG-gahl), is held in January, and Nigeria's New Yam Festival falls in July or August.

Some countries hold elaborate harvest festivals that include rituals and ceremonies that are centuries old. Czechs and Slovaks celebrate the harvest with a folk festival called Obzinky (pronounced OB-zen-kih), which was originally held to celebrate the completion of the harvest and to honor landowners, who in turn treated their farm servants to a feast.

For other cultures, celebrating the harvest is considered a sacred time. For instance, India's Pongol festival, which is held for several days, includes many Hindu rituals. The ceremony known as Incwala (pronounced TDLICKH-wah-luh) is the most important traditional holiday in Swaziland. It not only celebrates the harvest, but it is also a national holiday that binds the nation of Swaziland to its king.

Harvest festivals are part of some countries' New Year celebrations, because in agricultural societies the new year traditionally began after the harvest. In India, some consider Pongol as their New Year's Day.

In the United States, the harvest festival known as Thanksgiving is celebrated on the fourth Thursday in November. Because the United States is no longer a country based on an agricultural economy, the festival only symbolically celebrates the harvest. The highlight of Thanksgiving Day is sharing a large meal that includes traditional foods. The holiday usually extends through Thanksgiving weekend when families attend church services, watch sports, and attend parades.

History

Since people first began to cultivate crops, thousands of years ago, they have held ceremonies and rituals to give thanks

Holiday Fact Box: Thanksgiving and Harvest Festivals

Themes

Giving thanks for the earth's gifts; bidding goodbye to summer and welcoming winter; relaxing after summer's hard work; remembering the dead.

Type of Holiday

Thanksgiving and harvest festivals have both religious and agricultural significance. Because they were first celebrated by ancient cultures, their origins are often difficult to pinpoint.

When Celebrated

Harvest festivals are usually held at the end of the growing season, when the last of the fruits and vegetables and other crops have been gathered and stored. In the Northern Hemisphere, this is usually between September and November. In the Southern Hemisphere, harvest times for different crops vary widely.

for a good growing season when plenty of fruits, vegetables, and grains were produced. The ancient Egyptians, Syrians, Mesopotamians, Greeks, Romans, Hebrews, and Chinese held harvest festivals. The Jewish festival Sukkoth (pronounced SUH-kus), during which people build small huts, or "booths," of branches and decorate them with fruits and vegetables, is one of the oldest harvest festivals, first celebrated about three thousand years ago.

Ancient peoples who lived near the Mediterranean Sea worshiped a goddess of agriculture. The Greeks called their goddess Demeter (pronounced dih-MEE-ter), and she was honored each year at two major festivals. These were times for feasting, games, and ceremonies honoring the goddess and giving thanks for a successful harvest. The Greeks also worshiped a god of wine, Bacchus (pronounced BA-kuss), to ensure a good grape harvest.

The ancient Romans held a harvest festival called Cerelia, to honor Ceres (pronounced SIR-eez), their goddess of grain. The word "cereal" comes from her name. This festival included offerings to the goddess of newly harvested grain and fruits, the sacrifice of a pig, as well as music, parades, games, sports, and a thanksgiving feast.

A Chinese harvest festival with ancient beginnings is the Harvest Moon Festival, which is held to celebrate the birthday of the moon. It includes a thanksgiving feast of roasted pig, newly harvested fruits, and moon cakes stamped on top with a picture of a rabbit, which the Chinese imagine is on the face of the full moon. The ancient Chinese believed that flowers would fall from the moon during this festival and that anyone who saw them would have good luck.

Celebrating the harvest in Africa and India

The people of Africa have long celebrated the harvest by making offerings to the spirits of the earth, including sacrificial animals and the first vegetables and grains gathered at the end of the growing season. These ceremonies were solemn but were followed by feasting, singing, and dancing. For example, the ancient Egyptian harvest festival in

A Colonial American family using scythes to harvest wheat. Since people first began to cultivate crops, ceremonies and rituals have been held to give thanks for a good growing season.
Reproduced by permission of the Corbis Corporation (Bellevue).

honor of Min, the god of crops and fertility, included a procession, a great feast with music and dancing, and sports and games.

Many ancient farmers believed spirits that made the crops grow would be released, or even killed, when the crops were harvested. Early Egyptian farmers pretended to cry as they harvested their grain so that its spirit would not be angry with them. In both Africa and India, as well as in many American Indian cultures, people have traditionally been forbidden to eat of the newly harvested foods, called "first

fruits," until thanks has been given to the gods or spirits for providing them.

The New Yam Festival of Nigeria is an ancient tribal "first fruits" celebration that is still widely celebrated today. The people of Swaziland continue to celebrate their first fruits ceremony, Incwala, whose origins have survived only in legend.

In India, which has one of the world's longest histories of civilization and farming, the grain harvest has been celebrated for thousands of years. Some historians believe the harvest festival Pongol evolved from the combination of a southern Indian harvest festival and a winter solstice celebration introduced by the Aryans. The Aryans were northern peoples who spread from the colder climates of southern Russia and eastern Europe through Mesopotamia, Asia Minor, and India.

Harvest festivals in Europe

One of the earliest harvest festivals in western Europe was Samhain (pronounced SOW-en), the Celtic harvest festival held in November and December, when food was gathered in and preparations were made for the long winter.

The Celts (pronounced KELTS) lived in Ireland, Scotland, England, Wales, and northern France more than two thousand years ago. They believed that ghosts roamed the earth at Samhain, and Celtic priests performed certain rituals to keep the mischievous spirits from doing harm. Some writers believe that Samhain, considered the Celtic New Year, later contributed to some traditions associated with both Halloween and New Year celebrations in Europe.

As Christianity became widespread in Europe and replaced earlier pagan (worshiping many gods) religions like that of the Celts, Europeans began giving thanks to the one Christian God rather than to various spirits or gods associated with the harvest. They also introduced Christian rituals that blended with traditional harvest customs.

Some of the earliest Christianity-influenced harvest festivals began during the Middle Ages (about 500 to 1500). People went to church to seek God's blessing on the harvest, but feasting, music and dancing, and some pre-Christianity customs were still held outside of church ceremonies.

During the Harvest Home Festival, popular in England, a girl crowned as the harvest queen, wearing a wreath of grain and flowers, rode home from the fields on a wagon. Afterward, the farm workers feasted, danced, played games, and dressed in costumes, a custom that probably had its roots in the ancient Samhain celebrations when people wore animal skins to disguise themselves from roaming spirits.

The Festival of Lammas, or "Loaf Mass," was held a few days after the Harvest Home Festival and marked the baking of the first loaves of bread from newly harvested grain. Lammas included a religious ceremony in which loaves were blessed in church and thanks given to God for the wheat harvest.

The Harvest Home Festival survived into the 1600s in England, and some English settlers brought these customs with them to the American colonies, where they later influenced the celebration of the American harvest festival, Thanksgiving.

During the Middle Ages, French, German, Dutch, Swedish, Irish, and English Catholics began celebrating the Feast of Saint Martin of Tours (316–397), also called Martinmas, on November 11. This feast was held in honor of the Hungarian saint who, legend says, hid in a barn when he heard he had received an appointment as bishop because he did not believe he was worthy of such an honor. A honking goose is said to have revealed his hiding place, so roast goose became the main dish for the traditional Martinmas feast, along with wine made from the grape harvest.

Early Saint Martin's day folk celebrations included elements of Halloween, with children marching in parades carrying homemade lanterns, sometimes carved from turnips or gourds, like jack-o'-lanterns. Protestants in Germany and other European countries later came to celebrate the Feast of Saint Martin in honor of the German religious leader and founder of Protestantism, Martin Luther (1483–1546), who was born on November 10 and was named for Saint Martin of Tours.

In the eighteenth and nineteenth centuries, Protestant churches decorated with harvested pumpkins, flowers, and loaves of bread made from new grain. In England, Harvest Thanksgiving became an official religious festival, held on a Sunday in September or October. Some churches held harvest services on the Sunday nearest Saint Michael's Day, September 29, the feast of Saint Michael the archangel. This festival fell at the end of the harvest season in Great Britain and was also a time for settling debts. It occurred at the time of year when geese were fattest and ready to eat.

Many of the customs of the Czech and Slovak folk harvest festival Obzinky may have originated with pagan ceremonies in honor of the gods of the fields. Farmers offered them a sheaf of wheat from the harvest as thanks for their gift of grain. Obzinky has been celebrated since about the tenth century, with singing, dancing, and feasting. It has kept many of the customs and folklore from earlier times, such as decorating a wreath or sheaf of grain and giving it a place of honor in the home. The Czech and Slovak church harvest festival Posviceni (pronounced POS-vih-tsee-nih), also hundreds of years old, includes a service for giving thanks to God and asking a blessing on the harvest.

Harvest holidays in the Americas

The Thanksgiving harvest festival celebrated in the United States today combines elements introduced both by American Indians and European settlers. The American Indians had celebrated harvest festivals for centuries prior to the first colonizers who settled in America from Spain, the Netherlands, and England. An especially important festival was, and is, the Green Corn Ceremony, celebrated by American Indian tribes in the Northeast and Southeast, and among tribes in the Southwest, including the Pueblo.

The festivals celebrated both the ripening of the first corn of the season and the harvesting of the first corn. The tribes shared many of the same rituals, but the actual festivals were celebrated at different times of the year depending on when the harvest occurred in the various regions of the country.

When English colonizers began arriving in America during the early 1600s, they brought their customs with them. As early as 1607, Thanksgiving celebrations were held in the Jamestown, Virginia, colony. They featured many of the English Harvest Home traditions, including guising (pronounced GUY-zing), or dressing in costume. But, history usually upholds that the very first American Thanksgiving was held at Plymouth Colony, and was attended by members of the Wampanoag (pronounced wahm-puh-NO-ag) tribe and British colonists, who would later be known as the Pilgrims.

In 1621, after they had spent their first year in the New World, the Pilgrims held a feast of thanks. Chief Massasoit (pronounced MASS-uh-swah) and some ninety of his Wampanoag Indian men came to the

Massasoit feasting with the Pilgrims. For the first Thanksgiving dinner, Massasoit and ninety of his Wampanoag Indian men brought five deer they had killed to add to the Pilgrims' wild game and harvested crops. Reproduced by permission of the Corbis Corporation (Bellevue).

settlement, bringing five deer they had killed to add to the Pilgrims' wild game and harvested crops. A handful of Pilgrim women and girls cooked for the crowd, and the feast lasted for three days. It was customary for American Indians to feast for three days during their celebrations. The Pilgrim men and boys played games and sports with the Indians, and a small band of Pilgrim soldiers paraded and shot blanks from their muskets.

After that "first" thanksgiving, the various colonies continued to celebrate with feasts of thanks. In 1789, U.S. Presi-dent George Washington (1732–1799) issued a Thanksgiving Proclamation for the United States declaring Thursday, November 26, as a day to give thanks. It was not until 1863, however, that Thanksgiving was declared a national holiday in the United States by President Abraham Lincoln (1809–1865), to be held the last Thursday in November.

Because some months contained five Thursdays, there was confusion over the day to celebrate Thanksgiving for another eight decades until, in 1941, the U.S. Congress declared Thanksgiving—to be celebrated on the fourth Thursday in November—a legal public holiday in the United States.

Folklore, Legends, Stories

Every country with harvest traditions has its own folklore, legends, and stories surrounding these observances. Some date back to ancient times when people believed in sun gods and rain gods who made the crops grow.

In India, where the majority of people follow the Hindu religion, many ancient myths about the gods are taught as part of children's religious training. One is the legend of the bull Basava (BAH-sah-vah), a messenger of the god Shiva (pronounced SHEE-vuh). Because Basava mixed up Shiva's instructions to the people on Earth—telling them to eat daily and bathe once a month instead of bathe daily and eat once a month—Shiva decreed that bulls would plow the fields for man forever to help keep him supplied with food. To this day, bulls and other cattle are honored during the Hindu festival Pongol for their help in planting and harvesting.

Crops that are important to a culture often feature prominently in harvest legends. For instance, rice in India and yams in Africa have their own spirit legends that have been told for centuries. The Ibo people of Nigeria tell the story of a brother and sister that explains how the yam and the cocoyam, a similar starchy root vegetable, became staple foods for their people. Long ago, during a time of famine, a man named Ibo was told by a powerful spirit to kill his son and daughter and cut their bodies into pieces and bury them in hills of soil. He did so, according to the legend, and when the hills sprouted green leaves of the yam and the cocoyam, the spirit told Ibo and his remaining children to farm the crops. The two root crops saved the people from starvation and have been staple foods for centuries in Africa.

Swaziland's harvest festival Incwala is based on an ancient tale about a Swazi queen mother who was banished from the tribe. She fled to the open grasslands with her infant son and the tribe's rainmaking materials. There they lived on wild foods and relied on the branches of a shrub for shelter. The boy grew up to be king of his people. The foods and the shrub later became important parts of the Incwala first fruits ceremony.

Throughout Europe, many superstitions were associated with the harvest, because the amount of food produced in a season could mean either prosperity or starvation for the people. Reapers sometimes rolled on the ground before a harvest for two reasons: the direct contact with the earth was believed to give them great strength for the long hours of hard work ahead, and the rolling represented the number of sheaves (bundles) of harvested grain that would be rolled into the barn when the work was done. The last sheaf of grain gathered in the fields was said to have healing powers and the ability to bring fertility to households and to the farm.

Two well-known poems about the harvest by European writers are "John Barleycorn" (c. 1790), by Scottish poet Robert Burns (1750–1796), who writes about the spirit of the grain as if it were a man, and "The Hock-Cart, or Harvest-Home" (c. 1648), by English poet Robert Herrick

(1591–1674), who describes the ceremony of cutting the last load of grain in the fall and bringing it in for the Harvest Home Festival.

One of the most well-known stories from U.S. history is that of the Pilgrims, who celebrated the first Thanksgiving with the Wampanoag Indians at Plymouth Colony in 1621. Very little was written about this harvest celebration by the colonists themselves, but historians have been able to reconstruct the event using the information from Pilgrim journals and combining it with knowledge about the land and the American Indians of the period.

Customs, Traditions, Ceremonies

For farmers, harvest is a time to rest and be rewarded for a long season of hard work. In many parts of the world, the completion of harvest is a bustling time and is celebrated with music and dancing. In some cultures, the harvest marks the end of an old year and the beginning of a new and so is also considered the New Year, as at Pongol, a rice harvest festival in India.

In the Northern Hemisphere, fall harvest is a time to say goodbye to summer and prepare for winter by bringing in crops and storing food. This time of plenty is celebrated by feasting, as at Thanksgiving in North America. For some people, harvest is a time to remember their ancestors, as the Ibo people of Nigeria do during the New Yam Festival.

Some harvest customs are common to cultures around the world. Among these are giving thanks to God or other deities and spirits for a plentiful harvest, feasting on special foods, sharing with others, and reuniting with family members. In India, farmers even show their thanks to the cattle that help with plowing and harvesting by decorating them with flowers and paint and allowing them to roam freely in the streets.

Among other harvest customs are cleaning homes and businesses and burning old clothing, blankets, ceremonial objects, and utensils on a bonfire. These customs are common to cultures as widely separated as the Tamil people of India during Pongol, the American Indians in their Green Corn Ceremony, and the people of Swaziland following their Incwala ceremony.

Harvest traditions might include taking hay rides, especially in North America and Europe, and attending dances, as during Obzinky in the Czech and Slovak Republics, the Green Corn Ceremony of various American Indian tribes, and Nigeria's New Yam Festival. Watching parades and sporting events is especially popular in North America at Thanksgiving.

People of different cultures might attend plays or reenactments of special events associated with the harvest. Two examples of these are plays and reenactments about the Pilgrims who celebrated the first Thanksgiving at Plymouth Rock in 1621 and a reenactment of the killing of the boy Ahiajoku, who later became known as the god of yam, a legend on which the origin of the Nigerian yam crop is based.

Some African cultures hold elaborate "first fruits" ceremonies that take days of careful preparation in order to bless the newly harvested crops and purify the people before they eat these foods. In Swaziland's Incwala ceremony, these include the ritual preparation of the king, who is the first to taste the foods. American Indians once carried out similar strict cleansing rituals before their Green Corn Ceremonies.

Special church services are held to bless the harvested crops, as at Posviceni in the Czech and Slovak Republics. Meetings centered around keeping peace between nations are also held around the world at Thanksgiving. Harvest time is a time of joy and plenty and of giving thanks. It is an occasion for showing kindness and generosity toward all people.

Clothing, Costumes

Although Thanksgiving is not usually thought of as a time for dressing in costumes, children and adults performing special dances, rituals, or plays during this time wear costumes associated with the ceremony or performance. For example, children reenacting the first American Thanksgiving in a school play dress as Pilgrims and American Indians. During the Incwala ceremony held in Swaziland, the king paints his body and wears a costume made from animal skins and grass. When a large holiday gathering is part of the harvest celebration, people usually put on their nicest clothes for the occasion.

Foods, Recipes

Thanksgiving and harvest festivals center around food, especially crops that provide a major portion of the people's diet. For instance, corn has always been an important food for cultures and countries in North and South America and is often featured at harvest festivals. Indian corn is also used to decorate during Thanksgiving and other harvest celebrations.

Cartoon character Betty Boop floats in the Macy's Thanksgiving Day Parade in 1986. The giant helium balloons are kept earthbound and guided through the streets by handlers holding cords attached to the giant characters. Reproduced by permission of the Corbis Corporation (Bellevue).

In India, rice is a particularly important food, and a special dish of boiled rice sweetened with raw sugar is prepared for Pongol, the rice harvest festival. In Nigeria and other African nations, yams are a dietary staple year round, and people rejoice and hold a two-day ceremony to bless the new yam crop and to make offerings to the spirits for a successful harvest.

Grains such as wheat, rye, barley, and oats are harvested in European coun-

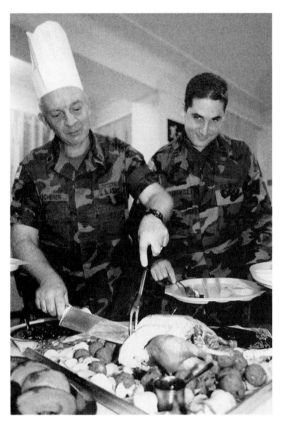

U.S. soldiers stationed in Sarajevo, Yugoslavia, in 1998, enjoy a traditional American Thanksgiving dinner of roast turkey with all the trimmings. Reproduced by permission of AP/Wide World Photos.

dressing, cranberry sauce, vegetables, and pumpkin pie. Other feasts throughout the world might include roast goose, roast pig, ham, sausages, fish, or vegetarian dishes.

Arts, Crafts, Games

People everywhere love to decorate for festivals, and harvest festivals are no exception. In India, for example, women make colorful designs on the floor or ground of the area where a special pot of rice will be boiled for the festival called Pongol. They also decorate the pot itself with leaves and flowers. On one day of this festival, families paint the horns and hooves of their cattle and release them to walk through the streets with flowers, fruit, and beads adorning their necks. People in some African cultures carve intricate designs into gourds called calabashes and use them to make offerings of new yams.

Orange, red, and yellow are colors associated with the brilliant fall season in North America. Homes, schools, and businesses are often decorated in these colors. Common harvest holiday decorations include pumpkins, corn, squash, fall leaves, nuts, and apples. Drawings of the wild turkey, the Pilgrims, and the American Indians are also used to decorate for Thanksgiving.

Games and sports have traditionally been a part of Thanksgiving and harvest holidays. During Pongol festivities in India, farmers sometimes tie bags of money around the necks of bulls, and village youths compete to see who can "take the bull by the horns" and retrieve the money.

tries, and bringing home the last cutting of grain from the fields is an occasion for celebrating. In other countries, celebrations are observed for harvesting new crops of apples, grapes for wine making, nuts, sugarcane, hops for making beer, and for many other vegetables, fruits, and grains.

Sharing a special feast is a universal custom during harvest festivals, and the feast is usually based on particular foods or meals. In North America, Thanksgiving dinner often includes roast turkey and

In early America, people gathered for corn-husking bees at harvest time. These were community parties where everyone participated in removing the outer layers of husk from the ears of corn. Because everyone helped, the work was finished faster. After the work was done, people played games such as rolling an egg or a small pumpkin across a room with a spoon. Some of these games are still played today.

In the United States, watching football games on television has become a favorite pastime on Thanksgiving Day. In some countries, horse or dog racing and bullfights or cockfights are popular harvest holiday pastimes.

Symbols

Because harvest festivals are about the gathering in of crops, specific foods are often considered symbolic of harvest festivals. But some of these foods, such as corn and other grains and the yam of Africa, are also sacred symbols that represent the spirit of the earth and nature. Offering thanks to these spirits was an important religious practice in many early cultures. People often believed that the spirits lived in the crops themselves—especially the first of the season or the last to be harvested—so these crops became very important. Also associated with the harvest are the full moon; the cornucopia, a symbol of plenty; and, in the West, the Thanksgiving turkey.

Corn

Corn, also called maize, was an important food to the native Indians of the Americas. They honored the corn spirit, corn mother, or corn goddess for helping them grow this vital crop.

Archaeologists have found that hundreds of different kinds of maize were grown by native Americans over a seven-thousand-year period and that maize was a staple food from Argentina to southern Canada. The Maya Indians of Mexico and Central America cultivated maize to feed the thousands of people in their cities, and they worshiped a corn god. The Aztec Indians of central and southern Mexico, who controlled the land from the fourteenth to the sixteenth centuries, made human sacrifices to the corn goddess, believing this would ensure a successful harvest.

Widespread legends were told about the corn spirit. For example, the Pueblo Indians of the southwestern United States believe the corn mothers brought the first corn with them from the world of the spirits, giving life to all people. Mothers placed a fetish, or good-luck charm, made from corn next to their newborn infants. People kept their corn fetishes all their lives.

Among the Apache Indians of the southwestern United States, the women did the farming, calling on the "corn people" to help guarantee a good crop. Farming women among tribes in the east central United States believed each corn plant had a spirit and liked to hear the women sing as they cultivated the crop.

During the Green Corn Ceremony, held in honor of the newly ripened corn at the beginning of each harvest season, North American Indians from many different tribes honored the corn spirit by ritually purifying themselves before eating the new corn. This first corn of the season was believed to be sacred because it held the spirit of the corn and would feed a person's body and spirit. The Indians considered giving thanks an important part of living, and thanks were offered to the Great Spirit during the Green Corn Ceremony.

The American Indians introduced corn to European settlers from Great Britain, Spain, Portugal, France, Germany, and other countries who migrated to the Americas beginning in the 1500s. When the Pilgrims arrived in what is now Massachusetts in 1620 and established Plymouth Colony, they settled at the site of an abandoned Indian village and found multicolored seed corn left by the Patuxet (pronounced puh-TUX-it) Indians. Neighboring Indians taught the Pilgrims how to plant corn in hills, using dead fish as fertilizer. Through early European explorers, corn made its way to Europe, Africa, and around the world and is still a major world grain crop.

Sheaf of grain

To European peoples, grains such as wheat, rye, oats, and barley have been important foods for centuries, and hunger or plenty depended on the success of the grain harvest. The ancient Greeks and Romans paid tribute to their goddesses of grain, Demeter and Ceres, with large festivals at harvest time.

Early Europeans believed the spirit of the grain lived within the grain itself. To prevent the spirit from abandoning their fields, farmers left at least one sheaf, or bundle, of grain standing in the field after the rest was harvested. A sheaf of grain was often decorated and presented to the landowner as protection for the household during the winter and to ensure a successful crop the following year. Grain was sometimes woven into wreaths and used to bless a new marriage, ensure a safe childbirth, or make hens lay more eggs. Grains

from the last sheaf were saved and planted with the first seeds to go into the ground the following spring to guarantee another bountiful harvest.

Like the American Indians, Europeans believed that an earth mother, or grain mother, protected them and made their crops grow. After corn was introduced into Europe in about the seventeenth century, farm women began making "corn dollies" from corn husks, similar to the corn fetishes made by American Indians of what is now the southwestern United States. These were woven in distinctive local patterns and kept above the hearth to keep the spirit of the corn alive and warm throughout the winter.

In some regions, a large corn dolly was dressed with flowers and ribbons and one of the last sheaves of harvested grain was tucked under her arm. She was then hung in the barn until the following year's harvest to ensure a good crop. At the end of the harvest, a pretty girl was crowned with a wreath made from grain woven with flowers. She was called the corn maiden and represented the spirit of the harvest.

The sacred yam

The yam, a root vegetable similar to the sweet potato, is an important food for many peoples of Africa, and its cultivation is as ancient as the legends told about it. Many Africans consider the first fruits of the yam harvest to be sacred, and certain rituals and ceremonies have traditionally been performed before these first yams can be eaten.

Africans who still practice native tribal religions continue these rituals, but the majority of Africans have adopted either Islam or Christianity and combine ceremonies to honor the land and crops with giving thanks to Allah or God for the harvest. Yam festivals are therefore both cultural and religious festivals for African people today.

Some Yoruba people of Nigeria believe the sacred yam can be used to predict the future of the people and the success of the following year's crop. Tribal priests perform special rites during the New Yam Festival to make these predictions. Yorubans who still practice their native religion believe that spirits of nature called *orisa* control the success or failure of crops and must be offered a sacrifice of new yams before the people eat them.

The moon

The cycles of the moon play an important role in many of the world's holidays. For most harvest festivals, it is the full moon at harvest time that is considered part of the ceremonies. The American Indian Green Corn Ceremony, the Chinese Harvest Moon Festival, and the Jewish harvest festival, Sukkoth, are celebrated during the time of the full moon, as are many other harvest festivals.

The full moon plays a critical role in Swaziland's Incwala festival, and the time of the festival is carefully determined by tribal astrologers so that the full moon will give strength to the Swazi king, who is central to the ceremonies. The Swazi believe disaster will befall the people if the wrong date is chosen for the sacred festival. Preparations for Incwala begin when the moon is in its new phase, but branches from a sacred shrub used to build a shelter for the king as part of the ceremony must be gathered only during the full moon.

The full moon nearest to the time of the fall equinox (about September 23 in the Northern Hemisphere) is called the Harvest Moon because it occurs at the traditional time of harvest. This moon appears larger and brighter than the usual full moon seen each month and has a slightly rose color. During the harvest moon cycle, the moon is full for an extra night, giving farmers more time to harvest crops because they can work until long after dark for a few nights in a row. Harvest moon is also a perfect time for nighttime hay rides and harvest parties.

Cornucopia

The cornucopia is most often depicted as a curved, horn-shaped basket overflowing with fruits, flowers, ears of corn, and fall vegetables. Also called the horn of plenty, it is a prominent symbol of Thanksgiving. In many homes throughout the United States and Canada, it is the featured table decoration for the large Thanksgiving Day meal.

The word "cornucopia" is a combination of the Latin words *cornu* and *copia,* which mean "horn of plenty." It is often associated with Greek and Latin myths about a goat's horn. It is also said to have once represented early America, with its abundant land, forests, wild game, and native foods. Today, the cornucopia is a symbol of abundance, fruitfulness, and thanksgiving for a plentiful harvest.

Turkey

The plump tom turkey with its tail feathers in full spread is often depicted as a symbol of the U.S. Thanksgiving holiday.

Roast turkey has been at the center of the Thanksgiving dinner table in the United States and Canada since the mid-1800s, but the wild turkey was a native of North America for about eight million years before the first humans came. The turkey is a variety of pheasant and is a large bird, weighing about twenty to thirty pounds. The male, or tom, turkey has greenish-bronze feathers, and the female, or hen, has brownish-gray feathers.

Because they were too heavy to be good flyers, turkeys were easily captured for breeding. Native peoples in Mexico, Central America, and Latin America domesticated wild turkeys and made them an important part of their diet long before the arrival of the Spanish explorer Christopher Columbus (1451–1506) in 1492.

Columbus and his crew members called the large bird *tukki,* the Hebrew word for "big bird." They also referred to it as *tuka,* the Indian word for "peacock," because they mistakenly believed the land they had discovered was part of India.

Columbus and other Spanish explorers took turkeys back to Spain, where they were bred and raised for food as early as 1511. Farmers in France and England soon began raising turkeys as well. The English confused the turkey with the guinea fowl—brought from the Turkish empire during the mid-1500s—and named it "turkey," as well.

The Pilgrims who celebrated Thanksgiving at Plymouth, Massachusetts, in 1621 were introduced to the turkey, and other wild game, by members of the Wampanoag tribe. It is not certain, but turkey may have been served at this early feast.

Music, Dance

In most cultures, the time after the new harvest has been blessed and declared ready for eating is an occasion for celebrating with feasting, music, and dancing. Some European and American farming communities today gather for folk dancing after the harvest is in. These traditional dances are accompanied by music played on fiddles, guitars, and perhaps accordions, flutes, or other instruments.

An Obzinky tradition in the Czech Republic and Slovakia was a moonlight dance and feast on the landowner's property. Today, many farmers come together at a community center for dancing.

In India and Africa and in American Indian communities, dancing is usually accompanied by drums and other percussion instruments with many different sounds. During Pongol in India, Hindu folk singers stroll through the streets playing traditional Tamil instruments such as the *tharai,* an S-shaped horn, and the *thambattam,* a type of drum.

The Yoruba people of Nigeria play "talking drums" that sound like the human voice. The Nigerian Ibo people hold a dance in the streets on each day of the New Yam Festival. The festival includes drumming and singing of traditional African songs. American Indian tribal dances such as the Corn Dance and the Great Feather Dance are often performed during the Green Corn Ceremonies in North America.

Ritual songs and dances are a major part of the Incwala ceremonies in Swaziland. The people sing songs about their king, his enemies, and his greatness. They perform ritual dances with the king at the center of a circle. On the final day of Incwala, he makes up a spectacular dance for his people.

Early English farmworkers sang the traditional "Harvest Home" song as they were bringing in the last wagon load of harvested grain. In the United States, people sing traditional Thanksgiving hymns such as "Come, Ye Faithful People, Come" (1858), by Henry Alford and George Job Elvey, as well as popular songs like "Thanksgiving Day," a poem by Lydia Maria Child (1802–1880) that was set to music and is known as "Over the River and Through the Wood."

Special Role of Children, Young Adults

Children and young adults often have special roles to play in preparing for a harvest celebration and in the celebration itself. In cultures where the ceremony is of a religious nature—the Hindu festival of Pongol, for example—it is considered important for children to learn specific rituals and the religious teachings that go with them.

Children are sometimes given certain tasks, such as gathering firewood and tending the fire, making decorations, and helping prepare meals. In India, families exchange gifts during Pongol. Harvest and Thanksgiving festivals are fun for children everywhere, who take part in the dancing, singing, sports and games, parades, and, of course, the feast.

Czech Republic and Slovakia

Name of Holiday: Obzinky

Introduction

The Czech Republic and Slovakia, which formerly comprised the country of Czechoslovakia, have for hundreds of years held two traditional harvest festivals in late August or early September. One is called Posviceni (pronounced POS-vih-tsee-nih). It was held in churches to thank God for a successful harvest and to bless the grain. The other was Obzinky (pronounced OB-zen-kih), a folk festival held to celebrate the completion of the harvest and to honor landowners, who in turn treated their farm servants to a feast. Rituals and customs associated with these traditional festivals are often reenacted by Czechs and Slovaks during folk festivals at home and by those who have immigrated to other countries.

History

From about the eleventh through the seventeenth centuries, much of the farmland in the Czech Republic and Slovakia was owned by wealthy nobles from neighboring countries, such as Hungary and Germany. Many people farmed the land for these nobles and received a small plot of land, a house, and food for their families in return. This type of land ownership and servitude was called the feudal (pronounced FEW-duhl) system.

Throughout this period, the farming peasants held a fall harvest festival to celebrate the gathering in of grain such as wheat, oats, flax, rye, corn, and barley, and to pay tribute to the feudal landlord, who then honored them with a feast. This ceremony was called Obzinky, and although the peasants did not own the land on which they worked, the harvest was one of the happiest times of year.

When feudalism was finally abolished in 1848, many peasants migrated to Hungarian farms to work during the harvest season. They brought with them the custom of celebrating Obzinky when the grain was harvested. After World War I (1914–18), farmers stopped celebrating Obzinky for several years. Following World War II (1939–45), it was revived in collective farms under Communist rule in what is now eastern Slovakia and in other areas throughout Europe.

The Communist government was overthrown in 1989, and the Czechs and Slovaks declared themselves two independent nations in 1993. On the cooperative farms of today, harvesters still carry out some traditions from the past. As a show of respect, they sing traditional folk songs and bring an Obzinky wreath to the farm manager. Afterward, an Obzinky feast is held at a local tavern or at a community center.

Folklore, Legends, Stories

Many superstitions were associated with the harvest, because the amount of food produced in a season could mean either prosperity or starvation. Reapers sometimes rolled on the ground before a harvest for two reasons: the direct contact with the earth was believed to give them great strength for the long hours of hard work ahead; and the number of rolls represented the number of sheaves, or bundles, of harvested grain that would be rolled into the barn when the work was complete.

The last sheaf of grain gathered in the fields was believed to have the power to both heal and to bring fertility to households and the farm. Parts of the sheaf were woven into wreaths and given to a new bride and groom or placed in a new mother's bed to ensure a safe childbirth. They were also hidden in hen houses to make the hens lay more eggs. Grains from the last sheaf were saved and planted with the first seeds to go into the ground the following spring to guarantee another bountiful harvest.

Customs, Traditions, Ceremonies

Most of the traditions associated with current Czech and Slovak harvest festivals were first established during feudalism, when the peasants held ceremonies to honor the fruits of their labor.

Leaving the *boroda* in the field

Some Czech and Slovak reapers have traditionally left a single shock of wheat standing in the field after the harvest is complete. This shock is tied up with ribbon or straw cord and is called the *boroda* (pronounced BOH-roh-duh), which means "beard." It is said to help feed the field mice and keep them from coming into the barn for grain during the winter.

The grandfather and the *baba*

The last ears of grain to be harvested are traditionally tied with ribbon into a neat sheaf and decorated with wildflowers. One name for this sheaf is *dido* (pronounced DYIH-doh), meaning "grandfather." It is brought into the landlord's house and remains there until after Christmas. The dido is believed to bring good luck to the household.

In other areas, the harvest sheaf is known as the *baba* (pronounced BUH-buh), or "old woman." The bundle is dressed as an old woman and carried into the landlord's home, where it is displayed with honor until Christmas or until the following year's harvest. Like the dido, the baba "sits" in a special place at the dinner table on Christmas Eve. Sometimes, a living woman, often the woman who harvested the last sheaf of grain, is bound in the sheaf and carried home in a cart. She is teased and laughed at, and then cut loose.

Procession of the harvest wreath

At the end of the harvest, reapers make a large wreath from the last sheaf of grain, interwoven with wildflowers and ears of corn. The wreath traditionally is sometimes placed on a pretty girl's head for the harvest procession to the landlord's home, or, in modern times, to the home of the farm manager. It might also be carried through town on a tall pole or placed in a wagon decorated with sickles, rakes, scythes, and other farm tools.

During Obzinky commemorations, people wear their most colorful clothes. These folk costumes vary from region to region, but for the most part women wear gathered skirts and blouses with lace and embroidered trim, aprons, shawls, jackets, and special bonnets or scarves. Reproduced by permission of Helene Cincebeaux.

Clothing, Costumes

During Obzinky commemorations, people wear their most colorful clothes. These folk costumes vary from region to region, but for the most part women wear gathered skirts and blouses with lace and embroidered trim, aprons, shawls, jackets, and special bonnets or scarves. Men's costumes consist of embroidered white shirts, with full sleeves gathered at the wrists, colorful vests, and white pants, or dark woolen pants and caps. Both men and women wear boots. Dyes made from indigo and other plants are sometimes used to color the clothing.

Foods, Recipes

After the harvest procession and the presenting of the wreath or sheaf to the landowner, the farm workers are treated to a harvest feast, called Obzinky Oldomas (pronounced OLE-duh-muss). This feast includes

Sausage and Barley Stew

Ingredients

1 pound pork sausage, cut into bite-size pieces

1 large onion, coarsely chopped

3 cloves garlic, finely chopped

1 cup celery, finely chopped

2 cups chopped mushrooms

2 cups cooked barley

1 cup water or chicken broth

salt and pepper to taste

Directions

1. In a large skillet, fry sausage over medium heat for about 3 minutes.

2. Add onion, garlic, celery, and mushrooms and cook for about 5 minutes, stirring often.

3. Stir in cooked barley, water or broth, and salt and pepper. Cover and cook over low heat for about 30 minutes. Serve hot as a main dish or a side dish.

foods such as roast pig or goose; pastries filled with prunes, sweetened cottage cheese, poppyseed filling, or apricot jam; beer; and a prune liquor. After dinner comes music and dancing until late at night.

Music, Dance

Singing and dancing play an important part in Obzinky celebrations, as it does in all Czech and Slovak folk festivals. Folk tunes are played on string instruments resembling the fiddle and the dulcimer, bagpipes, a large shepherd's flute called the *fujara* (pronounced FOO-yuhr-uh), drums, and the more modern accordion, clarinet, and trumpet.

Here is one example of a harvest song sung by farm workers in eastern Slovakia, who in times past often served wealthy foreign nobles:

> We work on our master's fields from sunup to sundown,
> And our master says it can't be helped.
> Because of hard labor, our hands are losing strength,
> While the masters help themselves to a good drink.

From Czechoslovakian harvest traditions came some of the many popular folk dances for which the Czechs and the Slovaks are known, including the polka, the shepherd's dance, and a group women's dance called the *chorodový* (pronounced KOHR-oh-dohv).

Special Role of Children, Young Adults

Young men and women who helped with the harvest are usually given special parts in the Obzinky ceremony. Sometimes the most popular boys are allowed to carry the harvest sheaf or wreath in the procession to the farm manager's house. Pretty girls often wear the harvest wreath. Boys and girls also enjoy folk dances after the Obzinky feast. Children dress in Czech or Slovak traditional costumes and participate in folk festivals that re-create the Obzinky customs of other centuries. These folk festivals help keep their heritage alive, to be passed along to future generations.

For More Information

"Folk Customs of Carpatho-Rusyns." [Online] http://www.carpatho-rusyn.org/customs/stand.htm (accessed on February 19, 2000).

India

Name of Holiday: Pongol

Introduction

Because there are many different languages in the various regions of India, the rice harvest festival has many names. In southern India, especially, it is known as Pongol (pronounced PONG-gahl). Usually falling during mid-January, the three-day thanksgiving festival gives thanks for the rains and sunshine that produce the harvest. The festival also honors cattle for their help in plowing and harvesting the fields. Non-farming families thank the farmers for producing food.

Pongol is the name of a sweet boiled rice dish that is prepared to celebrate the rice harvest. The word comes from *pongu* or *ponga,* meaning "to cook" or "to boil." Some cultural groups celebrate Pongol as New Year's Day. Pongol brings people together to share and give thanks and to have fun. Social and economic differences are forgotten, and everyone—rich and poor, landowner and peasant—comes together for a time of thanksgiving and friendship.

History

India was first populated approximately six thousand year ago. Because it has one of the world's longest histories of human habitation, historians know that the harvest has been celebrated in some way for thousands of years. It is believed that many of the harvest traditions were introduced to India in about 1500 B.C. by Aryans, northern peoples who migrated to India from colder climates in central Asia. These people eagerly awaited the return of spring after long, cold winters when food was scarce.

Aryan customs mingled with the early religions of the people of India to eventually form the religion known as Hinduism (pronounced HIN-doo-IZ-uhm). The majority of people living in India today are Hindu, and their harvest festivals include traditional elements of Hinduism.

Folklore, Legends, Stories

Hinduism is one of the oldest religions in the world, dating back to 3,000 B.C. It also carries a rich tradition of storytelling and is filled with legends about the gods. A number of them are related to farming and the harvest and are told during Pongol celebrations.

Legend of the bull

According to legend, the god Shiva (pronounced SHEE-vuh) once asked his bull, Basava (BAH-sah-vah), to visit Earth and give people this advice for good health: have an oil massage and a bath every day and eat once a month. Basava mixed up Shiva's instructions, telling everyone to eat daily and bathe once a month. Shiva was so angry that he cursed Basava, and sent him to Earth to plow the fields to help people produce more food. Bulls have helped man in the fields since that time, and so they are honored on the third day of Pongol for their help with the planting and harvest.

The sacredness of firsts

Many Indians believe that "firsts," such as the first crop, the first catch or kill of a season, or the firstborn of a domestic animal, are sacred. These "firsts" should not be touched by man until a ceremony is performed and an offering is made to the gods and to the ancestors. This sort of ceremony is similar to the First Fruits Ceremony in Swaziland and similar rituals around the world.

People in India also believe that no crop should be gathered until it is ready. Pongol symbolizes the sacredness of the first harvest, so cutting the crop before it is time is forbidden. Farmers perform a special ceremony before cutting the rice in the paddy, or rice field. They bless their plows and sickles by rubbing them with sandalwood paste from the native sandalwood trees, and then use these tools to cut the new rice. This ceremony is performed not only for traditional ritualistic purposes, it is also practical: sandalwood has insect-repelling properties.

A Pongol prayer

For Hindus, an important goal of religion is to help people achieve their greatest spiritual growth, which will in turn lead to peace in the world. To that end, they say a special prayer during Pongol:

> Lead me, O Lord, from untruth to Truth
> from darkness to Light
> and from death to Immortality.

A Pongol greeting

Indian literature includes many stories and poems about Pongol. Indians may greet the festival with the following verse:

> May the pot of prosperity boil over
> May the Pongol that we cook,
> the fragrance of turmeric
> the taste of sugarcane, ginger and honey
> Bring the joy of Pongol into our homes
> May the blessings of the Sun God flood our lives.

Customs, Traditions, Ceremonies

Pongol is most often celebrated for three days: Boghi Pongol, Surya Pongol, and Mattu Pongol. Several customs and ceremonies are associated with each of these days.

Boghi Pongol: A day of cleansing

The first day of Pongol, Boghi Pongol, is the day that people make things right and complete. They buy gifts for relatives and pay off debts to ensure a fresh start. In a symbolic washing away of sins, they scrub their homes from top to bottom and sweep the streets and roads. Farmers clean out their barns, and businesspeople clean their shops, factories, and offices. Orthodox, or very traditional, Hindus also bathe in the Ganges River to wash away their sins.

On this day, people also put old clothes, mats, rugs, and other items to be discarded on a bonfire made from wood and dried cow dung. Girls dance around the bonfire, which is said to represent the appearance of the sun. They sing songs in praise of the gods, springtime, and the new harvest. Boys beat drums made of water

In Varanasi, India, Hindus bathe along the banks of the Ganges River. On the first day of Pongol, very traditional Hindus bathe in the river to wash away their sins. Reproduced by permission of Cynthia Bassett.

buffalo hides throughout the night as the bonfire is kept burning.

Surya Pongol: A new beginning

The second day of Pongol is the main celebration, and it is the only day declared a public holiday. This is the day for making the rice dish pongol and for offering thanks for the harvest to the sun god, Surya; hence the name Surya Pongol.

On Surya Pongol, each family rises early, bathes, and puts on new clothes. Many people take a sesame-oil bath. Then they go to an open courtyard in front of the house or to a sun room or garden facing east and in full sun. This is where the pongol-cooking ceremony will take place. Prior to the ceremony, a special area has been prepared. The women in the family sweep the ground or floor, and decorate it with colorful designs and patterns called *kolam*.

The cooking begins by putting a new, decorated clay pot on the fire, filled with cow's milk or coconut milk. An adult member of the family, often the male head of the house, cooks the pongol, while the other family members watch or help. When the milk comes to a boil, a family member puts three handfuls of newly harvested rice into the pot in a special ritual. Then the rest of the rice is put into the pot. Other ingredients are then added, such as jaggery (raw brown sugar) or katkandu (sugar candy), beans, sesame seeds, dried coconut, raisins, cashew nuts, and cardamom (a spice).

As the pongol continues to cook, the milk boils up and spills over the sides of the pot. This is the most exciting part of the ceremony. When the milk boils over, everyone shouts, "Pongolo, Pongol!" several times. Sometimes they light firecrackers or blow horns or conch shells to announce that the pot has boiled over. The boiling over is a symbol of abundance and prosperity. All day on the streets, people greet one other with the question, "Is it boiled?" or "Has the milk boiled over?" They answer, "Yes, it is" or "Yes, it has."

When the meal is ready, the first serving is put on a banana leaf, and the family prays to thank the sun god, Surya, who is said to love offerings of flavored rice. Then the meal is served directly from the pot and eaten with fruits, like banana and mango. It will later be shared with neighbors, friends, and relatives, because sharing is an important part of the celebration. Gifts are often exchanged after the meal.

In cities, people spend the evening going to exhibits, concerts, or plays and visiting relatives and friends. Traditional events like ox-cart races are held in villages. Other games, music, and plays are also popular. Many people travel home to be with their extended families during Pongol. It is considered unlucky, however, to travel far during the days of the festival, so once home, people stay at home with their families or at least within the city or community. Many Indians send Pongol cards or write

letters for the holiday.

Mattu Pongol: Decorating the cattle

Cows, bulls, water buffalo, and oxen get special treatment during Pongol to show they are appreciated for helping with planting and harvesting the rice crop. The third day of Pongol—Mattu Pongol—is devoted to these cattle, or *mattu*. Cattle are never killed for their meat and are always respected and treated like family members. These animals provide milk and manure, which, when mixed with water, is often used as a disinfectant. They also help with transporting crops, plowing, and harvesting.

On the morning of Mattu Pongol, cows and bulls are bathed and their horns are cleaned, polished, and painted with red saffron or bright blue or gold colorings. The tips of the horns are sometimes covered with shining metal caps. Multicolored beads, tinkling bells, feathers, ribbons, ties, streamers, sheafs of corn, and flower garlands may be tied around their necks. Their hooves may also be painted bright blue or gold, and jangling silver ankle bracelets may be fastened about their lower legs.

Then the cattle are led out into the streets to music and drumming. Young men sometimes race one another's cattle. People walk through the neighborhoods, admiring the beautiful animals. After an offering of pongol is made to the sun god, cattle are fed the pongol and stalks of sugarcane. They are given a day of rest and freedom to roam where they please.

Jellikattu: Wrestling money from the bulls

In some villages in Tamil Nadu, farmers tie bundles of money to their bulls' horns or around their necks on the evening of Mattu Pongol for a competition called *jellikattu* (pronounced jell-ee-KAH-too). Young men try to catch the bulls and win the money. Sometimes they make the bulls stampede by beating drums and rattling noisemakers to make the game more challenging.

The youths who catch the bulls are considered very brave and in addition to winning the money are invited to the farmers' homes for dinner. Jellikattu is sometimes an occasion for young men to win their brides through a show of bravery.

A blessing for brothers

Another Pongol tradition is the sisters' blessing of their brothers. This is done by sisters of all ages for their brothers, wherever they might be. The women of a family gather in the courtyard for a ceremony using large banana leaves, pongol, colored rice, betel leaves and nuts, sugarcane, turmeric leaves, and fruit.

A little of the pongol, rice, smaller leaves, and fruit are placed at the four corners and in the center of the banana leaf. An oil lamp is also placed in the center of the leaf. Then the women say a prayer that the homes and families of their brothers might prosper. They also perform a ritual to keep away evil by sprinkling turmeric water, limestone, and rice on the colorful designs drawn in the courtyard.

If their brothers are present, the sisters apply a paste to their brothers' foreheads to protect them and then give them fruit, sweets, sesame seeds, and jaggery, brown sugar. The brothers thank their sisters by giving them money and gifts.

Kites and paper lanterns

In the state of Gujarat, the International Kite Festival is held during the three days of Pongol. People come from many cities for a friendly kite-flying competition, which continues after the sun goes down. Paper lanterns are fastened to the kites and fill the night with flickering lights.

Bathing in sacred waters

Hindus believe it is very beneficial to bathe in sacred rivers and other bodies of water during Pongol. Many thousands of Hindus go to rivers, lakes, and to the sea to bathe. Every twelve years on Pongol, a major Hindu religious festival and fair is held in the holy city of Allahabad in northern India, where the Ganges and the Yamuna Rivers meet. This most holy festival, during which some five million people bathe in the rivers, is called Magha Mela or Kumbha Mela.

Clothing, Costumes

Indians buy or make new clothing for Pongol, and burn or throw away their old clothes. This custom is very similar to the American Indian tradition of burning old clothes and making new ones when they prepare for their Green Corn Ceremony. In many villages in India, newly married couples are given new clothes by the bride's parents on Surya Pongol, because the marriage is a symbol of joy and new beginnings. In more wealthy homes, servants are also given new clothes at Pongol, in addition to their share of the newly harvested grain.

Foods, Recipes

The special rice and milk dish cooked on the morning of Surya Pongol is

Sweet Pongol

Ingredients

3 quarts milk

handful of almonds, chopped

1½ cups rice

¼ cup mung beans

¼ cup cashew nuts, chopped

1½ cups brown sugar

¼ teaspoon nutmeg

¼ teaspoon saffron (optional)

1 teaspoon cardamom powder

2 tablespoons melted butter for frying

Directions

1. Pour the milk into a large pot and heat to boiling.

2. Wash rice and mung beans and fry for a few minutes in butter.

3. Quickly fry cashews and almonds.

4. When milk begins to boil, add rice and beans. After they have cooked for about 30 minutes, add chopped nuts, brown sugar, and spices. Bring to boil again and cook until rice and beans are tender. Serve with fruit.

called sweet pongol, or, simply, pongol. It is cooked in a new pot outdoors in the sunlight, over a fire, or is cooked indoors and brought outdoors or to a room that faces the sun. Pongol is made from newly harvested rice cooked in either cow's milk or coconut milk and sweetened with jaggery, a raw brown sugar made from the sap of palm trees. Beans, called *dhal* in India, are also added.

Today, newly harvested rice is not always available to families who are not involved in farming, so they use the rice they have on hand in cooking pongol. Once the pongol has been offered to the sun god and served to the family, it is shared with friends and neighbors so that everyone has plenty to eat.

Sesame sweets

"Have a sesame sweet and say only sweet things" is a greeting heard everywhere on the evening of Surya Pongol, as mothers and daughters give out candies made from sesame seeds and molasses. Sugar figurines made using wooden molds are also a popular treat. Pongol is considered a time to say only kind words, to refrain from telling anyone "no," and to renew friendships. The sweets are said to keep the mouth busy, so a person is not able to say any "unsweet" words.

Sharing a feast

In some villages, the evening of Mattu Pongol is an occasion for a community thanksgiving feast. Meals are prepared using ingredients from the new harvest, and everyone, no matter their class, occupation, or status, is invited to come and share the food. This custom brings young and old, rich and poor, landlord and servant together in peace and brotherhood to share a delicious meal and give thanks.

Arts, Crafts, Games

Two important and sacred parts of celebrating Pongol are preparing the courtyard or room where the pongol will be boiled, and decorating the new clay pot that will be used for cooking it.

Making the kolam

The women and girls of each household trace special designs called "kolam" to define and decorate the area where the pongol is to be prepared. They first sweep the area and then "freshen" it by sprinkling it with cow-dung water. Then the kolam is drawn with a white paste made from finely ground rice and water or limestone and water. The outlines are drawn with red mud.

Brightly colored powders are used for coloring the kolam. Yellow pumpkin flowers or marigolds are pressed into balls of cow dung and set in the center of each pattern, resembling flowerpots. Young girls then put on costumes and walk around the kolam singing songs.

Decorating the pongol pot

Every family gets a new clay pot called a *pongapani* (pronounced PON-gah-PAH-nee) for cooking pongol each year. Pots decorated with beautifully artistic designs can be bought in markets at village fairs. On the day before the ceremony, the pot is trimmed with flowers and fresh greenery, like mango leaves, for prosperity; fresh ginger saplings with young leaves for putting spice into life; and turmeric leaves and roots, symbols of good luck. The ritual of decorating the pot is called *Pongol Panai*.

Games for Pongol

In addition to jellikattu, the bull-chasing game played to win money tied to the bull's horns, other rowdy games and sports are enjoyed during Pongol. Some of these are bullock (a young bull) cart races, ram fights, and cockfights.

Music, Dance

The Pongol festival is a time for singing and dancing. People sing traditional Hindu songs and play music on Mattu Pongol after the cattle have been decorated and fed and turned out into the streets for a day of leisure.

Some men train oxen to dance in front of houses during Pongol in exchange for gifts of grain and clothes. These oxen wear multicolored saddle blankets and canopies over their horns with colorful streamers and scarves attached. Folk singers walk through the streets and sing traditional Hindu songs to entertain people. Songs are played on instruments such as the *tharai,* an S-shaped horn, and the *thambattam,* a type of drum.

Special Role of Children, Young Adults

Children are included in all Hindu religious ceremonies to help them understand and pass on their religion and the culture of their people. Spending time with the family is important, and older family members such as grandparents are especially honored. Both children and adults visit their elders throughout Pongol. While visiting, they sit touching the feet of their older relatives in order to receive a blessing from them. People exchange gifts during Pongol to show love and unselfishness.

Holiday sweets

In addition to all the fun and activities that occur during Pongol, children love this holiday for the sweet foods they get to eat. Some families shower children with sweets and coins on Boghi Pongol, believing this will protect the children from evil.

Offering food to the birds

On the third day of Pongol, in a ceremony called Kanu (pronounced KAH-noo) Pongol, young girls prepare colored balls of sweet rice, sour rice, rice with coconut, and other special dishes and take them to riverbanks or ponds. They put the rice balls out to feed the birds (especially the crows), the fish, and other animals. As they offer the rice balls to the birds and animals, the girls say a prayer for their brothers' happiness.

Kanu Pongol is a way of acting out the belief that everyone should share whatever they have with all living things. It is also a day for brothers and sisters to remember one another wherever they might be.

For More Information

Corwin, Judith Hoffman. *Harvest Festivals Around the World*. Parsippany, N.J.: Julian Messner, 1995.

McNair, Sylvia. *India: Enchantment of the World*. Chicago, Ill.: Children's Press, 1999.

Web sites

"Hindu Festivals: Pongol." [Online] http://www.ashram.net/hindu_festival3.htm (accessed on February 19, 2000).

"Indian Festivals." [Online] http://www.indiancultureonline.com/Festival (accessed on February 19, 2000).

"Thai Pongol." [Online] http://www.sangam.org/CULTURE/pongal.htm (accessed on February 19, 2000).

Nigeria

Name of Holiday: New Yam Festival

Inroduction

The New Yam Festival is a two-day cultural festival that marks the beginning of the harvest season in southern Nigeria. It is held sometime between the end of June and the beginning of September, after the rainy season, when the yam crop is ready to harvest. Yams are root vegetables similar to sweet potatoes and are an important food of the people of southern Nigeria. They can be cooked and eaten or dried and made into flour.

The yam festival marks the end of one farming season and the beginning of another, a season of plenty. It is chiefly celebrated by members of two large cultural groups: the Ibo (pronounced EE-boh) or Igbo people of southeastern Nigeria, and the Yoruba (pronounced yoh-ROO-bah) people of the southwest. The Ibo call the festival Iri Ji (pronounced eer-EE-jee); *ji* means "yam." The Yoruba call it Eje (pronounced EE-jee).

The New Yam Festival also has religious meaning for those who still practice the native tribal religions. Even though most Nigerians of today are either Muslim or Christian, many still honor the spirits of the land and the souls of their ancestors in their everyday lives and in their ceremonies.

History

Tribal peoples of Nigeria practiced their native religions for centuries before Islam was introduced into the country during the Middle Ages (about 500–1500), and then Christianity during the seventeenth century. The New Yam Festival was one of several yearly celebrations held as part of these early religious observances.

Yams are a staple food in Nigeria and have been since very early times. During the 1500s to 1700s, thousands of native Nigerians and other Africans were taken to new lands that are now South America, the Caribbean, and North America, where they were sold as slaves. Yams were one of the main foods taken on board the slave ships as provisions, along with other African staples such as peanuts, plantains (a kind of banana), limes, peppers, and palm oil.

Folklore, Legends, Stories

According to Ibo myth, a man named Ibo, or Igbo, gave the tribe its name. A very old legend explains how the yam and the cocoyam, another starchy root vegetable, became such important foods for the Ibo.

During a time of terrible famine, a tribesman named Ibo was told by a powerful spirit that he must sacrifice his son Ahiajoku (pronounced ah-HE-uh-JOE-koo) and his daughter Ada to save his other children from starvation. After Ahiajoku and Ada were killed, the spirit told Ibo to cut their bodies into many pieces and to bury the pieces in several different hills of soil.

Ibo did these things, and, in a few days, yam leaves sprouted from the hills containing pieces of Ahiajoku's flesh, and leaves of the cocoyam sprouted from the hills where Ada's flesh was buried. The spirit told Ibo and his living children to farm these two crops. They did so, and when the

A woman cleaning grain in Gumel, Nigeria. The New Yam Festival celebrates the transition from a time when food is scarce to a time of plenty. Reproduced by permission of the Corel Corporation.

yams and cocoyams were harvested, they provided food that kept the family from starvation. Because of this, Ahiajoku is worshiped as the god of yam. He is greatly honored during the New Yam Festival.

Customs, Traditions, Ceremonies

The New Yam Festival celebrates the transition from a time when food is scarce to a time of plenty. During the time before the yam harvest, people fast, pray, seek forgiveness for wrongdoing, and mourn for the dead. The festival itself brings a time of hope and plenty, a time for joy. Just before the festival, any remaining yams from the previous year's harvest are destroyed.

New yams are sold in the markets before the yam festival, and Christians and Muslims sometimes eat new yams in either June or July. But many families in southern Nigeria consider it taboo to eat the newly harvested yam before the harvest has been blessed in festival ceremonies.

The Ibo once considered the new yams to be so sacred that a person would be put to death for stealing them before the ceremonies. In more modern times, yam thieves have been sent away from the tribe.

Preparing for the New Yam Festival

Several days before the festival, villagers clear major roads and collect plenty of firewood for cooking the feast. At the marketplace, people are busy buying chickens, rams, and goats for the sacrifice and for the special dishes that will be prepared in addition to the yams. Young men perform magic displays and dance in the bustling marketplace.

Then, the harvesting of the yams begins. Some yams are not harvested whole but are cut in two, leaving part of the tuber in the ground to sprout new plants. Women wash all the household utensils that will be used to prepare offerings and meals for the festival, including the calabashes, large gourd-like fruits that are hollowed out and used for cooking and holding water. These will be used to hold cooked yams soaked in palm oil as offerings to the spirits. The women also wash pots, wooden bowls, and the mortar in which the yams will be pounded to make yam balls during the festival.

Villagers clean their houses and paint them white, yellow, or dark green. Women sometimes paint special designs on their bodies and shave their children's hair in beautiful patterns. Because new yams may be hard to digest, many people take medicine to prepare their stomachs for New Yam feasting.

Celebrating the harvest

The New Yam Festival is celebrated by gathering, blessing, and then feasting on the new yams. In Nigerian villages, most families grow their own yams in small fields near their homes. Large fields are farmed for crops that go to the marketplace. Village women often harvest the family's yams and carry them home in large baskets balanced on top of their heads.

In many villages, the unwashed yams are placed on the roofs of the houses. In this way, villagers can see which families had good or poor harvests. Those with more yams will share with families whose harvest was less bountiful.

At the beginning of each new harvest, the ritual of eating the first yam is performed by the oldest man in the community, the king, or a priest, to express the community's thankfulness to the spirits of the land and nature for making a good harvest possible. After this sacred rite is performed, a celebration begins, and the people feast, sing, dance, and exchange gifts.

Ritual sacrifice and "handing round of fowl"

For the Ibo, an important part of the New Yam Festival is a thanksgiving ritual in which a chicken is sacrificed. This ritual is held in each family and is a closed ceremony to which guests are not invited. An elder of the family kills the chicken and sprinkles its blood on the family symbol, giving thanks to the spirits of the family's ancestors for watching over the household. The chicken's feathers are scattered over the threshold as a sign that the family members will stay away from all evil in the coming year.

Other chickens are killed and prepared for the first day's feast, but one chicken is kept aside for the second day of the festival. On that day, all members of the extended family gather at the house of the eldest family member for a special ritual called the "handing round of fowl."

In this ritual, certain members of the family receive specific parts of the roasted chicken. The father cuts the meat and gives the head to the youngest member of the family. The liver and gizzard go to the father, and a thigh goes to the first daughter. After the meat is divided, the family stands to say a prayer of thanks for the blessings of life and for coming together for another New Yam Festival. This practice is similar to saying prayers at Thanksgiving dinner in the United States.

Reenacting the legend of the god of yam

An old custom was the reenactment of the myth of Ahiajoku, known as the god of yam because he was sacrificed so that his people could live. During the New Yam Festival, the head of each household placed four to eight new yams on the ground near the shrine of one of the nature spirits, called the *erosi* (pronounced eh-ROH-see). These sacred yams were dug from the ground by hand, using no tools, and were kept hidden until the ceremony.

After saying a prayer, the head of the house cuts small portions off the ends of each yam to symbolize the sacrifice of Ahiajoku, whose body was cut into pieces, according to legend. In a ritual that may have been adapted from the lessons of Christian missionaries, the yams were then cooked with palm oil, water, and chicken to make a soup that represented the body and blood of Ahiajoku. Family members ate the soup, symbolic of eating the flesh and drinking the blood of the god of the yams.

Gift giving and the ancestors

The New Yam Festival is also a time for giving gifts. Men give presents to their wives and children and give yams to the parents of all their wives. (Men may have more than one wife in this culture). When a woman and her children go to her parents' home, her father and mother bring out yams and call on the family's ancestors, known as *ale* (pronounced AH-lay). They offer pieces of kola nut to the ancestral spirits, and the father asks God to give his daughter more children.

In some families, the daughter is asked to put her hands on the yams and the father spits on them as he asks for blessings. The father may give his son-in-law a bottle of whiskey or some money to thank him for the yams he brought.

Yoruba celebrations of New Yam Festival

The Yoruba celebrate the New Yam Festival, or Eje, for two days after the yam harvest. In addition to fasting and giving thanks for the harvest, they use new yams in special rites to predict the future of the community and the abundance of its crops during the coming year.

To Yorubans who still practice the native religions, the success or failure of the crops is believed to be controlled by guardian spirits or forces of nature called *orisa* (pronounced oh-REE-sah), by the ancestors, and by the families themselves. The New Yam Festival involves sacred ceremonies that are performed to offer the new yams to the spirits before the people are allowed to eat them. These ceremonies are held at sacred shrines and sacred groves, which have been purified for the ritual. A shrine can be a natural landmark such as a rock, a river or pool, a special tree, or other place where the spirit is believed to dwell.

Purification and offering

On the first day of the festival, the site where it will be held is purified through a ritual performed by the *Oba* (pronounced OH-bah), the Yoruban king or traditional leader of the village. The newly harvested yams are then taken to the village leader's farm. The people gather at the shrine of the sea spirit, and the priest of the shrine prays for a good year to come. All night, the people stay outside the shrine, making offerings of palm wine and kola nuts to the spirits and to the ancestors.

In the morning of the second day of the festival, the village leader, dressed in a white robe, makes an offering of a white kola nut and a white pigeon and joins the priest in praying to the sea spirit. Later, the people and the priests go to the leader's palace, and he leads them in a procession and dance through town. The procession stops at each shrine along the way, where sacrifices of the new yam are made to the orisa, or nature spirits.

The sacrificial yams are boiled, then cut into slices and placed in calabashes. The yams are covered with palm oil, and the calabash is taken into each shrine, where priests offer bits of yam to the spirits.

The feasting begins

After all the spirits have received the yams, the village leader and the priests break their fast. The priest prays for a better harvest in the coming year, then eats yams that have been cooked and pounded until soft. A soup is made from the meat of a goat that has been sacrificed to the spirit of the harvest. After the village leader and the priests eat the new yams, a celebration begins, at which the people may eat all the yams they like. In some villages, when everyone has eaten their fill, the people throw yams at one another in a gesture of abundance and joy.

Using yams to predict the future

A special divination, or fortune-telling, ceremony is held at both the sacred shrine and the sacred grove where New Yam rituals are held. A newly harvested yam is sliced in half, and the priest throws the two halves into the air. If one part lands face up and the other face down, it is believed to be a sign of a good year and a good harvest in the following year. If both halves land either face up or face down, it is considered an omen of ill fortune for the village.

Clothing, Costumes

Although people dress in their best clothing for the New Yam Festival, there are no special costumes for this day. A few weeks before the yam harvest, a Yoruba masquerade festival called the Egungun (pronounced ee-GOON-goon) Festival is held to honor the ancestors and the dead. This festival includes street dancers in elaborate ancestral masks and long multicolored robes, who visit houses where family members have recently died.

Foods, Recipes

Yams are an important food year-round in Nigeria, and people depend on the success of the yam crop for their survival. A favorite dish made from yams is *fufu*. The yams are boiled, peeled, pounded, and then shaped into a loaf or little balls. Another dish popular during the New Yam Festival is *futari* (pronounced foo-TAR-ee), a soup made from yams, squash, onions, and coconut milk, seasoned with cinnamon and cloves. Palm wine is a popular beverage during the festival.

In many households, yams are cooked and served on oval-shaped dishes. All members of the family sit around the table and eat from the same dish. Many Nigerians eat from baskets placed on the table and instead of using a fork, they use their right hand to break off pieces of food. The left hand is never placed on the table because it is used for washing and grooming the body.

Arts, Crafts, Games

One art form evident during the New Yam Festival is decorating the calabashes, large gourd-like fruits that are cut in half lengthwise, hollowed out, and used as bowls or dippers. Calabashes are used as containers for the sacred yam slices soaked in palm oil that are offered to the spirits at village shrines.

A calabash is sturdy enough to boil water in, so the dried skins are hard enough

Fufu (Yam Balls)

Ingredients

2 pounds yams or sweet potatoes, boiled in skins and cooled

salt and pepper to taste

1¼ teaspoons nutmeg

Directions

1. Peel boiled yams or sweet potatoes, cut into small chunks, and mash with a potato masher or fork until smooth.
2. Add nutmeg and salt and pepper to taste, mixing well.
3. Wet hands and shape yams into a loaf or into balls about the size of a plum.
4. Serve alone or serve the balls in soups or stews as dumplings.

to be carved with designs. These designs can be intricate or simple, depending on the craftsman. Calabash vessels may be purchased in the marketplace before the New Yam Festival and are sold in craft shops in the cities.

Music, Dance

The New Yam Festival is a time for celebration, and this includes lots of drumming, tribal dancing, and singing. The Yoruba play special drums that sound like the human voice and are called "talking" drums. Each cultural group in Nigeria has created its own instruments, and most have been played at festivals for hundreds of years.

An Ibo dance called the *ikoro* (pronounced ih-KOH-row) is held on the evening of the first day of the New Yam Festival and again on the second day after the giving of gifts and sharing of yams.

Special Role of Children, Young Adults

Children participate throughout the New Yam Festival and have a few special roles. Yoruba children are given the task of tending the fire on the first night of the festival. They may stay up all night keeping the fire burning and are given tiny yams to roast and eat while they poke the fire. Children play tom-toms and other small drums at the festival and perform team dances. They practice year-round for these dances. Young Ibo men participate in wrestling matches on the second day of the festivities.

For More Information

Levy, Patricia. *Nigeria.* New York: Marshall Cavendish, 1996.

Markham, Lois. *Harvest: World Celebrations and Ceremonies.* Woodbridge, Conn.: Blackbirch Press, 1998.

Owhonda, John. *Nigeria: A Nation of Many Peoples.* Parsippany, N.J.: Dillon Press, 1998.

Web sites

"The Igbo Home Page." [Online] http://www.lioness.cm.utexas.edu/I-files/Igbo (accessed on February 19, 2000).

"The Yoruba Page." [Online] http://www.yoruba.com (accessed on February 19, 2000).

Swaziland

Name of Holiday: Incwala

Introduction

Swaziland is a kingdom in southeastern Africa bordering Mozambique and the Republic of South Africa. Because of its natural beauty, the mountains that surround it, its small size, and its similar name, Swaziland is sometimes referred to as the Switzerland of Africa. The people of Swaziland are known as the Swazi (pronounced SWAH-zee).

The sacred Incwala (pronounced TDLICKH-wah-luh), or "First Fruits" Ceremony, is the most important traditional holiday in Swaziland. It is held at the king's capital near the cities of Mbabane and Lobamba. In 1999, more than ten thousand Swazi people attended the festival. It is both a harvest thanksgiving festival and a "kingship" festival that serves to bind the king and the nation together.

Traditionally, the king of Swaziland is more honored by his people than kings in other monarchies, governments in which power is held by one person. He is a symbol of the nation's strength, and his virility is believed to protect the people and provide for their well-being. The Incwala is the annual ceremony to renew the king's powers.

The festival is a time for the ritual cleansing of the king and for the renewal of the strength of both the king and the country for the coming year. Incwala also serves to "sanctify" (give moral or religious approval to) the king's ability to father many children. The Swazi are polygamous (pronounced puh-

LIG-uh-mus), meaning they can have as many wives as they want. The last king fathered more than six hundred children.

Incwala also includes spectacular parties filled with intriguing traditions and notions, singing, dancing, and military reviews to kick off the harvest season and the new year.

History

The origins of the First Fruits Ceremony are somewhat hazy, but the festival is believed to center on the Queen Mother of an ancient Swazi clan that lived near the sea. She and her son supposedly ran away from their clan. They took with them the tribe's rainmaking medicines and lived in the veld, a grassland area with few trees. The Incwala stems from this incident and the tribe's ensuing history.

Folklore, Legends, Stories

Many of the rituals associated with Incwala symbolize the wanderings of the ancient Queen Mother during the time she stayed in the veld. According to legend, she lived mostly on whatever foods grew in the wild—sugarcane, maize (corn), roots, and a sort of wild pumpkin. She used the branches of the now sacred *lusekwane* shrub to comfort and shelter her son. Today, these foods and the sacred shrub play a large role in the First Fruits Ceremony.

Customs, Traditions, Ceremonies

The Swazi are named for a former chief of long ago. The traditional name for the Swazi king is Ingwenyama, which means "Lion" or "King." The king is the central political figure in Swaziland. In an area of little rain, where water is all-important, the king is believed to have the power to make rain for his people. The queen, who is also powerful, is known as the Indlovukati, or "She-Elephant." The queen is the caretaker of the rainmaking medicines.

Incwala is the most sacred ceremony of the Swazi. It takes place around the time of the summer solstice, in December or early January. Tribal astrologers set the date when the position of the sun and the phase of the moon are exactly right. The Swazi believe the full moon ensures strength and vitality and a waning moon brings weakness. The timing of the ceremony is therefore crucial, for it is believed that a national disaster will befall the country if the wrong day is chosen. The festival must begin when the sun appears to rise and set in the same location for several days— when it is said to be "resting in its hut."

Preparing for Incwala

Incwala is divided into two parts— Little Incwala, which precedes the new moon, and Big Incwala, which starts at the time of the new moon. Before the festival can begin, however, certain ceremonial items must be gathered.

A few weeks before the ceremony, Incwala councilors locate a pitch-black ox that will be sacrificed for Incwala. Parts of the ox will be used to decorate urns used to carry sacred water from the sea for the ceremony. Other parts will be used to prepare medicine to strengthen the king.

The councilors drive the ox to a byre, or cow barn, and kill it with a special spear. Warriors skilled in butchering animals then carefully dismember the ox. The skin and the tail are taken into a sacred enclosure called the *inhlambelo*. There, priests cut the skin into strips and twine them like wickerwork around the handles of the two urns that will be used to carry the sacred water. They tie the tail of the ox around the neck of the urn as a handle.

Sacred waters of the world

When the sun reaches its southern point, it is said by the Swazi to be "resting in its hut." During this time, the king also goes into seclusion for a while in a special hut used during the festival. At the time of "no moon," priests known as "the People of the Sea" begin their journey to collect sacred water and plants. One of the groups walks miles to the Indian Ocean (the location of the Swazi ancestral home) and the other to major rivers in the region. Before they leave, they are given the meat of the black ox.

Special beer and snuff are also prepared in the home of the She-Elephant, the Queen Mother. The priests and their helpers squat on the ground and partake of the snuff before beginning their journey. Wherever the priests stay on their trip, they are served meat and beer.

When they reach the ocean and the rivers, the priests must collect "the waters of all the world" and sacred plants, which will be used to purify and strengthen the king during the Incwala ceremony. They collect only the foam of the waves, believing that is where the strength of the sea resides. When they have filled the urns and found the plant medicines, they return, waiting at a village near the capital until

they are called by the councilors to bring the medicines for Little Incwala.

Little Incwala

When the priests return from collecting the medicines of the sea, Little Incwala begins at the royal *kraal,* or village. This is the village of the Queen Mother. The Swazi people, dressed in traditional costume, perform sacred songs and dances.

Surprisingly, most of the songs, which are forbidden at any time other than Incwala, are about how the king's enemies hate him. The words are mournful and accompanied by dancing and miming. The costumes, which include the feathers of certain birds and animal skins, indicate the importance of the wearer and also have religious significance.

As the sun goes down on a moonless night, the head councilor shouts, "Silence!" The singing stops as the king spits powerful medicines, first to the east, then to the west, and the people shout, "He stabs it with both horns!" The king has symbolically broken off the old year and prepared for the new.

To end the opening ceremony, the people sing a final song similar to a national anthem that praises the king as "our bull" and "lion." After this ceremony is repeated on the second day of Little Incwala, the warriors go and weed the Queen Mother's garden and then enjoy a feast of meat.

Big Incwala

When the moon is "ripe" (full), Big Incwala begins. This six-day ritual starts when unmarried young men walk more than twenty-five miles to a special hillside to gather branches from the sacred evergreen shrub, the lusekwane. They gather the branches by the light of the full moon. According to legend, on the journey back to the capital, the branches will remain fresh unless a boy has committed impure deeds.

The sacred branches are used to build a special enclosure where the Swazi king will go into seclusion to prepare for the final ceremony. He will be ritually bathed and "doctored" with medicines made from green herbs to renew his powers. This ritual is performed so that he may eat of the new harvest and close out the old year, making way for the new as a strong leader.

On the third day of Big Incwala, the king strikes a bull with a special wand, and young men catch and kill the bull with their bare hands. It is taken into the king's enclosure, where it is sacrificed according to ritual.

On the fourth day, the king emerges from the enclosure in an elaborate and frightening costume of animal skins and feather plumes. The people sing songs about his life and do a dance to encourage him to come back to them from seclusion. Then the king begins to dance. Toward the end of the dance, he eats part of a pumpkin from the first harvest and throws the rest to his warriors. This is the ceremony for blessing the new harvest and is a signal to the people that they may begin to eat the new corn and other "first fruits" of the harvest.

At the end of his dance, the king throws a special green gourd that represents the past year toward his warriors, who have been holding out their shields in anticipation of this ritual. The gourd must not touch the ground.

In a final Incwala ceremony on the sixth day, all objects associated with the festival are burned on a bonfire, including the king's costume, discarded blankets and clothing from the past year, last year's green gourd, and remains of ritual items. This "burning the filth of the old year" to make way for the new is similar to the cleaning and burning rituals performed during the Indian Pongol festival and other African harvest festivals.

Clothing, Costumes

Traditional Swazi ritual dress for Incwala includes three stages of costume for the men. They wear kilts (skirt-like wraps) made of leopard skins, black and red feather headdresses, and tied fluffed-out ends of tails from slaughtered cattle around their wrists and ankles. They wear special headbands and neckbands of animal skins and carry shields and ceremonial walking sticks. The men wear only certain parts of the costume during the first rituals, adding more of finery as the ceremonies progress, until they are in full Incwala dress for the last ritual.

The Swazi king has the most elaborate costume of all. For the final ceremony, his face is covered with a black ointment and he wears a full headdress made from long, black feathers. Underneath the headdress is a headband made from lion's skin. He wears a long cloak made from bright green grass and evergreen branches that trail along the ground. Around his waist is a loincloth made from silver monkey skin. He carries a shield and a long black wand and wears the inflated gall bladder of the pitch-black ox. Each part of the king's costume has magical and ritual significance in the ceremony.

People of Swaziland participate in the Reed Dance in celebration of the Harvest Festival. Ritual songs and dances are a major part of the Incwala ceremonies. Reproduced by permission of Jason Laure.

Everyone dresses in their finest clothing for the final day of Incwala. The Queen Mother wears a leopard-skin cloak, and other women in her family wear less-striking hide cloaks. Women remove their cloth shawls and wear ceremonial skirts and aprons made from leather, with black feathers tied over their ears. The young princes and princesses wear red feathers in their hair and special costumes. The final Incwala ceremony is a time to display magnificent native costumes.

Foods, Recipes

Incwala is a ceremony for blessing and eating the "first fruits" of the harvest, and these foods play a major part in Incwala rituals. Herbs and roots used as medicines are cooked with *mealie* (corn), *luselwa* (pumpkin), and *imfe* (sugarcane) in the sacred "water of all the world," sea foam. This dish is used during the Little Incwala ceremony as a powerful medicine to strengthen the king for the coming year. He chews a mouthful and spits it first to the east, then to the west.

The meat of a black bull slaughtered on the third day of Incwala is eaten by the young warriors who captured and killed it. During the Luma, or "Bite," ceremony on the fourth day of Incwala, the pumpkin, sugarcane, and herb dish is again prepared and chewed. The chief and his assistants rub some of it on their bodies, believing it will make them strong.

Pumpkin and sugarcane are honored in the Incwala ceremonies because, according to Swazi legend, they are the main foods the ancestral Queen Mother and her young son had to eat when they ran away from the tribe. These foods originally grew in the coastal areas of the Indian Ocean, where the Swazi culture began.

In the final Incwala ritual, the king eats part of a pumpkin from the newly harvested crop. When he is finished, he throws the rest to one of his warriors to let the people know they can begin eating corn, pumpkin, and other vegetables from the new harvest. After the final Incwala ceremony, the people gather to feast on meat and drink traditional Swazi beer. This is a time of joy and merrymaking.

Music, Dance

Ritual songs and dances are a major part of the Incwala ceremonies. During the Little Incwala, the people sing mournful songs about the king such as this one:

Shi shi ishi ishi—you hate him,
ishi ishi ishi—mother, the enemies
are the people.
Jjiya oh o o King, alas for your fate
Jjiya oh o o King, they reject thee
Jjiya oh o o King, they hate thee.

This song is about the enemies of the king, who are sometimes family members envious of his great status. Songs about the king's life are sung during the Little Incwala ceremony. At the end of the ceremony, after the king has spit the sacred foods to the east and west, the people sing the final Incwala anthem, which is also known as the Swazi national anthem:

Here is the Inexplicable,
Our Bull! Lion! Descend.
Descend, Being of heaven,
Unconquerable.
Play like tides of the sea,
You Inexplicable, Great Mountain.
Our Bull ye ye.

The Swazi perform dances throughout the Incwala festival, but the most spectacular is the one made up by the king when he appears on the final day of the ceremony. This dance has been called a dance that only a king could create. It is not learned but is a series of instinctive movements that come to the king at the time of the ceremony.

Swazi ceremonial dances include stomping the feet in unison and chanting. These dances can last for two or three hours. During Incwala, the dances include miming and gesturing toward the king to persuade him to come back to the people after his seclusion in the sacred hut.

For More Information

Blauer, Ettagale, and Jason Laure. *Swaziland: Enchantment of the World*. Chicago, Ill.: Children's Press, 1996.

Thompson, Sue Ellen, and Barbara W. Carlson, compilers. *Holidays, Festivals, and Celebrations of the World Dictionary*. Detroit, Mich.: Omnigraphics, 1994, p. 153.

Web sites

"Incwala." [Online] http://www.africasouth.co.za/swaziland/people/incwala.htm (accessed on February 19, 2000).

"Incwala: Festival of the First Fruit." [Online] http://www.whatsgoingon.com/coolest/1998 1215 (accessed on February 19, 2000).

United States

Name of Holiday: Thanksgiving

Introduction

Thanksgiving is celebrated in the United States on the fourth Thursday of each November. It is a time for giving thanks to God—not only for a successful harvest but for many other blessings, such as peace between nations, prosperity, good health, and being together with family. Thanksgiving is a day for feasting and offering hospitality, renewing family ties, watching football games and parades, and sharing with people who are less fortunate.

History

When English families first began to settle the Jamestown Colony (in what is now Virginia) in 1607, they celebrated the traditional English Harvest Home Festival, also called the Feast of Ingathering. This was an occasion for English landowners to hold a feast and share food with their servants and the farming families of the parish. Guising (pronounced GUY-zing), or dressing in costume, was popular at Harvest Home celebrations, as were making humorous speeches and telling jokes, and, for the young people, teasing and flirting.

The Festival of Lammas (Loaf Mass) followed the Harvest Home Festival in medieval (about A.D. 500–1500) England and marked the baking of the first loaves of bread from newly harvested grain. These loaves were blessed in church, and a special service was held to give thanks to God for the wheat harvest.

A small group of English settlers held a day of thanksgiving to God on December 4, 1619, when they arrived safely at the Berkeley Plantation on the James River, in what is now Virginia. In drafting the charter for governing their colony, they declared that the date of their arrival be set aside each year as a day of thanks.

But the English colonists known as the Pilgrims—with members of a neighboring American Indian tribe, the Wampanoag (pronounced wahm-puh-NO-ag)—are credited with holding what some consider the first true American Thanksgiving.

The first Thanksgiving

The first observance of Thanksgiving in the New World was in the fall of 1621. The feast was proclaimed by Governor William Bradford (1590–1657) of Plymouth Colony (in what is now Massachusetts) to give thanks for the survival of the colony through its first difficult year. It was also meant to celebrate the bounty of crops the colonists had been able to produce with great assistance from the American Indians.

These early settlers called themselves the First Comers, and they were known to their descendants as the Forefathers. Writers of the late 1700s gave them the name by which they are known today: the Pilgrims. They were members of a religious group called the Puritans, from England, who had left their own country in search of a place where they could be free to live and worship the way they wanted.

The Pilgrims lived in Holland for twelve years before setting sail for the New World. When their ship, the *Mayflower,* landed at Cape Cod Bay on November 11, 1620, the settlers on board numbered 102.

The First Thanksgiving at Plymouth, Massachusetts, a painting by Jennie Brownscombe. The feast was proclaimed in part to celebrate the bounty of crops the colonists had been able to produce with great assistance from the American Indians. Reproduced by permission of The Granger Collection, New York.

Only fifty-five were still alive by the spring of 1621. Most had died from pneumonia and scurvy, a disease caused by a lack of vitamin C, found in fresh fruits and vegetables.

The Pilgrims established Plymouth Colony on the site of an abandoned Patuxet (pronounced puh-TUX-it) Indian village. The Indians had all died from disease, probably smallpox, that had been brought by earlier European explorers. There was one surviving member of the village, a man named Squanto.

As a boy, Squanto had been captured by European slave traders and taken to Spain, returned to his village, and then captured again and taken to England. While living in Spain and England, Squan-

to learned to speak English and had adopted the Christian faith. Returning home for the second time and finding his village deserted, Squanto went to live with the Pilgrims. He taught them how to hunt and fish and cultivate corn and other crops that were native to the New World. Serving as a translator for the Pilgrims and for the large and powerful Wampanoag tribe, Squanto helped established friendly relations between the English settlers and their Indian neighbors.

When the Pilgrims were planning their feast of thanksgiving, they invited the Wampanoag chief Massasoit (pronounced MASS-uh-swah) and some of his people to come and share the feast. They were sur-

Thanksgiving in Canada

Canada lays claim to an even earlier beginning for its Thanksgiving than the United States. English explorer Martin Frobisher set out in 1576 to find a northern passage to China. In 1578, he and his men celebrated a day of thanksgiving in the eastern Canadian Arctic, on what is now Baffin Island, Canada, where they had been mining for gold. This is said to have been the first Thanksgiving in North America.

Canadians also say that the practice of celebrating Thanksgiving started by the Pilgrims at Plymouth Colony, Massachusetts, was brought to Nova Scotia, Canada, by settlers during the early 1700s. In 1763, Canadians in Nova Scotia celebrated the ending of the French and Indian Wars, or Seven Years' War, with a special day of Thanksgiving. As Canadian settlement spread, people carried the celebration with them.

Thanksgiving celebrations occurred sporadically, but tradition usually set the observance for the third Monday in October. In 1879, the Canadian Parliament in Ottawa declared November 6 a national Thanksgiving holiday. On January 31, 1957, Parliament set the second Monday in October as Canada's official national Thanksgiving Day. It is proclaimed each year as "a day of general thanksgiving to almighty God for the bountiful harvest with which Canada has been blessed."

Canadians celebrate Thanksgiving in much the same way that people in the United States do, with a feast that includes turkey and dressing, cranberry sauce, pumpkin pie, and other dishes. To many Canadians, ensuring that no one goes hungry at Thanksgiving, or at any time of year, is very important. Nearly five hundred food banks across Canada distribute millions of pounds of food each year to feed the hungry. Thousands of Canadians volunteer at the food banks.

prised when Massasoit and some ninety of his men came to Plymouth Colony as guests. The Indians stayed for three days, their customary period of feasting. In addition to the game killed by the Pilgrims and the food offered from their fall harvest, Wampanoag hunters killed five deer for the feast.

While the women and girls cooked, the Pilgrim men and the Indians competed in marksmanship, the Indians using bows and arrows, the Pilgrims their muskets. The men also competed in jumping and racing and played a game called stool ball, which is similar to croquet. A small band of Pilgrim soldiers led by Captain Miles Standish (c. 1584–1656) marched, shot blanks from their muskets, and blew their bugles.

The Pilgrims held no Thanksgiving feast the following year, because their harvest was too poor. On July 30, 1623, however, rain fell, breaking a long drought. The Pilgrims also received news that the ship *Anne* was coming into harbor bringing fellow Pilgrim settlers. For this good fortune, Governor Bradford declared a day of thanks and prayer to God.

The Washington proclamation

It was more than two hundred years before Thanksgiving became an established holiday in the United States. During that time, however, separate colonies set aside special days for giving thanks, feasting, and showing hospitality toward others.

New Amsterdam, now New York, celebrated "Thank Days" in 1644 for the safe return of their soldiers from a battle with Indians. In 1665, Connecticut named the last Wednesday in October as a day to give thanks for good harvests. The U.S. Continental Congress declared the first national day of Thanksgiving, to be celebrated on December 18, 1777, during the American Revolution (1775–83). In 1784, a special Thanksgiving day was held to celebrate the ending of the revolution.

In 1789, President George Washington (1732–1799) issued the first Thanksgiving Proclamation for the United States of America. He set aside Thursday, November 26, of that year as a day to give thanks to God for his:

> kind care and protection of the People of this country previous to their becoming a Nation, for the single and manifold mercies... which we experienced in the course and conclusion of the late war, for the great tranquility, union, and plenty, which we have enjoyed... and in general for all the great and various favors which he hath been pleased to confer upon us.

President Washington and Governor John Jay of New York called for another Thanksgiving in 1795. Between 1789 and 1815, U.S. presidents proclaimed days of thanksgiving three more times. The 1815 proclamation marked the ending of the War of 1812 (1812–14).

Holding some type of Thanksgiving feast, on whatever day they chose to celebrate, became a tradition among most families, and pioneers who moved westward took the custom with them. Farmers celebrated when the last crop was harvested and stored, dairymen when the cows were safe in the barn for winter.

Thanksgiving celebrations were observed occasionally by different states on different dates. Historians say the first Thanksgiving celebration in California was held in July 1769. New York officially adopted a Thanksgiving Day in 1817. In 1855, Virginia proclaimed Thanksgiving as an official state holiday, and other southern states soon followed.

Hale's Thanksgiving campaign

Sarah Josepha Hale (1788–1879), editor of the popular Philadelphia women's magazine *Godey's Lady's Book,* has been called the Mother of Thanksgiving Day because of her efforts to establish an annual Thanksgiving celebration for the United States. She began to promote Thanksgiving as a national holiday in 1827 by writing about the idea in her novel *Northwood; or Life North and South.*

As editor of the *Ladies' Magazine* of Boston, which later merged with *Godey's Lady's Book,* Hale wrote essays and editorials promoting the holiday to the public. She became editor of *Godey's* in 1846 and con-

Sarah Josepha Hale, the Mother of Thanksgiving.

tinued her campaign, gathering wide support from her many readers.

She also wrote hundreds of letters to prominent people all over the United States, to state governors, and even to President Abraham Lincoln (1809–1865). She sent the president a copy of George Washington's Thanksgiving Proclamation of 1789. She finally spoke personally with President Lincoln, convincing him of the importance of establishing a national time of Thanksgiving.

The Lincoln proclamation

On October 3, 1863, during the American Civil War (1861–65), Lincoln proclaimed the last Thursday in November an annual, national Thanksgiving Day. In his proclamation, he first named the many

things for which the United States could be thankful, in spite of the Civil War, then said:

> No human counsel hath devised, nor hath any mortal hand worked out these great things. They are the gracious gifts of the most high God, who, while dealing with us in anger for our sins, hath nevertheless remembered mercy.
>
> It has seemed to me fit and proper that they should be solemnly, reverently, and gratefully acknowledged as with one heart and one voice by the whole American people. I do, therefore, invite my fellow citizens in every part of the United States, and also those who are at sea and those who are sojourning in foreign lands, to set apart and observe the last Thursday of November next as a day of thanksgiving and praise to our beneficent Father who dwelleth in the heavens.

Congress declares Thanksgiving Day

With Lincoln's proclamation, Thanksgiving Day became a legal holiday on which banks, shops, offices, and schools closed and families joined together to share a feast and give thanks to God for the year's many blessings. But Thanksgiving celebrations remained somewhat unstable during the years to come. It was sometimes celebrated on the fourth Thursday in November unless there were five Thursdays—then it was celebrated on the fifth. A few presidents and governors objected to the holiday outright.

In 1939, President Franklin Delano Roosevelt (1882–1945) proclaimed the *third* Thursday in November as Thanksgiving after being pressured by merchants, who complained that the interval between Thanksgiving and Christmas was too short for the December holiday shopping rush. The American people were divided on the issue, and about half continued to celebrate on the fourth Thursday. Two years later, the fourth Thursday was again declared the date for Thanksgiving.

Finally, in 1941, a joint resolution of the U.S. Congress provided that the fourth Thursday in November be known as Thanksgiving Day, a legal public holiday in all states and U.S. possessions. A Thanksgiving Proclamation to that effect is still issued each year by the president and the governors of the states.

Folklore, Legends, Stories

Because Thanksgiving has been an American tradition since the 1600s, hundreds of stories and poems have been written about the holiday and its celebrations. One of the most well known is "The Courtship of Miles Standish," a poem written by Henry Wadsworth Longfellow (1807–1882) in 1858. The poem is about the Pilgrim Captain Miles Standish, John Alden, and Priscilla Mullins, who came to America on the *Mayflower* in 1620. It describes the events that took place during the first Thanksgiving feast.

Customs, Traditions, Ceremonies

Rituals and ceremonies to celebrate the harvest have been held in the Americas for centuries. North American Indian tribes whose economy was based on agriculture celebrated the Green Corn Ceremony. This was a harvest festival and a sort of New Year combined. Many of the rituals associated with the Green Corn Ceremony are still practiced today by various tribes.

When English colonists came to the New World, they brought their own customs, such as guising, or dressing in costume. These customs continued to be practiced in very early thanksgiving celebrations. In 1621, when the Puritans of the Plymouth Bay Colony held what is considered the first American Thanksgiving feast, they started an American harvest tradition of giving thanks for the bounty of the land. This first celebration included prayers, feasting, military parading, and playing games.

Many of the traditions of this "first" Thanksgiving are still carried out, although they have been adapted over the centuries as more and more people came to the United States from other countries. And, although the United States has moved away from an agricultural economy, people still symbolically remember the harvest when decorating for the season.

Today, Thanksgiving Day in the United States is marked by feasting, attending parades, spending time with family, giving to the less fortunate in the community, and giving thanks for the bounty of all things.

Green Corn Ceremony

The Green Corn Ceremony, also called the Green Corn Dance, or Festival, is a traditional American Indian harvest festival celebrating the early ripening of the year's first corn, still standing green in the fields. A corn harvest festival was held some weeks later when the mature corn was harvested from the stalks.

The Green Corn Ceremony was celebrated in similar ways by Indians throughout what is now the northeastern and southeastern United States and by the Pueblo Indians of today's Southwest. Tribes of eastern Woodland Indians, especially the

Squanto teaching the Pilgrims to plant corn. The Green Corn Ceremony is a traditional American Indian harvest festival celebrating the early ripening of the year's first corn, still standing green in the fields. Reproduced by permission of The Granger Collection, New York.

Iroquois (pronounced EAR-uh-kwoy), Seminole, Cherokee, Creek, and Yuchi (pronounced YOO-chee), celebrated the Green Corn Ceremony.

Typically a three- or four-day festival, the Green Corn Ceremony was held during the full moon at different times of the year by different tribes, depending on when the corn was ready to eat. New corn, considered food for both body and spirit, was not to be eaten or even touched until thanks was given to the Great Spirit and a ritual was performed. The Indians considered giving thanks an important part of living, and they believed that trouble would come to those who did not give proper thanks to the Great Spirit.

The Green Corn Ceremony was a kind of New Year's celebration. It was a time for cleaning out households, piling trash onto a common bonfire and burning it. People destroyed old clothes and made new ones, broke old cooking pots and utensils and made new. Old fires were put out and the ashes discarded. New fires were kindled with coals from a ceremonial fire made in the center of four large logs pointing in the four directions: north, south, east, and west. It was also a time for renewing faith in the Great Spirit.

Rituals and dances made up a big part of the ceremony. One was a ritual of purification in which chiefs, medicine men, tribal elders, and young warriors drank a stimulating beverage called the Black Drink, made from cassine, a type of holly that grew along the eastern coast. It was often drank from cups made from sea shells, carved with sacred writing and pictures. The Black Drink was believed to purify those who drank it and to strengthen relationships and communication among members of the clan.

The men then participated in a ritual called "scratching," in which their backs, legs, or arms were scratched with thorns or with snake fangs attached to a comb-like implement. This was supposed to make them pure and renewed and worthy to eat the new corn, which was believed to be sacred because it contained the spirit of the corn.

Depending upon the tribe, the sweet, milky under-ripe corn was prepared in a variety of ways. The kernels could be cut off the cob and steamed in the green husks, or the corn could be boiled on the cob; made into different types of bread; roasted over a fire; or scraped off the cob, parched, and ground into meal. The Indians also made corn milk by boiling the ears and then letting the "milk" sit for a few days until it soured.

The Great Feather Dance and other dances, prayers, and council meetings were also held during the Green Corn Ceremony. At the council meetings, old wrongs and arguments between individuals or clans were forgiven and settled. This was also a time for naming ceremonies for babies and for boys and girls who were becoming young men and women.

Playing a ball game was popular. Boys and girls hit a buckskin ball against a tall tree or pole to see who could hit a mark high on the pole. The Yuchi still play a game in which players try to throw the ball into a basket at the opposite end of a field. Young people and warriors of different clans competed in games after the ceremonies. Once the fasting, purification, and religious ceremonies were completed, the people feasted on meat, corn soup, beans, and squash.

The Green Corn Ceremony today

The Seminole Indians of Florida are among the tribes that still celebrate the Green Corn Dance today. Their ceremony is held in May. The Cherokee and Creek still hold the ceremony for curing and healing. The Iroquois celebrate the Green Corn Festival for four days in September, holding the Great Feather Dance and the Corn Dance.

The Pueblo Indians of New Mexico hold the Green Corn Dance on their saints' days or in August, when the corn ripens.

Dancers dressed as *koshares* (pronounced koh-SHAR-ehs), sacred clowns representing the spirits of the ancestors, participate in the ceremony. Other dancers carry evergreen branches as symbols of the growing corn.

The Mohegans of Uncasville, Connecticut, gather each year for a Green Corn Festival at which they tell stories, honor the Great Spirit, and renew their connection to the earth. This is a weekend of ancient ritual, native art, and history.

Thanksgiving dinner

A large Thanksgiving feast is at the center of Thanksgiving Day celebrations. The traditional American Thanksgiving dinner includes roast turkey or ham, dressing, gravy, cranberry sauce, corn, green beans, peas, sweet potatoes, creamed onions, mashed potatoes or potato salad, deviled or pickled eggs, rolls, and pumpkin, mince, or fruit pies for dessert. People from various ethnic backgrounds may also introduce traditional foods that have been passed down through the generations.

Most of the dishes commemorate the Pilgrims' first Thanksgiving and the bountiful harvest of field and garden. Although turkey may or may not have been eaten at the first Thanksgiving, the turkey is a native, wild bird of North America that was often used for food by early colonists. Today, millions of turkeys are raised on farms in the United States, not just for Thanksgiving dinner, but as a healthy, lean meat to be consumed at any time of year.

When families and friends finally sit down to the big Thanksgiving feast after hours or days of preparation, mouths water with the anticipation of tasting the delicious food before them. But in many homes,

A Would-be National Symbol

After the U.S. Congress named the bald eagle the official United States bird in 1784, American statesman Benjamin Franklin (1706–1790) wrote in a letter to his daughter: "I wish the Bald Eagle had not been chosen as the Representative of our Country; he is a Bird of bad moral Character.... The Turkey is a much more respectable Bird, and withal a true original Native of America."

before anyone picks up a fork, it is a tradition to join hands and say a prayer of thanks for all the blessings of the year, especially for being together again at Thanksgiving.

Traveling "home" for family reunions is an American Thanksgiving tradition, and more people go home at Thanksgiving than at any other time of year. This can mean many hands to help prepare the turkey or ham, dressing, vegetable dishes, and special desserts for the Thanksgiving table—and many hands to help clean up afterward.

Sharing with the less fortunate

Americans in every city and town volunteer to help out at food banks and pantries that distribute food to the hungry on Thanksgiving and throughout the year. A special effort is made during the Thanksgiving and Christmas seasons to collect canned goods and nonperishable foods so that every family has something to eat at

these special times of year. Grocery stores and businesses may also donate turkeys to be given away. Many churches and community organizations prepare a complete Thanksgiving dinner and invite anyone who needs a meal to come and eat.

Thanksgiving Day parades

Thanksgiving Day parades are held in large cities and small towns throughout the United States. Thanksgiving marks the arrival of Santa Claus, and the Christmas decorating and shopping season begins the day after Thanksgiving. The first big Thanksgiving Day parade was the Gimbel's Department Store parade held in 1920 in Philadelphia. It remains a tradition today.

Macy's New York City Thanksgiving Day Parade, first held in 1924, is the most famous. The parade route follows some of New York's major streets: Central Park West, Broadway to Times Square, 35th and 34th Streets. It is held on Thanksgiving morning. Gigantic helium balloons representing favorite cartoon and storybook characters, lavishly decorated floats, and marching bands entertain the thousands of spectators who attend the parade. Those who cannot be in New York City on Thanksgiving watch the televised version at home as the Thanksgiving turkey is roasting in the oven.

Macy's parade balloons are created at a large studio in New Jersey, staffed by full-time sculptors, artisans, and welders who work on them year round. In 1996, there were eighteen giant balloons and twenty-three smaller ones in the parade, along with more than two dozen floats. The balloons are kept earthbound and guided through the streets by some 1,200 handlers holding cords attached to the giant characters.

Wild turkeys, not the official bird of the United States, but an official symbol of Thanksgiving.
Reproduced by permission of Field Mark Publications.

Reenacting Thanksgiving in Plymouth

People in Plymouth, Massachusetts, reenact the first Thanksgiving in an annual ceremony. Wearing Pilgrim costumes and each representing one of the original fifty-one colonists, they gather on Leyden Street, the colony's first street, and walk to the base of Plymouth Rock for prayer. They march in a procession, the men carrying old-fashioned muskets, to Burial Hill, where the Pilgrims who died during the first winter after the landing of the *Mayflower* are buried.

After a procession back to the First Parish Church, they hold a memorial and a Thanksgiving service. A feast featuring foods shared by the Pilgrims and the Wampanoag is held in town afterward. This event draws thousands of visitors to Plymouth each year.

Tourists also come to visit Plimoth (the Pilgrim spelling of Plymouth) Plantation, a living-history museum of Plymouth as it was during the seventeenth century. A replica of the *Mayflower*—called *Mayflower II*—a 1627 Pilgrim village, and a Wampanoag campsite are the main exhibits.

International Thanksgiving

In 1909, William T. Russell, rector of Saint Patrick's Catholic Church in Washington, D.C., planned a Pan American Feast Day on Thanksgiving Day. He invited representatives from all North, Central, and South American countries to Washington for a special mass and feast in honor of

Members of the group Volunteers of America serve Thanksgiving dinner to the hungry in Columbus, Ohio, in 1997. A special effort is made during the holiday season to ensure that every family has something to eat. Reproduced by permission of AP/Wide World Photos.

peace and brotherhood. The Pan American celebration became an annual tradition.

The Center for World Thanksgiving at Thanks-Giving Square in Dallas, Texas, was established in 1981 after nearly ten years of meetings between world religious leaders to discuss the importance of giving thanks worldwide. Since then, the center has held Convocations of World Thanksgiving at Thanks-Giving Square and holds a yearly meeting in Dallas of leading scholars from the world's five major religions. Today, an annual Declaration of World Thanksgiving is signed by twelve world leaders in the arts, religion, philosophy, and science.

The Center for World Thanksgiving sponsors conferences around the world where leading scholars, philosophers, and religious leaders discuss the importance of gratitude and thanksgiving to all humans. Its Thanksgiving World Advisors talk with international organizations like the Atlanta Olympics Committee and the United Nations 50th Anniversary Commission about giving thanks related to their specific projects.

In addition to the United States, seven other nations—Brazil, Canada, Japan, Korea, Liberia, Switzerland, and Argentina—have declared national Thanksgiving days.

Clothing, Costumes

People in the United States usually wear their best clothes to attend church services and the big family reunions that take place on Thanksgiving Day. If children or adults participate in plays or pageants that reenact the first Thanksgiving, they may wear outfits that recall what the Pilgrims and the American Indians wore during the early 1600s.

What the Pilgrims and American Indians wore

The Pilgrims who attended America's first Thanksgiving are often pictured wearing long black capes, black suits, black dresses with white aprons, tall black hats with silver buckles (for the men) or bonnets (for the women), and shoes with buckles. According to historians, they did not actually dress this way.

Although the men might have worn black suits and hats for religious or town meetings, they wore blue, gray, or brown linen shirts to work in the fields, and wool or leather pants with long, knit stockings. In cold weather they wore sleeveless jackets and woolen sock caps called Monmouth caps, with sleeveless cloaks. The buckles on the shoes were likely an artist's invention.

The women wore long dresses in bright colors, like green, blue, red, or purple, with a different-colored top called a "stomacher," and a bodice that laced to fit. In winter, they wore waistcoats and hooded cloaks.

For many months, the Pilgrims made do with the clothes they brought with them on the *Mayflower,* patching as needed to make them last. It would be some time before they had sheep for wool or planted flax to use in weaving linen.

The Wampanoag Indians wore little clothing in summer, probably only a breechclout (loincloth) for the men, and moccasins. The women wore dresses and leggings made from deer or other animal skins. In winter, the Wampanoag wore clothing and robes made from animal skins with the fur worn inside to keep them warm. They used beads and paint for ornamentation, and the men are believed to have worn a single feather in their hair.

Thanksgiving mumming

Dressing in costumes and walking from house to house performing or begging for treats or money—called mumming—is an old European tradition. Long before Hal-

Descendants of the Pilgrims who arrived in America on the *Mayflower* gather in Winter Park, Florida, in November 1999, and discuss what life was like for the Pilgrims on the first Thanksgiving Day. Reproduced by permission of AP/Wide World Photos.

loween trick-or-treating began in the United States, maybe as early as the late 1700s, children in New England put on masks and ragged costumes or painted their faces and walked the streets on Thanksgiving Day, begging for money or sweets from passersby. This Thanksgiving tradition continued until the early 1900s in some areas.

Foods, Recipes

With the help of Squanto and the Wampanoag Indians, the Pilgrims who set-tled Plymouth Colony learned to hunt, fish, and cultivate native crops that provided them with plenty of food for a three-day Thanksgiving feast in the fall of 1621. Among the guests at the feast were ninety Wampanoag.

Historians say the Pilgrims and their guests ate venison (deer meat); fowl such as wild geese, ducks, swans, and most likely wild turkeys; codfish and sea bass; and corn. The feast probably also included wild fruits like gooseberries, strawberries, plums, blueberries, crab apples, and cherries, either fresh or picked during the summer and dried.

The Pilgrim women might have cooked some of these dried fruits or mixed them with a type of dressing, which later colonists called "pudding in the belly" when it was stuffed inside a turkey. Cranberries should have been plentiful in nearby bogs, and the Pilgrims might also have used a few of these, although there is no mention of them in journal entries about the first Thanksgiving.

Other foods that may have been on the first Thanksgiving table were walnuts, chestnuts, and hickory nuts; corn bread; hoe cakes and ash cakes; and corn soup. The Pilgrims might also have served beans, squash, leeks, onions, carrots, cabbage, turnips, beets, watercress, and greens. Pumpkin was a native gourd (not the variety grown today), and the Pilgrims might have prepared it. Later colonists found countless uses for the pumpkin, which some called "pompion" or "pompkin."

The Pilgrims made wine for the first Thanksgiving from wild grapes, and they also served beer made from barley malt and a liquor called "aqua vitae" (water of life), which they had brought from England. There was no milk and probably no tea or coffee.

The Thanksgiving feast was prepared by the four wives remaining in the Pilgrim village, two teenage girls, and a few children. The food was cooked outdoors on spits over an open fire, roasted in the coals, or simmered in iron kettles. Everyone probably sat on benches at cloth-covered plank tables. The Pilgrims and American Indians most likely ate using small wooden plates

and a few spoons and knives. They may also have used clam shells or wooden scoops as utensils and ate some foods with their hands.

Thanksgiving dinner today

What many Americans think of as the traditional Thanksgiving dinner of today—roast turkey and dressing, gravy, cranberry sauce, mashed potatoes, green beans or peas, corn, sweet potatoes, cornbread or rolls, and pumpkin pie—really is an American tradition. A menu from a Thanksgiving Day dinner in 1863 sounds very much the same: Roast Turkey with Dressing, Cranberry Sauce, Cranberry Juice, Sweet Potatoes, Creamed Onions, Squash, Pumpkin Pie, Plum Pudding, Mince Pie, Milk, Coffee.

Although families can serve any feast they choose on Thanksgiving, turkey and ham are the meats most often chosen. Recipes for dressing vary from region to region and from ethnic group to ethnic group throughout the United States. Turkey and the most popular trimmings are often combined with Italian, Polish, German, French, or Latin American dishes or seasonings.

About 95 percent of Americans prepare turkey for Thanksgiving Dinner. This means that about forty-five million turkeys are eaten at this time every year. Turkey is most often roasted, but other ways of preparing it include injecting the meat with spices and deep frying it in hot oil or roasting turkey on the grill. Turkey is a low-fat meat that is increasingly popular with today's health-conscious families. Some, however, are choosing vegetarian Thanksgiving feasts and replacing meat with soy or

Cornbread Turkey Dressing

Ingredients

¼ cup butter

3 onions, finely chopped

4 stalks celery, chopped

2 cloves garlic, minced

2 teaspoons sage

1 teaspoon thyme

½ cup chopped fresh parsley

4 cups day-old cornbread, crumbled

1 or 2 slices dry white or wheat bread, broken into small pieces

1 cup turkey stock or broth

2 eggs, beaten

½ cup each, chopped walnuts and water chestnuts (optional)

salt and pepper to taste

1. In a large bowl, mix together crumbled cornbread, broken-up sliced bread, sage, and thyme.
2. Sauté onions, celery, and garlic in butter in a large skillet until translucent (clear).
3. Add the eggs, turkey stock, and parsley, stirring to combine.
4. Pour hot mixture over the crumbled bread mixture. Add walnuts and water chestnuts if desired. Mix well and season to taste with salt and pepper.
5. Stuff the turkey loosely with dressing and bake remainder in a baking dish, at 350 degrees for 1 hour.

wheat products, beans, grains, and dairy products.

Arts, Crafts, Games

Colorful Thanksgiving decorations for church, homes, schools, and businesses are made from fall leaves, grapevines, pine cones, red berries, and other natural materials. A cornucopia, or horn of plenty—a horn-shaped basket filled with the fruits and flowers of autumn—is often used to decorate the table at the big Thanksgiving Day feast. Ears of dried, multicolored Indian corn, gourds, squashes, and bright orange pumpkins also set the mood for Thanksgiving.

Thanksgiving games old and new

The following games were popular during the late 1700s:

Cranberry contest. The older boys, each with a large needle and long, coarse thread, stood around a bowl filled with raw cranberries. At a signal, each boy threaded as many cranberries as he could in three minutes. The one who strung the most won a prize and got to hang the necklace around his favorite girl's neck and give her a kiss.

Corn game. Five ears of dried corn were hidden throughout the house. These five ears were a tribute to the five grains of corn which, according to legend, were the daily food ration of the Pilgrims during their first winter at Plymouth. The children who found the ears then competed to see who could strip the kernels off their ear of corn the fastest. The winner received a prize.

Pumpkin race. Boys and girls raced to a finish line, each rolling a small pumpkin along the floor with a wooden spoon. This was a funny sight, because the pumpkins were not perfectly round and wobbled all over the floor, sometimes rolling away from the child. A prize was awarded to the boy or girl who got their pumpkin to the finish line first.

Corn-husking bees (parties) were popular in America during the mid-1800s to early 1900s. These were big gatherings at which many people worked to pull the outer coverings, called husks or shucks, off the ears of corn. The work was completed quickly, and the families made a party out of the occasion. To make the work go faster, workers sang traditional songs that repeated certain lines to make them last as long as the chores did. Each family brought a dish to the husking bee, so plenty of food was available.

Among the games played at corn-husking bees was one in which the boy who found the first ear of red corn would throw it to the prettiest girl at the party. He then chased her until she was caught, and kissed her. Afterward, they shared a dance.

Around the end of the nineteenth century, attending bicycle races and horse races were popular ways to spend Thanksgiving Day. Today, watching football games on television, taking walks through the fall leaves, and playing games both indoors and out are all considered Thanksgiving traditions.

Music, Dance

Among the most well-known Thanksgiving poems set to music is "Thanksgiving Day," by Lydia Maria Child (1802–1880). This poem sets the theme of the traditional American Thanksgiving in the northern states during the 1800s, with snow on the ground, a sleigh ride, and pumpkin pie in Grandmother's oven. It eventually became a popular song to sing in the car while driving to visit family and friends during the holidays.

> Over the river and through the wood,
> To grandfather's house we go;
> The horse knows the way
> To carry the sleigh
> Through the white and drifted snow....
>
> Over the river and through the wood
> Trot fast, my dapple-gray!
> Spring over the ground
> Like a hunting hound,
> For this is Thanksgiving Day....
>
> Over the river and through the wood—
> Now grandmother's cap I spy!
> Hurrah for the fun!
> Is the pudding done?
> Hurrah for the pumpkin pie!

Another traditional Thanksgiving song is "Come, Ye Faithful People, Come" with words written by Henry Alford in 1844, and set to music by George J. Elvey in 1858:

> Come, ye thankful people, come,
> Raise the song of harvest home;
> All is safely gathered in,
> Ere the winter storms begin;
> God, our Maker, doth provide
> For our wants to be supplied:
> Come to God's own temple, come,
> Raise the song of harvest home....

Special Role of Children, Young Adults

Unlike Christmas, Halloween, and Easter, Thanksgiving in the United States is not considered a special children's holiday. Instead, it is a holiday for the entire family, in which grandparents often play important roles, especially if they host family gatherings for the holidays. Gifts are not given, but many people send Thanksgiving cards.

A time for learning America's history

Schoolchildren all over the United States have performed Thanksgiving plays for generations. They dress as Pilgrims and American Indians and bring to life the historic days when some of the earliest Americans feasted together in peace.

Thanksgiving is also a time for students to learn about the early history of their country. They learn about the pre-history of colonization and about American Indians. Teachers plan lessons on different tribes, and students might build models of American Indian villages or bring family artifacts to share with classmates. Students also study how early settlers lived and worked and how they colonized various parts of America.

For More Information

Greenwood, Barbara. *A Pioneer Thanksgiving: A Story of Harvest Celebrations in 1841*. Toronto: Kids Can Press, 1999.

Pennington, Daniel. *Itse Selu: Cherokee Harvest Festival* Watertown, Mass.: Charlesbridge, 1994.

Sechrist, Elizabeth Hough, and Janette Woolsey. *It's Time for Thanksgiving*. Detroit, Mich.: Omnigraphics, 1999.

Smalls, Irene. *A Strawbeater's Thanksgiving*. New York: Little Brown & Co., 1998. (story based on U.S. slave narratives)

Web sites

"The First Thanksgiving." [Online] http://www.pilgrims.net/plymouth/thanksgiving.htm (accessed on February 19, 2000.)

"Green Corn Dance." [Online] http://www.seminoletribe.com/culture/dance.shtml (accessed on February 19, 2000).

Schwalbe, David. "American History: Our Day of Thanksgiving." [Online] http://americanhistory.miningco.com/library/weekly/aa112497.htm (accessed on February 19, 2000).

Sources

Booth, Alan R. *Swaziland: Tradition and Change in a Southern African Kingdom*. Boulder, Colo.: Westview Press, pp. 47–48.

Cohen, Hennig, and Tristram Potter Coffin, eds. *The Folklore of American Holidays*. 2nd ed. Detroit, Mich.: Gale Research, 1991, pp. 212–13, 398, 403–04, 406–10, 415–16.

Dickson, Paul. *The Book of Thanksgiving*. New York: Berkley, 1995, pp. 5–20, 66, 85, 111, 124–25.

Fisher, Robert B. *West African Religious Traditions*. Maryknoll, N.Y.: Orbis Books, 1998, pp. 21–22.

Gall, Timothy L. *Worldmark Encyclopedia of Cultures and Daily Life*. Vol. 4: Europe. Detroit, Mich.: Gale Research, 1998, pp. 117–20, 355–59.

Gay, Kathlyn, and Martin K. Gay. *Encyclopedia of North American Eating & Drinking Traditions, Customs & Rituals*. Santa Barbara, Calif.: ABC-CLIO, 1996, p. 247.

Griffin, Robert H., and Ann H. Shurgin, eds. *The Folklore of World Holidays*. 2nd ed. Farmington Hills, Mich.: Gale, 1999, pp. 98–99, 525, 536–47.

Kuper, Hilda. *An African Aristocracy: Rank Among the Swazi*. New York: Holmes & Meier, 1980, pp. 197–225.

Kuper, Hilda. *The Swazi: A South African Kingdom*, 2nd ed. New York: Holt, Rinehart & Winston, 1998, pp. 71–76.

Levy, Patricia. *Nigeria*. New York: Marshall Cavendish, 1996, pp. 71–73, 109–111.

Owhonda, John. *Nigeria: A Nation of Many Peoples*. Parsippany, N.J.: Dillon Press, 1998, pp. 85–89.

Thomas, David Hurst, Jay Miller, Richard White, Peter Nabokov, and Philip J. DeLoria. *The Native Americans: An Illustrated History.* Atlanta: Turner Publishing, 1993, pp. 103–05.

Umeasiegbu, Rems Nna. *The Way We Lived: Ibo Customs and Stories.* London: Heinemann Educational Books, 1969, pp. 34–35.

Webb, Lois Sinaiko. *Holidays of the World Cookbook for Students.* Phoenix, Ariz.: Oryx Press, 1995, pp. 28–29, 88.

Web sites

Bisen, Malini. "Bawarchi: Indian Festivals: Pongal." [Online] http://www.bawarchi.com/festivals/pongal.html (accessed on February 19, 2000).

"Pongal." [Online] http://www.tntech.edu/www/life/orgs/indian/Pongal.html (accessed on February 19, 2000).

"Sankranti." [Online] http://www.andhratoday.com/festival/sank.htm (accessed on February 19, 2000).

"Thanksgiving in Canada: A Holiday Stuffed with History." [Online] http://www.mb.sympatico.ca/Features/Thanksgiving/history.html (accessed on February 19, 2000).

Thanks-Giving Square. "Thanksgiving in the World." [Online] http://www.thanksgiving.org/html/traditions/world.html (accessed on February 19, 2000).

Tush, Bill. "Macy's Parade Celebrates 70 Years of Hot Air." CNN, November 28, 1996. [Online] http://cnn.com/EVENTS/1996/thanksgiving (accessed on February 19, 2000).

Index

Index